Golding: The Law and Practice of Reinsurance

GOLDING: THE LAW AND PRACTICE OF REINSURANCE

by
C. E. Golding, LLD, FCII

edited by K. V. Louw, MSc, FCII

LONDON
WITHERBY & CO. LTD
32–36 Aylesbury Street
London EC1R OET

Published 1937
1st Edition 1937
2nd Edition 1948
3rd Edition 1954
4th Edition 1965
5th Edition 1987

MONUMENT
SERIES

ISBN 0 948691 14 X

Printed in Great Britain by
Witherby & Co. Ltd. London

FOREWORD

For a long time reinsurance was deemed to be the exclusive domain of the practician. Impatient young reinsurers were generally told that the essentials of the business could only be learned through many years of professional experience.

C. E. Golding's "The Law and Practice of Reinsurance", first published in 1937, showed, however, that it was possible to describe the fundamental theory of reinsurance concisely and with practical relevance and thus to provide the reinsurer with a most valuable tool for his day-to-day work. Golding's readers demonstrated their gratitude over the years. The book was reprinted several times and served as an example for a number of others. No author of the younger generation could ignore the views expressed in the Golding "classic". On the contrary, anyone who was able to quote Golding in support of his arguments was always sure of gaining wide acceptance for them throughout the reinsurance world. And this has remained so to the present day.

On the other hand, it is clear that in our day and age reinsurance – like other aspects of economic and social life – has undergone a profound transformation. Many of the resulting problems were completely unknown a few years ago or their full implications at least were not realized. They affected both the extent of the capacity that international reinsurance markets have to provide nowadays and the qualitative changes in risk factors that have taken place as a result, for example, of rapid technological development and the altered economic, legal and social environment. The current situation in the US liability market offers a striking example of the dimensions that the consequences of such changes can assume for insurers and reinsurers. And finally, it seems, even the traditional very close relationship between insurers and reinsurers has not remained unaffected by this general transformation.

The challenge of having to find new solutions to new problems makes it more essential than ever to remind ourselves of the way in which reinsurance basically functions, to become aware of what is needed for it to function and to have a thorough knowledge of the entire range of tools available to bring this about.

It is therefore scarcely a coincidence that Golding's standard work should be reissued just now, after a gap of many years. We owe a debt of gratitude to Mr K. V. Louw for undertaking this task as editor and for updating the text wherever it seemed necessary without touching the substance of it, which remains and will continue to remain valid beyond all short-lived developments.

Having been privileged to know Dr Cecil E. Golding for many years – as a teacher and friend above all – I consider it a great honour and pleasure to contribute this foreword recommending this new edition of his book to the reader.

Habent sua fata libelli – I wish the new "Old Golding" the best of all possible fortunes.

Dr Klaus Gerathewohl

Member of the Board of Management
of the Munich Reinsurance Company.

PREFACE TO THE FIFTH EDITION

When a new edition of a book such as this, which has been out of print for some twenty years, appears, then some explanation is due to the reader.

Its reappearance will undoubtedly be welcomed by many of those of us of an older generation of reinsurance professionals. But, such welcome on the grounds that "This book taught me all I know about reinsurance" or "Dr Golding is still the best book on reinsurance" may be due to little more than nostalgia for a lost youth when all the underwriters were wise, all intermediaries honourable, and all statistics reliable.

More importantly, this edition appears at a time when the reinsurance business is making efforts to recover from what seems to have been an interminable period of adverse reinsurance underwriting results. There is therefore a pressing need to take this opportunity to return to the fundamental principles of the reinsurance business and, thereby, hope to avoid future underwriting cycles of an even more extreme nature whereby the upturn in an underwriting cycle becomes of a shorter duration, while the downturn becomes longer—and deeper.

Dr Golding believed in the often derided theory that reinsurers should operate at an underwriting profit. He also believed that the fundamental insurance principles of "utmost good faith" should apply likewise in contracts of reinsurance as between reinsured and reinsurer. Re-reading this book in an altered underwriting climate shows how much is still valid and how transitory were the hothouse improvements generated by the soft markets. One of the prime qualities of this book, in this now more honest and (hopefully) more professional reinsurance age, are the remarks scattered throughout the pages concerning the fundamental principles of Reinsurance. By way of selection, the following are noteworthy—

"The doctrine of good faith is of universal application as much to reinsurance as to direct insurance." (Chapter 2 Page No. 8)

"It may be convenient at this point to set out some observations on the true principles which underlie the operation of this function of reinsurance, for though a logical analysis makes these principles abundantly clear, in practice they are apt to become obscured, or to be so operated as to depart from what is strictly right and proper. It may be stated very definitely that the true function of reinsurance is to dispose of surplus risks, but not to dispose merely of bad risks." (Chapter 3 Page No. 19)

"Whatever may be said as to the function of reinsurance in easing the strain imposed on a direct office by the acceptance of hazardous risks, there is never any doubt in the mind of the reinsurer that the aggregate business must be made to pay. This is only as it should be, for not only could no insurer be expected to engage in business which persistently produced losses, but if it did it manifestly could not build up that position of financial security which is essential to its continuance." (Chapter 3 Page No. 20)

"It is, however, a well-established reinsurance principle that it is not wise, except in very special circumstances, to accept liability for the whole of a claim or series of claims, the settlement of which is left entirely in the hands of the ceding company. Such a condition of affairs, without any reflection whatever on the honesty of the ceding company, is likely to lead to some relaxation in the methods of claim settlements to the prejudice of the reinsurer." (Chapter 9 Page No. 196)

"In this, as in all forms of reinsurance, the gross account must provide a reasonable chance to profit for both ceding company and reinsurer, which must of necessity involve a possibility of loss from time to time equally to both parties and cannot guarantee a profit to either of them." (Chapter 9 Page No. 199)

Despite the alterations which might be needed in matters of detail, statements of the basic principles of reinsurance are still as true today as they have ever been.

In summary I have attempted to adhere to the following principles:—

(1) To preserve as much of the original text as possible, preferring to keep the original flavour of "proper practice" as between professional practitioners both in insurance and in reinsurance. Obviously, there have been certain developments (such as the growth of excess of loss reinsurance) in the last 20 years, when the last previous edition was published, which do affect the proper practice of the business. These have been incorporated in the text. Specifically the treatment of Excess of Loss forms of reinsurance has had to be extensively rewritten. Not only has the form become more widely used, but there are specialist variations in approach and practice as between liability excess of loss and property excess of loss. Thus the treatment of excess of loss is now spread over three Chapters, Nos. 7, 8 and 9. Furthermore, much Facultative reinsurance is now transacted on an excess of loss basis. However, since Chapter 4 is concerned mainly with facultative procedures equivalent changes have not been made thereto. Because of the increase in

the use of reinsurance intermediaries, reinsurance brokers and underwriting agencies, it has been felt necessary to add a specific chapter on this topic. However, certain practices and clauses, which have developed in various markets in the last couple of years, are patently of a transitory nature and have therefore been ignored. On the other hand, certain parts of the previous text have been maintained (even though subsequent developments may have rendered such prior approach out-of-date) so that reader can understand the background to the more modern treatment of a topic.

(2) To avoid an overly mathematical treatment. Although, in recent years, various statistical and actuarial approaches and techniques have benefited the business, a full explanation thereof would unnecessarily burden a text of this nature.

(3) To follow the original method of punctuation, even though the modern usage is to use far fewer punctuation marks—such as commas—than in the past.

(4) To follow the original method of the classification of the classes of insurance. Over the past twenty years descriptions of the business written have necessitated many changes in the usage in, for example, the United Kingdom as a result of the newer definitions contained in the various Insurance Companies Acts. This is mirrored by the changes in practice in insurance markets in other parts of the world whereby a greater range of perils is covered within the scope of a single insurance policy. However replacing "fire" by "property" does not change the tenor of the text.

The writing of a book is never an easy task and, in some ways, it is even more difficult for an editor. This one is very, very grateful to Peter Allen for bringing the whole project to fruition, to Peter Smith for reading an earlier draft and, above all, to Mr. R. J. Kiln for the benefit of his perceptive comments on the manuscript.

LONDON, 1987 Ken Louw

CONTENTS

Chapter 1
Origin and History

The place of reinsurance within the orbit of the great business of insurance is of considerable importance. In the main this is due to an increased demand arising out of the advance, both in volume and range, of direct business, which advance is itself a result of the development of modern conditions of social and economic life. Reinsurance, as its name implies, draws all its substance and vitality from insurance, and though the extent of its use will depend not only on the amount, but also on the character of the risks which direct insurance is called upon to assume, it is yet true to say that the volume of reinsurance business which can usefully be transacted depends in the main on the volume of direct business available at any given time. The records of this century show plainly how great has been the expansion of direct insurance business and it gives no cause for surprise that the demand for reinsurance has followed along the same lines. By an apparent natural law this has led to the creation of a greater supply of reinsurance facilities, and has raised the business to an important plane in the scheme of insurance matters. This in its turn requires a more intensive study of the nature and characteristics of reinsurance by those who are interested in the technical side of the subject and are desirous of observing all its tendencies and implications.

The purpose of this book is to set out in compendious form the law and practice of reinsurance, primarily as transacted in the United Kingdom. In this connection, however, it has to be borne in mind that reinsurance is essentially an international business, so that its practice differs somewhat according to the customs of different countries, though its fundamental principles are universal. The subject is dealt with in this book with that point of view in mind.

In investigating the origin and historical development of reinsurance, it is not possible to say with unimpeachable authority when it first began. No record which can be pointed to as beyond all question the first essay in reinsurance is available, though it is possible to assume with a fair degree of accuracy that reinsurance followed very closely after the earliest beginnings of insurance itself. As will presently appear, the idea of reinsurance is rooted in the same human instinct that brought insurance into being—the desire that the loss of one shall be shared amongst many—and just as this leads a member of the public to insure with a direct insurer, so the insurer in turn is moved to reinsure part of his risks with a reinsurer. But obscure though the origin of reinsurance may be, there is nevertheless certain information existing on the subject.

Many years ago, the author had access to a vast mass of extremely valuable and exhaustive information on the early records of reinsurance, which had been gathered together through the indefatigable energy of Mr A. Rendtorff, Chairman of Sterling Offices Ltd, and which led in due course to the publication of a work entitled "A History of Reinsurance" which was issued by that firm in 1927 in commemoration of its jubilee. Sadly the book has not only been long out of print but remains also the only work in the English language on this subject. The major part of the brief historical sketch which follows is taken, with the fullest acknowledgments, from that authoritative work, and supplemented with details of later research on the subject.

The transaction of insurance business by organisations working on the lines known at the present time, has been practised for about three hundred years, but there are records of isolated examples of insurances dating back much further for five or six hundred years. The basic idea upon which insurance rests is, of course, much older than that, and can be traced in some form or another back to the dawn of civilisation itself. It seems a reasonably safe asumption that reinsurance began to be practised soon after the beginning of insurance itself, for though the earliest underwriters—who were concerned with the early pre-company era—would not at first make a habit of accepting a greater risk than they were prepared to keep, yet in course of time they no doubt began to do so, whilst other reasons for laying off a share of an acceptance are not difficult to divine. Indeed, what is perhaps the earliest recorded example of a reinsurance—a marine case dated 1370, where on a voyage from Genoa to Sluys the underwriter reinsured that part of the voyage from Cadiz to Sluys and retained the part through the Mediterranean for his own account—was a reinsurance of the hazardous part of a risk, and this consideration probably weighed more with early underwriters than the need to reduce their insurance amounts. In looking into old records of reinsurance, care must be taken to distinguish between a reinsurance proper, i.e. a transaction which can be initiated only by an insurer, and the case of an insured insuring again because the first original insurer had gone bankrupt. This kind of a transaction is often referred to as a re-insurance though of course it is really a fresh insurance.

Much confusion of thought existed on this point, especially in the early days of marine insurance, so much so that when marine reinsurance was made illegal by an Act of 1746, an exception was made if the original insurer became insolvent or bankrupt or should die. But of course the exception could only enable a fresh insurance to be taken out by the insured, since the first insurance had become valueless. So the effect of the Act was to forbid the practice of reinsurance, using the word in its proper sense, but not to forbid insuring again in the circumstances mentioned.

It is clear from such records as are available that reinsurance was generally practised throughout the eighteenth century and had become well established by the beginning of the nineteenth century. The prohibition of marine reinsurance enacted by the Act of 1746 was not lifted until that act was repealed in 1864, but it nevertheless appears that cases of marine reinsurance were recorded in this country during the intervening period, while abroad the practice steadily developed. All these early instances of reinsurance were effected by facultative methods, as indeed was to be expected, since cover could be required only in individual cases, which could be quite properly considered by a facultative reinsurer each on its own merits and would not to be acceptable at that early stage by any other method. Facultative reinsurance was thus the earliest form of the business and for many years had the field to itself. But as the need for cover expanded, following the growth of direct insurance, it became necessary to devise some other method of reinsurance, giving to the original insurer some greater certainty as to the facilities for reinsurance which could be obtained. This was found in the treaty method of reinsurance, which, as will appear on a later page, is a means whereby a direct insurer can be secure from its reinsurer an obligatory cover, thereby enabling it to write its business on a wide basis and on a surer footing. The great growth of insurance companies and the tremendous expansion of their business made some such device a necessity, so that in modern reinsurance practice the treaty has, to a great extent, supplanted the older facultative method.

Yet even so the treaty is not a purely modern instrument of reinsurance, and it may be a little surprising to the student of the subject to discover that the first known reinsurance treaty of which we have the terms was concluded more than one hundred and fifty years ago—to be exact in 1821. This was made between the Compagnie Royale in France and the Compagnie des Proprietaires Reunis of Brussels and dated the 15th December 1821. The first treaty arrangement made by a British office was begun only three years later—in 1824—between the Imperial of London (now part of the Sun Alliance Group) and La Nationale of Paris. The treaty was made by an exchange of letters; from the minutes of the board of La Nationale this was considered as sufficient, "the good faith of the London company not permitting the anticipation of any infringement on its part of the agreement concluded between the two companies." It was however on the Continent of Europe that the reinsurance treaty was primarily developed and studied. It was likewise on the Continent that the first independent, specialist reinsurance companies were established. Thus, the first subsidiary reinsurance company was established in Germany in 1843, while the oldest reinsurance company still existing, the Cologne Reinsurance Company, was founded in 1846. The Swiss Reinsurance Company was organised in 1863 by three insurance and banking interests; the Allgemeine Versicherungs Gesellschaft Helvetia of St. Gallen, the Schweizer Kreditanstalt of Zurich and the Basler Handelsbank of Basle. The Munich Reinsurance Company was established in 1880. In the history of its reinsurance offices the United Kingdom presents a point of particular interest. Attempts were made to form such offices in England at a date not much later than the time at which the earliest companies in central Europe were formed, and, though some of these lasted for a time, and transacted a certain amount of business, not one of them was destined to survive. The major reason arose from the customary practice of the English direct insurance offices to place their reinsurance contracts with each other. This was directly linked to the attempts by certain offices to maintain agreement on minimum premium ratings and the avoidance of rate cutting. Thus in 1833 the Association of Managers of Fire Offices, established in Edinburgh, compelled the Caledonian Insurance Company to withdraw an offer of reinsurance to the National Insurance Company because the National shared profits with policyholders. Another company, the Western of Aberdeen was compelled to reduce its commission rates by the same methods. These rules were maintained by the successor organisation, the Fire Offices' Committee. This approach indirectly involved Lloyd's of London in the reinsurance business, where previously it had been purely a marine insurance market. In 1885 the underwriter, C. E. Heath, accepted a share of the reinsurances of the Hand-in-Hand Insurance Company which, being a non-tariff office, was precluded from reinsuring with the tariff companies.

These early treaty reinsurances were on a proportional basis and the form thereof was established at an early date, thus Cornelius Walford's Insurance Cyclopaedia, published in 1878, states that:—

"The principles which govern the business of fire reinsurance in France are much the same as prevail in England. They are usually embodied in the treaties between the parties to a contract, and are as follows;

(1) The reinsurance premiums shall be exactly the same as those of the direct policy.
(2) The direct company shall retain on the risk insured a sum equal to that given to the reinsurance company.
(3) The accounts to be settled every 3 or 6 months, as may be agreed.
(4) The losses below 2,000 or 3,000fr. are generally included in accounts, i.e. they are not claimed immediately, but are treated as a deduction from the current premium account.
(5) The larger losses are to be paid by the reinsurance company as soon as the direct company has paid.
(6) All differences to be adjudicated upon by arbitrators, and not by the Common Law Courts.

The mode of conducting the business now is that the risks offered are entered in a book (carnet), and the signature by the agent of the reinsurance company denotes acceptance of the risk.

The commission paid by the reinsurance companies is usually 25%."

However although the forms of reinsurance were established at an early date, so too were various forms of malpractice. Thus, for the year 1877, the Moskau Insurance Company reported that on a gross premium of 2,975,000 roubles 74.15% had been reinsured. The reinsurance commission received of 377,000 roubles exceeded the total original commission paid by 130,000 roubles. This led the Insurance Times of November 1878 to comment that, "This is a general practice now by all Russian companies, and shows how they can procure a net profit while all the other companies, chiefly English, transacting business with them suffer heavy losses on the same business. The greater part of the Continental companies who became familiar with this practice have declined to transact further business with Russian companies, and it would be a very good thing if the English companies would take the same course."

Throughout the nineteenth century the use of the treaty developed steadily, though not so as to supplant all at once the facultative method, for even as late as 1900 many offices conducted a great part of their reinsurance by that method, especially in fire and accident business. But the advantages of the treaty became increasingly apparent—and the more so by reason of the tremendous growth of insurance business which came in the twentieth century and which rendered the facultative method more and more inadequate for its purpose. The invention of the excess of loss basis of reinsurance gave an added impetus to the use of the treaty method of reinsurance. It is commonly accepted that excess of loss reinsurance was developed at

Lloyd's by C. E. Heath in the 1890s. But its use became widespread only from about 1906, after the San Francisco Earthquake, when insurance companies began to see the need for a catastrophe protection against an accumulation of losses due to a major fire, etc. C. E. Heath's first treaty was written as a reinsurance of the Hartford Fire of Connecticut. So today the treaty has come into universal use as the main implement of reinsurance used in all classes of business and in all countries of the world.

Thus the technique of reinsurance has developed throughout the past two centuries or so from the early individual cases occurring only at rare intervals, to the elaborate system which modern practice has brought into being. In this way reinsurance has played its due part in the evolution of insurance business and has indeed done much to make possible the crucially important role which that business now fulfills in the commercial and industrial life of the world.

Chapter 2
The Law of Reinsurance

A reinsurance transaction is an agreement made between two parties, called the reinsured (or ceding company, a term also often used—especially in relation to reinsurances on a proportional basis) and reinsurer, respectively, whereby the reinsurer agrees to accept a certain fixed share of the reinsured's risk upon terms as set out in the agreement. Such an agreement is a contract and the law of reinsurance is based primarily on the law of contract. Nevertheless it has certain special features inherent in the matter by reason of the nature of the business and its connection with insurance.

The contract itself may relate to one particular reinsurance and be expressed in a reinsurance policy—or, as was often called in fire insurance, a guarantee policy but nowadays is more commonly referred to as facultative reinsurance; or it may provide for the reinsurance of a number of risks and be expressed in the form of a treaty. In either case the reinsurance derives its force from the terms of the contract and is subject to all its provisions and limitations.

The parties to the reinsurance contract are the "reinsured" (or "ceding company")—that is the original insurer who, having issued a policy to an insured to cover a certain risk, desires to relieve itself of a part thereof—and the "reinsurer"—that is the company who accepts that part of the risk which is reinsured. This gives the clue to the real nature of a reinsurance. It cannot exist without there first being a direct insurance, for the first party is the reinsured who has already issued a direct policy. Yet the insured under that direct policy has no interest in or right over the reinsurance. It has no privity of contract in the transaction and can make no claim thereunder. The reinsurer is certainly liable in respect of its share of any claim made by the insured, but its liability is to the insurer and to the insurer only, for the insurer alone is the other party to the contract. The insured may have an interest indirectly in knowing that its insurer is supported by sound reinsurers, since that goes to improve its security, but it has not and cannot have any direct interest in the reinsurance contract.

The consideration for the contract is the reinsurance premium paid by the reinsured to the reinsurer, which may be a share of the original premium subject to deductions such as for commission or otherwise as may be agreed at the time the contract was made. The wording embodying the terms of the agreement under the contract is signed by the party to be charged. In the case of a facultative reinsurance a policy would be issued and signed by the reinsurer. A treaty wording, which contains reciprocal undertakings, it signed by or on behalf of each party thereto. The practice which had developed over the past 20 years in parts of the London reinsurance market (and elsewhere) whereby the only evidence of a contract is either a signed "slip" or a broker's "Cover Note" has given rise to a number of legal cases which have not only reflected adversely upon the reinsurance profession, but also created some important precedents as to the correct legal practice.

It is well known that insurance business is transacted upon certain principles which are inherent in it and are grounded in ancient usage arising from the needs of public policy. These inherent principles apply in like manner to reinsurance and for the same reasons. These principles are:—

(1) There must be insurable interest.
(2) The contract is one of the utmost good faith (uberrimae fidei).
(3) The reinsurance contract is one of indemnity (though this many not necessarily apply to the original insurance contract).
(4) The subject matter of the contract must be in existence at the time the contract is made.

Insurable interest is vested in the reinsured and the fact that it has issued a policy and accepted liability to its original insured has been held to give it an insurable interest sufficient to enable it to reinsure (vide Lower Rhine & Wurttemburg Insurance Association v Sedgwick, 1899). The point is that although the reinsured has no actual legal interest in the property which is the subject matter of the original insurance, it has assumed responsibility in regard to it, and has therefore put itself into a position, recognised by law, in which it would be prejudiced by its loss. Hence its insurable interest must be circumscribed by the nature and scope of the liability which it has assumed, so that a company which has undertaken to insure property against (say) fire, would not thereby acquire an insurable interest which would enable it to reinsure against loss by burglary, for that is a loss by which it would not be prejudiced.

The doctrine of good faith is of universal application as much to reinsurance as to direct insurance. It calls for the disclosure by the reinsured to the reinsurer of every material fact relating to the risk to be reinsured. In the reinsurance transaction the reinsured is in the same position vis-a-vis its reinsurer, as its original insured was towards itself in the negotiations leading up to the issue of the original policy. Nevertheless, the duty of disclosure in reinsurance business is qualified by one important fact, that it is transacted between parties who are equally experts in their business. This will sometimes relax to a minor degree the duty imposed upon the reinsured, as for example, where the facts are such as the intending reinsurers ought to know, or which the reinsured is fully entitled to assume that they already know. Subject to this qualification and provided that even this is fully justified by the circumstances, the duty of good faith is no less important in reinsurance than in insurance. A fundamental rule of reinsurance is expressed as follows:—

The foundation of a reinsurance is—

(1) Full information, so far as possessed by the reinsured, as to the risk on which the reinsurance is requested.
(2) Full information as to the amount retained by the reinsured on the identical property on which the reinsurance is requested.

In recent years the increasing complexity of the business of reinsurance has focussed a greater degree of attention on the problems of disclosure and materiality. For many years the test of materiality was based upon the concept of the "prudent underwriter". The words of Kerr J in the case of Berger & Light Diffusers Pty Ltd v Pollock, 1973 may be regarded as a summary of this approach, "It seems to me, as a matter of principle, that the Court's task in deciding whether or not the defendant insurer can avoid the policy for non-disclosure must be to determine as a question of fact whether by applying the standard of the judgment of a prudent insurer, the insurer in question would have been influenced in fixing the premium or determining whether to take the risk if he had been informed of the undisclosed circumstances before entering into the contract. The effect of the non-disclosure may be so clear that the Court will require no evidence, or only little evidence, to decide in favour of the insurer. In doubtful cases, on the other hand, the Court may require evidence from the insurers themselves before being able to hold that the right to avoid the policy has been established. In my view, the underwriter concerned should have been called in the present case, and this should be the practice in all doubtful cases even if an independent underwriter or broker is called as well." This approach was followed in the case of Container Transport International Inc. v Oceanus Mutual Underwriting Association (Bermuda) Ltd, 1982 where Lloyd J introduced the term "some difference of action" to indicate what was required in order to establish materiality. What needed to be proved was not whether the non-disclosure would have influenced the prudent underwriter to act otherwise but simply if the judgment to accept or reject the insurance proposal was affected. On appeal this approach was overturned in Container Transport International Inc. v Oceanus Mutual Underwriting Association (Bermuda) Ltd, 1984 where all three judges agreed that a disclosure is material if it would have an impact on the formation of the insurer's opinion and on his decision-making process, and if it is proved then it is not necessary to prove that the mind of the insurer was so affected. Hence only the underwriting judgment or the assessment or the evaluation of the risk need be influenced and not the actual terms conditions or premiums or final decision. Thus, now, under English law an insurer is entitled to avoid a contract if there was undisclosed before the contract any circumstance which a prudent insurer would take into account when reaching his decision whether or not to accept that risk or what premium to charge; the yardstick is the prudent insurer and not the particular insurer. This latter judgment has recently been followed in the case of Highlands Insurance Company v Continental Insurance Company where the judge confirmed that a judgment applying to a case involving marine insurance applies equally to non-marine business.

Questions of materiality and disclosure involve both parties to the contract. The obligations of the insured (or reinsured) were listed in Anglo-African Merchants Ltd v Bagley, 1969 where it was decided that the defence of non-disclosure prevailed if:—

(1) the insured knew of the facts
(2) if as a reasonable man he should have realised that knowledge of those facts might be regarded as material by a prudent underwriter
(3) if those facts were not disclosed and
(4) if they would have been material; and a fortiori if the insured actually did realize that the facts of which he had knowledge might be regarded as material.

However it does seem that this duty was extended by Stephenson LJ in the case mentioned above of Container Transport International Inc. v Oceanus Mutual Underwriting Association (Bermuda) Ltd, 1984 where he stated that "Accordingly it is for the insured to give the underwriter the material; it is not for the underwriter to ask for it. It is not 'of itself a good answer to say "if it was material why did you did you not ask?" ' said Lord Justice Goddard in the Zurich case (1942). This is not a branch of insurance where the insurer shows what he regards as material by submitting questions in a proposal form to the insured."

Yet it will be obvious that the rule as to good faith can be applied strictly in the foregoing manner, only when every risk to be reinsured is dealt with separately, that is, by the facultative method. The growth of the treaty can give rise to a change in the application of the doctrine. A treaty is a contract, which by itself may give effect to no particular reinsurance, but which can provide a method whereby any number of risks may be reinsured at any time during the currency of the contract. Under this method it may not be possible for the reinsured to give full information as to the nature of the risk to be reinsured or its own retention, in respect of every cession to be made under a treaty. To have to do this would go a long way to defeat the objects for which this method of reinsurance was devised. Nevertheless, the duty of good faith still remains. It is incumbent upon the reinsured to make a full disclosure of all the material facts in the negotiations leading up to the completion of the contract. The information which should be put before an intending reinsurer who is contemplating entering into a reinsurance treaty is more fully dealt with in subsequent chapters. It suffices here to say that any failure to disclose such material facts would be sufficient ground to enable the reinsurer to avoid the contract.

The ordinary rule as to disclosure of material facts operates only up to the time the contract is concluded, but it may be submitted that under a treaty something more may be required. The mere completion of the contract is but the beginning, not the end of the reinsurance operations which are contemplated thereunder. Every time a cession is made under a treaty this initiates an actual reinsurance, and though the details which have to be communicated to the reinsurer may be limited, yet in the general operation of the treaty the reinsured is bound to exercise the utmost good faith towards its reinsurer, even though this must occur after the contract was concluded. In modern treaty practice this continuing duty of disclosure is normally expressly stated within the terms and conditions of the formal treaty wording.

The principle of indemnity is an integral part of the reinsurance contract and this will be so even though the original contract may not have been a pure indemnity. Thus a personal accident reinsurance is designed to indemnify the reinsured in respect of an amount it has been called upon to pay to its insured, although that payment was itself made not by way of an indemnity. There is nothing in this principle, however, which gives any right to an indemnity to any party other than the reinsured and it confers no rights on the original insured. A reinsurance operates to make good to a reinsured a share of an amount which it has paid or become liable to pay. This distinction is not ordinarily of much moment, since a liability to pay is generally followed by a payment, but the fact that the reinsured has not actually made payment to its insured would not enable a reinsurer to withhold its share. Nevertheless, the reinsurer is entitled to proof of loss and in case of dispute the reinsured must show that the loss has actually occurred and that it is one which rightly falls under the terms of the reinsurance contract (St. Paul Fire & Marine Company v Morice, 1906).

Nevertheless, there are occasions when the distinction between an actual payment and a corrresponding liability to pay may be of the utmost importance. It is a fundamental principle of reinsurance that the reinsurer is only liable for a share of loss for which the reinsured is also liable. This principle was affirmed in the case of Merchants Marine Insurance Company v Liverpool Marine & General Insurance Company (1928). In that case the reinsured had paid a claim for which it was not liable under its policy, and although the reinsurance policy issued by the defendants contained the clause "to pay as may be paid thereon," it was held that they were not liable. Those words must be constructed as meaning "to pay as may be liable to pay thereon." The indemnity which the reinsurer provides does not go beyond the range of the original insurance. Thus a reinsurer is not liable for a share of any costs incurred without its consent in defending a claim, even though the claim was one for which it would bave been liable if it had been well founded. This was laid down in Scottish Metropolitan Insurance Company v Groom (1924) on the ground that there was nothing in the reinsurance contract to make the reinsurer liable to contribute to the costs.

It should be emphasised that these conditions arise out of the strict application of the principle of indemnity as it exists at common law. They may be, and frequently are, overridden by express or implied conditions in the reinsurance contract. The cases quoted refer to marine facultative reinsurances in which no special terms were incorporated in the reinsurance policies. It is possible for a clause to be added giving the reinsured the right to settle or compromise all losses at its sole discretion and without interference from the reinsurer, or to contest or defend a claim and to hold the reinsurer liable for a claim for its proportionate share of any costs incurred in connection therewith. In that event the reinsurer would be liable for a claim even though it were settled ex gratia and without strict liability, and likewise for its share of any costs incurred in contesting a claim. So far as treaty reinsurances are concerned, a clause setting out an agreed procedure apportioning claims and expenses is almost always included in the contract wording. In facultative business the practice is not so common, but in fire facultative reinsurance, such provisions are contained in the rules of the Fire Offices' Committee and since all guarantee transactions between members of that body are specifically declared to be subject to those rules, those provisions are by implication imported in the reinsurance contract. In recent years the Reinsurance Underwriting Group, an association of reinsurers in the London Market, has developed a set of rules designed to govern the operation of facultative reinsurances placed with its members.

The distinction between a payment and a liability to pay is of importance also in cases where the reinsured may go into liquidation. In such case, once the insolvent company's liability to pay a claim has been established, the reinsurer is liable to pay its full share of such ascertained liability, even though in fact the reinsured may only pay a small dividend in respect of its liability to its creditors. (Law Guarantee & Accident Society v Munich Reinsurance Company, 1912). Payments made by a reinsurer in such an event do not go to the claimant on the risk which was reinsured, since there is no contract between claimant and reinsurer—but fall into the general assets of the reinsured in liquidation.

The subject matter of the reinsurance contract is in effect the reinsured's liability in the original insurance, and since that liability depends on the existence of the subject matter of the insurance, it follows that the validity of the reinsurance is equally dependent thereon. This is obvious, since if there is in existence no property answering the description set out in the original policy, the policy does not attach and any reinsurance made in respect thereof falls to the ground.

It may be convenient to devote a few words here to two points which affect the general law governing the transaction of reinsurance business. The first point relates to the question as to who may transact reinsurance business in this country; the second relates to the legal consequences following therefrom.

Since the 19th century the objective of the legislature in this country has been to seek to prevent insurance companies from running into difficulty by setting up a combination of authorisation, solvency and reporting requirements. For many years the practice of insurance business in this country was governed by the Assurance Companies Act, 1909, under which all those engaged in the business were required, inter alia, to make certain deposits with the High Court and to render accounts annually in a prescribed form. The Act was drafted to apply to certain specified classes of insurance only, and no mention was anywhere made of reinsurance. For this reason it was for a long time thought that companies which solely transacted reinsurance business were not subject to the provisions of the Act. This applied not only to the few British companies which carried on only reinsurance business, but to the much larger number of foreign companies which, though writing direct business in their own countries, confined their operations in this country to reinsurance. It was felt that the main purpose of the 1909 Act was to do something to protect the insuring public against loss due to unsound trading on the part of insurance companies, and as reinsurance transactions were carried on only between companies well acquainted with one another, no protection in this particular form was called for.

Nevertheless, in course of time the point was brought to the test and in 1925 in the National of Copenhagen case (Attorney General v Forsikrings Aktieselskabet National) it was decided that for the purposes of the legislation the term "insurance" included "reinsurance". However this case involved mainly the question whether, like direct insurers, reinsurers needed to lodge deposits with the High Court in order to transact business. Many of the other requirements of the legislation governing companies transacting insurance business in this country were not enforced against companies which transacted reinsurance business only.

In 1946 the legislation governing insurance companies underwent a profound change in moving from a system of attempting to guarantee the solvency of insurers (and reinsurers) by the making of deposits to a system of calculating solvency margins. In essence, this means that insurers need to comply with a stipulated legal minimum percentage of net worth to written premium (net of reinsurance ceded). Of course the commercially acceptable level of solvency would be very much higher than this legal minimum. A series of problems in the British insurance industry throughout the 1960s and 1970s led to a number of revisions in the legislation. In addition the accession of Great Britain to the European Economic Community brought about the implementation of the Second Directive on Insurance. Nevertheless, during this period certain differences still remained in the treatment in law as between companies writing insurance business and those solely writing reinsurance. Eventually the Insurance Companies Act, 1981, in the course of a general revision of the legislation governing the regulation of the insurance companies, removed most of the anomalies involving companies writing solely reinsurance business. The current legislation is embodied in the Insurance Companies Act, 1982, which is, essentially, a consolidating measure. Thus purely reinsurance companies transacting business in this country need to comply with the requirements relating to authorisation, categories of acceptable investment, reporting and maintenance of adequate solvency margins, etc.

This aspect of authorisation raises the other point. A company intending to undertake the business of insurance or reinsurance in this country must receive the necessary authorisation from the relevant supervisory body, The Department of Trade & Industry. This requirement applies equally to a company already authorised to write certain classes of business but which wishes to extend its activities to one or more further classes. The legal consequences of a company transacting business for which it is *not* authorised have recently been considered in a series of legal judgments which have important consequences for the business of reinsurance. Because of the important differences of legal interpretation which these judgments have exhibited, it is necessary to devote some attention to these cases. In The Bedford Insurance Company Ltd v IRB and Others, 1984, it was held that an insurer which carried on insurance business without the appropriate authorisation could not recover under reinsurances of that business. The judge held that the transacting of insurances without an authorisation was an illegal act and that since the principle is well settled that if a plaintiff requires any aid from an illegal transaction to establish its cause of action, then it shall not have any aid from the Court. In a subsequent case, Stewart v Oriental Fire & Marine Insurance Co. Ltd, 1984, it was held that a Lloyd's underwriter who was carrying on business lawfully, could recover from a reinsurer who was not authorised. This reasoning followed the principle that innocent parties should not suffer. These cases were closely followed by that of the Phoenix-General Insurance Company of Greece SA v Halvanon Insurance Company Ltd, 1985. The conflict arose from the Phoenix-General having underwritten aviation contingency business in London for a number of years and effecting reinsurance thereon. Under the terms of the Insurance Companies Act, 1974, the general definition of the different classes of insurance business meant that the company was authorised to write business of this nature. In 1977, regulations were made in accordance with the EEC harmonisation of laws whereby the categorisation of the different types of insurance business was altered. Under the transitional provisions allowed for, the existing authorisations were transferred to the new categories. However the new categories did not correspond exactly with certain aspects of the definition of "aviation contingency". There was a new category within which this class of business could have been included but the company was not authorised therefor. It was held that after the 1st January 1978 (when the revised regulations became operative) the Company was not authorised to write the business so reinsured. Although the reinsured had no deliberate intent, their conduct was nonetheless illegal. Thus the plaintiffs, in respect of that part of the business for which they had no authorisation, could not enforce the reinsurance contract. This latter, however, was overturned in the Court of Appeal in the related case of Phoenix-General Insurance Company of Greece SA v ADAS, 1986 where it was decided that the Transitional Provisions of the regulations under the 1977 Act did in fact allow for such authorisation. The Appeal Court, in addition, found that the decision in the Stewart case was untenable. Thus, under English law, an insurance or reinsurance contract made without authority is void and unenforceable, as is any subsequent contract of reinsurance.

For a long period legislators, in many parts of the world, avoided the problems arising from the writing of policies of insurance across State boundaries, both as to the rights of the buyers of such insurances and the enforceability of contracts against the issuers thereof. Reinsurance, being by its very nature not comprehensible to the generality of commerical life and international in scope, has therefore tended to escape the legislators' attention—other than as a possible source of revenue. The experience of recent years could show that the legal problems are of considerably greater importance.

Chapter 3
The Practice of Reinsurance

A description of the practice of reinsurance requires at the outset some explanation of the exact nature of the business and how it functions. Reinsurance is a method whereby an original insurer distributes its risks by giving off the whole or some portion thereof to another insurer, with the object of reducing the amount of its possible loss. As previously mentioned, the need which an insurer feels for reinsurance cover is strictly analogous with that which animates a member of the public to obtain the protection of direct insurance. An insurer who has made himself responsible for a large sum on one particular risk, does not think it safe to keep that liability for his own account. He looks about for a way of sharing that risk with someone else, so that in the event of a loss he shall not suffer too great a burden. This, although differing in degree, is the same in kind as a private person does who is not content to run the hazard of losing his property by a fire, for example, and who therefore by insuring throws a part of the burden on to someone else, i.e., the insurer. It is true that the private person rids himself of most of the burden, since his own share is represented by the comparatively small premium which he has to pay, whereas the insurer who in turn reinsures, is generally prepared to keep a substantial part of his liability. That is, however, part of his business, which consists of the acceptance of a large number of risks and averaging one against another. He is chiefly concerned with the size of his risks and to make sure that no one risk which remains at his own charge is too great in relation to the whole range of his business. The principle is the same, whether the purpose be to reduce the hazard in respect of a single risk, as in the case of a sharing reinsurance, or to limit the possibility of loss over a whole range of liabilities, as in the case of excess of loss reinsurance.

These reflections on the subject show clearly that the structure of reinsurance has to be regarded from two points of view, that of the reinsured and that of the reinsurer. Each of these plays a part in the making of the reinsurance transaction, but each approaches it from an opposite point of view. It is possible to arrive at a just appraisal of the nature and function of reinsurance only by examining these two points of view, noting their essential differences and observing how they are reconciled so as to produce harmony in the completed transaction.

The point of view of the reinsured from whom the reinsurance originates may logically be considered first. His purpose is to secure cover for a part of his risks and his primary outlook is directed to that side of the transaction. This raises the question of how and when to reinsure and introduces the broad issue of retentions. The fixing of retentions is an important part of the reinsured's side of reinsurance. This is not to say that it is not also of importance to the reinsurer, since the retention will very largely govern the quality of the reinsurance business. It is not practicable to lay down hard and fast rules to govern the manner of fixing retentions, though certain broad principles emerge. The retention is fixed in the first place with due regard to the amount which the reinsured can afford to lose by the happening of the insured event in regard to the particular risk insured. There is room for variation in opinion in fixing that amount, for it depends not only on the sum insured, but also on the likelihood of the loss being total or partial, a factor in the calculation which cannot be judged with exact precision. But experience acts as a guide in this matter and there is a law of probabilities which can be relied upon to some extent. Secondly, the amount of such probable loss may be assumed to vary according to the nature of the risk, so that the more hazardous classes of risk will produce losses greater in number and more costly in amount than the less hazardous. The proper classification of risks is an essential feature in the construction of a system of retentions. This has become an important feature in modern reinsurance, and one upon which the operation of the reinsurances largely depends. It can be described as "exposure to risk" or "estimated maximum loss" or "maximum probable loss," generally reckoned as a percentage of the total sum insured. If this percentage is accurately assessed, it may enable the nominal retention to be fixed at a figure much above what the reinsured is prepared to lose. Thirdly, the amount of probable loss which the reinsured fixes as suitable to retain for its own account must bear some reasonable proportion to its financial position, as reflected in its premium income and in its capital or other reserve funds. These are the broad principles upon which a table of retentions will be drawn and the quality of the reinsurance which emerges therefrom will depend upon the skill with which the various factors have been assessed. The function of reinsurance is to absorb those surplus amounts on each risk accepted by the reinsured which go beyond what it can safely retain for its own account.

The extension of large risks which is a feature of modern industrial life, has added greatly to the importance of the estimated maximum loss in the implementation of reinsurance affairs, an importance no less vital in sharing treaties than in excess of loss contracts. It is equally important to the reinsured in fixing its retention, and to the reinsurer in deciding what proportion of a reinsurance it will accept. It must be remembered however, that this estimated maximum loss is not capable of exact appraisal; it can be computed only approximately in the light of as full knowledge of the risk as may be available, and judged by experience of other similar risks. Even so the judgment may prove to be wrong. Thus, in recent years, in relation to insurances covering fire and associated property risks, many old ideas have gone by the board. The point has to be allowed for in reinsurance practice and some safeguards have been introduced in an attempt to counteract it, as will appear in a later chapter.

It may be convenient at this point to set out some observations on the true principles which underlie the operation of this function of reinsurance, for though a logical analysis makes these principles abundantly clear, in practice they are apt to become obscured, or to be so operated as to depart from what is strictly right and proper. It may be stated very definitely that the true function of reinsurance is to dispose of surplus risks, but not to dispose merely of bad risks. It is obvious that the general character of an aggregate portfolio of reinsurance risks will be of a less favourable nature than that of a portfolio of retained direct business. This is a natural and proper thing, since a reinsured is entitled to retain the whole of the small non-hazardous risks, a large proportion of the more non-hazardous risks, but a smaller share of the more hazardous risks. Yet it is important that the function of reinsurance should not be understood as providing a means whereby a very small proportion of good risks and a very large proportion of bad risks may be properly ceded. To do this is to destroy the balance of the business, to interfere with the operation of the law of average and to ensure with tolerable certainty that the business will produce a loss to the reinsurers. It needs no great discernment to see that such a state of affairs could not continue very long, and this shows clearly enough that the purpose of reinsurance is not to enable a reinsured to unload on to a reinsurer business too heavy to retain for itself. Its real and true purpose is to assist the reinsured to maintain its net account on a well-balanced footing, to prevent the results showing very favourably in one year, but perhaps very unfavourably in the next. Wide fluctuations in the original experience are inevitable at times and by the wise use of reinsurance, what have been described as the "high peaks" in the curve of the loss experience, are smoothed out and an atmosphere of stability is imparted to the net figures which increases the confidence of the insuring public in the office which produces them. It follows from this that a reinsured must be prepared to give away a certain part of its profits to its reinsurers, to surrender its surplus profits in good years, so as to be able to recover heavy losses in bad years. But, even over a period of years, on balance it must be prepared to forego a profit which it might have kept for itself, this being the reward which the reinsurer must earn in return for the liabilities it has assumed, and to enable it to continue in business and be able to meet its obligations when called upon to do so. All this is elementary, yet it is in danger of being lost sight of in the practical application of reinsurance by the reinsured, if only for the reason that this aspect of the business is so frequently concerned with the placing of the heavier risks. The key to the successful conduct of reinsurance seems to lie in the manner in which the reinsured operates its gross account. In that case if the reinsurers over a period of years incur a loss, this can only mean that the reinsured is securing an undue share of the profit. This in turn can only mean that the reinsurance operations are being improperly or unfairly manipulated. It may mean that only very small shares of good business are being ceded, or that substantial acceptances of hazardous business are being made and large proportions unloaded on to the reinsurers. This is the negation of sound reinsurance practice and must end by defeating its own object, since the results of the business must in time become so unfavourable that no reinsurer will be willing to accept it. By the avoidance of these errors, by the writing of gross acceptances and fixing retentions with a careful regard for the interests of its reinsurers as well of itself, the reinsured will contrariwise reap its due reward in that its treaties will be consistently good, will be in keen demand and will be able to command the most favourable terms. Thus it will be seen that the point of view of the reinsured, who must approach the subject of reinsurance for the purpose of determining how best to secure cover for its surplus risks, goes in its incidence somewhat beyond that simple thesis and involves the consideration of many different aspects and the careful weighing of various factors if it is to achieve the end in view.

It falls next to consider the point of view of the reinsurer, whose business it is to accept the risks which the reinsured has to reinsure. This is in many ways the converse of the point of view of the reinsured. The reinsurer is primarily concerned with accepting the risks reinsured in such a manner as will enable it to make a reasonable profit out of its business. Whatever may be said as to the function of reinsurance in easing the strain imposed on a direct office by the acceptance of hazardous risks, there is never any doubt in the mind of the reinsurer that the aggregate business must be made to pay. This is only as it should be, for not only could no reinsurer be expected to engage in business which persistently produced losses, but if it did it manifestly could not build up that position of financial security which is essential to its continuance. In its approach to the business therefore, the reinsurer has to keep certain broad principles in view and here it is necessary to bear in mind the distinction between facultative and treaty reinsurance. That distinction is fully dealt with in a later part of this book, and it is sufficient here to note that facultative reinsurance gives a very great measure of control to a reinsurer over the quality of its risks, which is not available under the treaty method. This being so, it is to the latter method that the following remarks mainly apply and these import a consideration of the methods of transacting reinsurance business according to present-day practice. The broad principles may be summarised as follows:—

(1) The characteristics of the type of insurance involved.
(2) The methods of the reinsured.
(3) The distribution of the business geographically.

The type of insurance

In constructing its portfolio of business the reinsurer must pay particular regard to the type of reinsurance it accepts. This can, of course, be looked at only by classes, since the treaty being an obligatory contract does not permit any discrimination of risks. In theory a reinsurer is more likely to secure stability in its business by accepting treaties in every class of insurance. The purpose of this is to assist the operation of the principle of average. It may be taken for granted that by reason of the less favourable selection of risk which falls to the reinsurer's lot, the margin of profit must in the ordinary way be lower on reinsurance business than on direct business. Further, the function of reinsurance is to take care of the extraordinary losses and a greater variation in the experience must be looked for, with sometimes a period of unfavourable results to eat into the profits of the good years. It follows that the reinsurer must do everything it can to minimise the effect of this factor on its business. This gives the clue to the wide distribution of its business which is the aim of every prudent reinsurer. One method of distribution is by classes of insurance. The experience in various classes of insurance is not always the same and there is always a chance that when one class is bad another will be good and so help to ease the strain. Nevertheless, though this theory is sound, the reinsurer's attitude towards its type of business must depend on the circumstances of the time and there may be times when the need for wide distribution of business may be overidden by the conditions under which some particular kind of reinsurance may be transacted at any given moment. A good example of this is provided by the unfavourable phase through which the whole of the reinsurance business has recently been passing, and which has been sufficiently serious to cause many reinsurers either to retire altogether from the marketplace or to withdraw from reinsuring particular classes of insurance, or at least severely to limit their acceptances, even though by so doing they have had perforce to narrow the scope of their operations. Such passing phases, however, do not affect the justice of the theory, indeed on occasions they may confirm it. However the operation may need to be qualified by the conditions of the moment.

In any event every class of reinsurance business must be dealt with according to its merits, bearing in mind the primary need of the reinsurer to earn a profit over the whole range of the business and over a reasonable period of time. It will appear, when the nature of a reinsurance treaty is considered, that the reinsurer who has once accepted a treaty has no control over the quality of the business being reinsured, nor where it comes from, nor its magnitude, except to the limited extent as may be laid down in the contract. The effect of the treaty method is to bring into prominence the second broad consideration enumerated above, viz., the methods of the reinsured.

Methods of the reinsured

When it is remembered that a reinsurer is bound to accept all business which may be reinsured to it under a treaty and has no power to criticise any risk, or to regulate the amount it will accept, it is obvious that the underwriting policy and general methods of the reinsured are of the utmost importance. A reinsurer will, of course, acquaint itself as far as possible with these matters before undertaking a treaty and this must be largely a matter of acquiring a general knowledge of the companies with which it is desired to do business. Certain factors can, however, be enumerated as furnishing some sort of guide in the matter:—

(1) The standing and reputation of the reinsured.
(2) The experience and quality of its management.
(3) The general underwriting policy of the company whether of the cautious type or whether with a broader outlook.
(4) The company's limits of retention and their relationship to the total premium income.
(5) The different areas from which the business is derived. The effect of this will be more fully dealt with under the succeeding heading.

These points will bear some examination for the light they throw upon this side of the reinsurer's business.

It is perhaps self-evident that where the reinsured is of high standing and with a great reputation, this is to be regarded as an extremely favourable point to a would-be reinsurer. Such a company will have high traditions and usually a long history behind it. It will have settled and established practices based on long experience, having stood the test of time and likely to have placed its business on a stable footing. Such a company is generally under the control of a sound and experienced management, composed of men who, though alive to the needs of modern times, are yet imbued with the fundamental principles of the business. The importance of such points as these to a reinsurer has been accentuated by modern methods of handling reinsurance business. These methods, in order to facilitate the smooth working of the business, tend to concentrate the control more and more in the hands of the reinsured, making the reinsurer correspondingly the more dependent, not only on the good faith of that company, but also upon its skill and aptitude for carrying on its business. It will be seen at a later stage how great are the powers of the reinsured under the modern form of treaty. Reinsurers in their own interest are bound to attach great importance to the manner in which those powers are likely to be exercised, whether with a continual regard for the reinsurer's interests, and whether with a just appreciation of the real functions of reinsurance business. It may be said here that reinsureds who fail in any of these particulars, do so in the great majority of cases from lack of foresight or expertise rather than lack of good faith, and this goes to underline the need for the reinsurer to be satisfied on these matters. These are of general import, while underwriting methods including the fixing of limits are of more specific import. Most companies have their own ideas as to methods of underwriting and it is outside the argument to judge as to the merits of each. Such methods are largely to be judged by past results, though this is not to be regarded as the perfect guide, since the future does not always reproduce the past. Yet a reinsured which is known to adopt very careful methods of underwriting, may be expected to produce reinsurance results, which, though possibly small in volume, will be of the best quality and not varying much from the normal. Such treaties are among the most attractive from a reinsurer's point of view. Where the underwriting methods are broader in character, consideration must be given to a number of different points. Retentions beome important, especially in the relation between the hazardous and non-hazardous risks. The extent to which other risks, apart from the main business, are accepted is also a vital point. Thus fire treaties for example may have considerable exposure to perils of nature such as storm, earthquake and hurricane. Under marine treaties a certain amount of "incidental non-marine business" may be included. The volume and nature of these risks and the extent to which they are concentrated in areas where the hazard is a predominant one, are factors in judging the effect of the underwriting.

Geographical distribution

The distribution of its business geographically is the second way open to a reinsurer to secure the greatest benefit from the law of average, so that in addition to writing its business as widely as possible by classes, it will endeavour to draw that business from as many different countries as possible. All the arguments which apply to the distribution by classes apply with equal force to distribution geographically, for, while all classes of business are not likely to be profitable at the same time, so even in one given class, one country is likely to produce profits at a time when another country is showing losses. In this way the essentially international character of reinsurance business is thrown into relief. It is international in the sense that it is most successfully conducted, not by confining it to one country, but by spreading it as far as possible among all countries. This would certainly seem to be true in regard to offices transacting reinsurance business only, generally known as professional reinsurers. Such offices, though legitimately looking to the support of their own national companies for the nucleus of their business and a valuable nucleus at that, cannot stop there, but must, if they are to grow large and prosperous and free from financial anxiety, extend their connections into foreign lands and play their part in the international markets of the world. Although reinsurers will always have a natural bias towards their own home market, which after all, is that which they know most intimately, yet it would seem that the wisest course is to seek business from far as well as near and not to allow a predilection for home business to overshadow the whole.

Yet here it is well to remember that the days of free trade for insurance and reinsurance have long since passed away, and many formalities may have to be complied with before a reinsurer can commence to transact business overseas. It may be necessary to obtain a licence to transact business in the foreign State, or to make deposits or otherwise comply with local laws. A reinsured giving off business in the foreign State may be at a disadvantage in dealing with an unlicensed reinsurer.

Yet in its approach to its business from the geographical standpoint, a reinsurer must be guided by circumstances rather than by a too slavish an adherence to theory, not matter how apparently sound. Thus some reinsureds, such as many major British, European and American offices, do not confine their business to their own home markets but actively engage in direct business on an international scale. A further number of companies, in other parts of the world, although they would not be termed truly international in scope, yet, do operate regionally rather than limiting themselves nationally. Reinsurance derived from such offices, though emanating from one particular national market, has nevertheless been geographically distributed before it reaches the reinsurer, and to that extent has already gone some way towards fulfilling the required purpose. Even so, however, this is not likely to achieve distribution in its most perfect form, for no matter how strong some offices may be in their foreign connections, the best business in each country is likely to go to the leading national companies and this tendency has undoubtedly increased greatly in recent years. So a reinsurer will best serve its purpose by accepting home treaties from leading companies in each country of the world, rather than by relying solely on the spread of business which may be obtained under general treaties including foreign business. This selection of business on these lines obviously calls for some discretion and an intimate knowledge of the relevant circumstances.

There is yet another factor which from time to time interferes with the free working of the theory of geographical distribution. Conditions may arise which may cause certain classes of business in certain areas to run unfavourably, or there may be certain reasons why business generally in some country may be rendered difficult. There have been many examples of such conditions during recent years. These have been either of technical or economic origin. Technical difficulties may arise through premium rate cutting or undue fluctuations in loss experience (such as are caused by natural perils) or increases in claim costs caused by legal or social pressures—matters which often seriously affect the experience in one or more classes of business. Economic difficulties are more general in their application. They are exemplified by currency inflation, restrictions on movements of currency, trade depression, general political and social unrest. Apart from the often unfavourable effect upon underwriting results, these combine to produce a feeling of insecurity which is inimical to the development of reinsurance connections. Such factors as these though often temporary in character and changing in their incidence must have due effect on the principles which a reinsurer would in the normal way follow in the building up of its account.

In carrying out this purpose the reinsurer has to consider the methods to be adopted in the investment of its funds. Apart from its capital, a reinsurer must accumulate reserve funds, partly to provide for unexpired risks and outstanding losses, and partly as surplus funds for contingencies. As a reinsurer grows large and powerful its funds may assume large proportions and the manner of their investment becomes of prime importance. To some extent the matter is complicated by delays in premium payment and the system of premium and loss reserve deposits, which are held by reinsureds and do not, therefore, fall to be handled by reinsurers.

So far as free funds are concerned the reinsurer must deal with its investments, so as to provide the best capital security with the highest interest yield which can be obtained, while at the same time keeping the assets reasonably liquid to meet any sudden demand for cash payments. How this is to be done may be a matter of opinion and may vary from time to time. But the success of a reinsurer in its investment policy, as disclosed in its annual accounts, will be a factor of prime importance in influencing a reinsured in choosing its treaty reinsurers. Indeed during the various phases of unprofitable trading which have afflicted many classes of insurance business of late, reinsurers have had perforce to rely more and more on their investment income to make both ends meet.

The foregoing analysis of the respective viewpoints of the reinsured and the reinsurer, presupposes a state of affairs in which each party sets out to fill its own particular needs—the reinsured to obtain satisfactory reinsurance facilities and the reinsurer to obtain profitable business on satisfactory terms—unaffected by any outside considerations, but following faithfully the fundamental rules governing the business. In practice, however, the matter is not quite so simple as that, for reinsurance arrangements are in fact affected by a number of extraneous factors, which have to do with the conditions under which the business is carried on at any given time. This leads us to a consideration of the various methods of conducting reinsurance business.

Chapter 4
Reinsurance Methods

As the business has developed the acceptance of reinsurance business is carried out by two distinct classes of companies, either by direct offices or by reinsurance offices. The direct office accepting reinsurance treats this as a department of its main business, and in premium volume it is generally but a subordinate part. The reinsurance office transacts nothing but reinsurance and undertakes no direct business. Its reinsurance business is no mere department, subordinate or otherwise, but is the beginning and end of its activites. Such companies are frequently called professional reinsurers, not that reinsurance is a profession properly so called, but because they hold themselves out to transact reinsurance business as their sole object and by implication to make themselves fully conversant with all its many-sided characteristics.

This division of reinsurance between direct and reinsurance offices has not always existed. In the early days of reinsurance the business was done solely by direct offices for the good reason that there were no other. In the history of the business it is clear that up to the middle of the nineteenth century reinsurance was effected between one direct office and another, at first on a facultative basis, subsequently by treaty and for a good many years by both methods concurrently. This was done in some form or other certainly from the middle of the eighteenth century, a good hundred years before any reinsurance office was founded. It is true that at that time the demand for reinsurance was small and the available business could easily be handled by the then existing direct offices. Reinsurance was then arranged very largely on the facultative system, under which, as will be seen later, each risk is offered separately to reinsurers, who may at their option accept or reject it. This business was done almost entirely on a reciprocal basis, particularly through the fire guarantee department. This is not to say that each facultative risk given off was given in return for another from the reinsurer, in the manner that reciprocity developed later under the treaty system. But each office in giving off its reinsurances took care to see that its business given to a certain company during the year was as far as possible balanced by the amount of reinsurance received by that company. This was done on the sound principle of supporting those who gave support in return, and it was one of the principle functions of the fire guarantee department to arrange its business satisfactorily in this respect.

In its facultative form, reinsurance in many ways resembles direct business. The reinsured takes the place of the original insured and has to a great extent the same relationship with its reinsurer, as the original insured had with the reinsured itself. The reinsurer receives full information of each risk and, though it must necessarily follow the reinsured in regard to such matters as survey, rating, policy conditions, and so on, yet it has the same opportunity to accept or decline the risk which the direct office had in the first instance. Except, possibly, in the matter of premium rating these principles apply even where the facultative reinsurance is arranged on an excess of loss basis. When confined to business of this nature reinsurance was eminently suitable for transaction by a department of a direct office, for it provided a convenient means of spreading the risks and by a judicious exchange of business avoided any reduction on the aggregate net account while maintaining a portfolio of business all more or less of the same texture. The system had the further advantage that it did nothing to derange a company's limits of retention, for exact records could be kept of all reinsurance acceptances in the same way as of direct insurances and, in accepting reinsurances, a company would always have strict regard to its existing commitments on the same risk.

But, though the methods of reinsurance continued for many years on these lines, the march of events brought certain inevitable developments which had a marked effect on the business. These were the introduction of the treaty system of reinsurance and the rise of the professional reinsurer, two factors not arising at the same time, yet having, it is submitted, a significant connection with the other. The transaction of reinsurance business has now become so familiar a phase of the business that it comes as something of a surprise that the first of such companies, the Cologne Reinsurance Company, was not founded until 1846. The foundation of that company and the various other offices which followed it, marked a definite stage in the evolution of reinsurance methods, and it is of interest to examine those factors in the matter which led to the formation of such companies and made it possible for them, as new entrants into business, to take their place with the direct offices already practising it and to make a success of their venture. In this matter two features emerge as having a dominating influence; one was an inherent disadvantage in the facultative method of reinsurance when carried on between direct offices and the other was the rapid growth of the treaty method of reinsurance which took place during the second half of the nineteenth century. Indeed, it is probable that the development of the treaty had more to do with the formation of reinsurance companies than any other factor in the situation.

The inherent difficulty in the facultative system, which in course of time became increasingly obvious, was the necessity which it imposed on the reinsured to disclose to its reinsurer all the material particulars relating to each risk. By this means each reinsurer gradually acquired a fairly extensive knowledge of the business connections of its reinsured, including details of the risks insured, rates of premium, and so on. Even though the offices concerned were of high standing and might be trusted to act in an honourable manner in their relations one with another, there were obvious disadvantages attached to this state of affairs, and a reinsurance office, carrying on no direct business, could very properly make a bid for a share of the facultative business, on the ground that it had no interest in the business connections of the companies which it reinsured and could not in any circumstances enter into competition with them. This supplies a reason why reinsureds might prefer to place their business with specialist reinsurance offices, but the introduction of the treaty might indicate a move in the same direction, by a change in the views of the direct offices accepting reinsurance business. Here it is important to note that the development of reinsurance methods is being considered, and what may have applied when the treaty idea was comparatively new, cannot necessarily be taken as representative of modern views on the subject. Treaties did not come into use all at once, but developed gradually, though by the middle of the nineteenth century they had become sufficiently well established to attract the attention of insurance companies as possessing certain undeniable advantages and likely to become even more useful as business increased and commitments became heavier.

But the treaty has certain characteristics not found in facultative reinsurance of a nature likely to raise misgivings in the minds of those controlling direct offices who had been accustomed to accepting their reinsurance business on a facultative basis. A treaty is an obligatory contract under which everything within the terms as agreed must be accepted and nothing can be declined unless outside such terms. No underwriting of the risks by the reinsurer is possible; no particulars are given other than in an abridged form by treaty bordereaux and sometimes not even that; and the effect on the reinsurer's limits of retention is difficult, if not impossible, to estimate. It is easy to understand that the acceptance of reinsurance by treaty would not all at once appeal to many direct offices who would quite freely have accepted facultative business where they would be able to exercise their own judgment. It seems a fair assumption that this fact gave rise to the idea of the formation of companies for the sole purpose of carrying on reinsurance business, having no direct business to accumulate with their treaty acceptances and able to devote their whole attention to the handling of their reinsurance business. It would perhaps be too much to enquire what motives were in the minds of the founders of the pioneer reinsurance companies, but it is to be supposed that they saw opportunities of carrying on a business which would produce them a profit and a fair return on the capital embarked in the venture, and it may well be surmised that they saw in the growth of the treaty method a very decided enlargement of those opportunities. However that may be, it is clear that down to the beginning of this century or thereabouts, speaking quite broadly, the treaty business was mainly held by reinsurance offices, while the facultative business remained largely in the hands of direct offices.

But this, which may be regarded as the second stage in the evolution of reinsurance methods, has already passed into a third stage, which is that existing at the present day and which is very largely a product of the twentieth century. The distinction is the set up of the business noted above has completely passed away. Facultative business is no longer regarded as a main method of reinsurance even though, for various reasons, it fulfills an important need. Furthermore the placing of facultative business by direct offices on a more less self-balancing basis has largely passed away, for facultative business in used nowadays in quite a different way and often for diverse purposes, as will be explained in a later chapter. The treaty on the other hand has developed until it has become overwhelmingly the predominant method of effecting reinsurance.

During the earlier part of this century, by reason of certain conditions attaching to the insurance business, the system of reciprocity became firmly established in the practice of reinsurance. Thus, just as there was a mutual exchange of reinsurances in the facultative method, so reciprocity also developed in treaty business. The modern system is to place treaties on a reciprocal basis one against another, so that a reinsured will only give a share of its treaty to a reinsurer who is able to offer another in return. This works rather differently from the older facultative method, where there was no setting of risk against risk, but only an approximation of the business passing between the parties during the year. It is not practicable to deal with treaty business in that way, for the treaty covers a whole portfolio of risks and the reinsured must make its bargain specifically at the time of placing the treaty and cannot reckon on acquiring an equivalent volume of treaty business in any other way. At one time there was an almost universal demand for reciprocity. But, in the view of the adverse underwriting results which have arisen in many countries over recent years, the demand has abated as companies became wary of ceding what they felt to be their profitable business in exchange for less desirable business. Nonetheless, a large proportion of reinsurance business is still ceded on a reciprocal basis.

The demand for reciprocity in treaty business was greatly stimulated after the end of the Second World War by the need to maintain the volume of the premium income. Various factors operate from time to time to depress the premium income such as depressions in trade, difficulties of monetary inflation and currency restrictions, and the spread of the national spirit in insurance leading to discrimination in favour of local companies and against foreign companies, factors which began to operate in the years immediately following the First World War. These go to reduce the yield of direct connections and turn the thoughts of direct offices towards the idea of keeping up the level of the premium income by a greater acceptance of reinsurance business. This idea is the more intensified because of the urgent need to keep down the level of the expense ratio, one of the most difficult problems of modern times. The advantage of treaty business in this respect seems obvious, when it is felt that such business can be obtained in substantial amounts at an acquisition cost of about 30% to 35%, whereas the cost of writing such business on a direct basis may be anything from 40% to 45%. This fact alone goes a long way to explain the former great spread of the system of reciprocity. It also partly explains the more recent tendency for large numbers of direct offices to write a small reinsurance account on a non-reciprocal basis. Thus many of the following paragraphs apply equally to "assumed" reinsurances written by direct offices on a non-reciprocal basis.

For there is another side to the picture, with certain inherent disadvantages. In the first place the acquisition of a substantial volume of treaty business must have an adverse influence on the claims ratio, since reinsurance business in the long run must produce higher claims than the net direct business retained by the company for its own account. This is due to the natural selection which must operate against the reinsurer. It is important to see that any saving on the expense ratio is not more than counter-balanced by the increase in the claims ratio. Secondly, the building up of an account of mixed direct and reinsurance business is likely to have an unsettling effect on the direct office's system of limits. This can be largely avoided by accepting treaties coming only from countries in which the accepting office has no direct interests, though when reciprocity is looked for on a large scale this cannot always be done. It is perhaps one of the chief disadvantages of reciprocity that it is apt to affect the judgment of the reinsurer in accepting the treaty, since it is concerned not only with the merits of that treaty, but also with the question of placing its own treaty in exchange. It must then look not for the most satisfactory market for its own treaty, but for the best opportunity to obtain a treaty in exchange, two differing points of view which will not always coincide. Finally, a widespread system of reciprocity can only work satisfactorily so long as the business continues to run on normally profitable lines throughout the world. Unfavourable runs of experience in any particular area at once give rise to difficulties, for such will mean that the results under reciprocal arangements will not be the same. This would lead to dissatisfaction and disturbance in treaty arrangements, which is not good for the business as a whole. It is the function of reinsurance to take the long view, to put aside its profits in good years to pay for the losses in the bad years, and not to be unduly disturbed by a temporary setback in results. When reinsurance is practised as a business, whether by direct offices or by reinsurance offices, this function is likely to be clearly understood. But when the position of a reinsurer who has incurred losses under treaties accepted is aggravated by the fact that its own treaties given in exchange are showing good profits, its patience is likely soon to become exhausted and it looks about to make other arrangments. This is natural enough and is indeed the obvious duty of that reinsured in its own interests. But it is an obvious inherent disadvantage in the system of reciprocity and is a major reason for the decline in the practice in recent years.

It is of interest to note that reciprocity is required mostly in respect of proportional treaties only. It was originally most common in fire business but has involved marine and certain classes of accident business. It does not usually operate in the excess of loss market, which is more highly specialised and the form of reinsurance written is not in the ordinary way so suitable to be exchanged on reciprocal lines.

A number of incidental effects flowed from the extensive use of reciprocity. The most obvious of these is that it tended to increase the amount of reinsurance treaty business which was accepted by direct offices, for though reciprocity can be practised by direct and reinsurance offices alike, the former have not only a greater volume, but generally also more favourable business to dispose of, and are able to command a larger proportion of the desirable reciprocity. This led in turn to a more widespread distribution of treaty business, both amongst reinsurers and throughout different countries of the world. Thus, every company with a treaty to give off became a potential reinsurer if it looked for reciprocity, and in consequence a far greater number of offices became engaged in accepting reinsurances than was formerly the case. At the same time the distribution was enlarged territorially, because reciprocity fulfills its purpose more effectively when treaties are exchanged between one country and another, and there is little doubt that the international spread of reinsurance business was promoted in this way. This has had an effect on the volume of international trade which is not without interest. Every time a reinsured gives a treaty to a reinsurer in a foreign country, it imports the cover granted by the reinsurer, being the commodity which the reinsurer has to sell. Similarly by the same transaction the reinsurer exports its cover, so that an arrangement of this nature adds to the invisible exports of one country and the invisible imports of another. Under a widespread system of reciprocity the exports and imports tended to counteract one another, so that while there may have been a substantial addition to the volume of international trade, the effect on the balance was greatly reduced. Of course the ceding of a treaty abroad, whether it be viewed as an import or an export, can only have its normal effect if it runs on profitable lines, for only then does the importer pay the price and the exporter receive it. If the treaty should produce a loss on the year's working, the reinsured, i.e. the importer, actually benefits financially, and the reinsurer, the exporter, loses. This is a reversal of ordinary trade procedure and illustrates the difference between insurance and other forms of commercial undertaking. This is of technical interest only, for in the long run reinsurance must produce a profit to the reinsurers or it cannot continue, and this is the price paid to the exporters for the cover which the reinsured imports.

Where a system of reciprocity is prevalent, it tends to work to the disadvantage of the purely reinsurance company which has no direct business of its own and can therefore only offer retrocession treaties, i.e. treaties which are a reinsurance of a reinsurance. Even at that it can scarcely afford to offer as much business as it receives, since that would generally be against its interests. As a general rule reinsurance companies cannot give more in reciprocity than 50 or 60% of the premium they receive. One effect of the growth of reciprocity was to cause the withdrawal of a certain proportion of treaties formerly held by reinsurance offices and to this extent their progress was hampered for a time.

One other indirect effect of reciprocity, which is of more general importance, may be noted. Reciprocity tended to a greater subdivision of the surplus to be placed under a treaty. The manner of allocating reinsurances is more particularly described in a succeeding chapter. It is sufficient here to say that in order that each reciprocal bargain may be arranged on appropriate lines, it is often necessary, especially for the larger ceding offices, to allot only a small proportion of the surplus to the particular reinsurer in question. In consequence the total number of reinsurers interested in one treaty may sometimes be very large, adding considerably to the complications involved in the matter. That is what has in fact happened in recent years—

another way in which reinsurance practice has altered. The work of administering the treaty is much increased thereby, not only for the accounting point of view, but also because of the necessity for the reinsured to keep a watch on the progress and stability of each one of its reinsurers. But the greater subdivision of the business to be reinsured has certain advantages to larger reinsureds in that they do not have to impose too heavy a responsibility on any one reinsurer. By the union of a large number of responsible reinsurers on the one treaty the reinsured adds strength to the undertaking.

The placing of treaties in small shares has had a further effect in the development of reinsurance methods, by expediting the practice of dispensing with bordereaux. As will appear on a later page, bordereaux are the means whereby the reinsurer is advised of the risks ceded under the treaty. In the early days of treaties bordereaux were universally used, and, by a proper system of indexing, the reinsurer kept a record of its commitments in much the same way as was done under the facultative system. In course of time, however in order to effect a saving in labour and expense, some reinsureds began to discontinue the use of bordereaux, though this practice did not begin until some time during the First World War, when there was a special need for it. During the period between the wars there was some tendency to revert to former practices, but since the Second World War the discontinuance of bordereaux has been greatly accelerated so that the absence of bordereaux may be said now to be the rule rather than the exception. Yet when a reinsurer receives only a very small share of a treaty, say one per cent., or even less, this does to some extent negate the importance of bordereaux, since it will be very seldom that the reinsurer will be heavily committed on any one risk. Many reinsurers, who, if they held a full line on a treaty, would wish to receive bordereaux thereunder, might be quite willing to dispense with the bordereaux if their share was only one-tenth of that line. This is what has happened very largely in practice and the majority of reinsurers receive their business without knowing any of its details and without being able to undertake any system of indexing to ascertain their commitments. A necessary consequence of this method of working in the dark is to throw upon the reinsured a strong duty to exercise the utmost good faith in its dealings with its treaty reinsurers—a duty inherent in the business in any event and fully recognised by all reputable reinsureds.

The effect has been to restrict the reinsurer's opportunities to keep any exact record of its commitments by a system of risk indexing. Under the facultative method, acceptances are invariably indexed, so that reinsurer may not accept more on one risk that it is able to deal with, either for its own account or with the aid of its retrocession arrangements. It has a power of selection in such acceptances and will exercise it with due regard to its existing liabilities. This adds to the expense of operating the business, but it enables the reinsurer to work with its eyes open. In the early days of treaties the same procedure was followed, but, with the gradual elimination of bordereaux, the system of indexing could not be carried through in its entirety, and most reinsurers have abandoned the system altogether. Indeed it may be doubted whether any reinsurers carry on a full system of indexing their risks as was common in the early days of the business. As the treaty system developed, certain difficulties in carrying through a complete indexing arrangement arose. A very large number of cessions come to the reinsurer under a surplus treaty, many of them very small in amount, especially when treaties are greatly sub-divided. Many provisional cessions never reach completion, and a host of alterations and cancellations must always be expected. To keep track of the many ramifications of the cessions under a modern surplus treaty, and to make sure that an accurate analysis of the risks has been made, involves an immense amount of labour and expense which in the opinion of many is out of all proportion to the advantage gained. Unless the indexing system is complete it loses much of its value, but to make it complete means entering a large number of very small risks, so that a great deal of work has to be done, much of which turns out to be irrelevant to the main purpose of the system, which is to find out where accumulation of hazard exists. Moreover, even this cannot be done unless bordereaux are supplied under every surplus treaty accepted, for if only one be omitted the analysis is not strictly correct. It was no doubt because of the introduction of the non-bordereaux treaty that reinsurers were led to discontinue the attempt to index their business. To hold to a complete indexing system would have meant declining certain desirable business, and the alternative thus presented may have expedited the move towards the more empirical methods.

The obvious purpose of an indexing system is to ascertain where a reinsurer is too heavily interested on any one risk, and to enable it to reinsure itself in its turn, so as to relieve its accounts of too heavy a liability. This is what is known as retrocession, an important part of a reinsurer's business. With an indexing system the reinsurer would set up a table of limits in regard to various classes of risk, and would retrocede only when its index showed those limits to be exceeded. This would be done under a surplus retrocession treaty and, as will be seen in a later chapter on the treaty, this is not a very popular form of reinsurance contract under modern conditions, having certain disadvantages for both parties. Another reason, therefore, for the decay of the indexing system in reinsurance business is found in the fact that it leads only to a system of retrocession which is not very readily arranged, and for which it is becoming increasingly difficult to find satisfactory facilities. Other methods have had to be adopted which, though involving the retrocession of business, which on any system of limits of retention could well have been kept, yet go a long way to reduce the administrative cost and are in a form to find a reasonably adequate market for the business.

Apart from these two major methods of effecting reinsurances, i.e.:—

(a) facultatively, where each risk to be reinsured is individually offered to and accepted or declined by the reinsurer, and
(b) by treaty, an agreement whereby the reinsurer will automatically accept a range of business up to agreed limits, without any option for declinature,

there are also two distinct forms in which such facultative or treaty reinsurances may be structured.

The form and function of each these types are described in greater detail in the following chapters. However at this stage we shall briefly characterise these forms as:—

(1) Proportional, or sharing, forms of reinsurance of which the principal types consist of surplus reinsurances and quota share reinsurances. Under this form the reinsured company cedes to the reinsurer a specified share of the insurance exposure he has accepted. The reinsurer receives a pro rata share of the premiums and pays a pro rata share of the losses. Under the "surplus" form of reinsurance, the ceding company will maintain different limits of retention for different types of risk and the amount ceded to the reinsurer will vary in accordance with the amount of the retention; under "quota share" reinsurances the ceding company will retain an agreed fixed share of all policies and will likewise cede an agreed fixed share of all such policies to the reinsurer.
(2) Non-proportional, or excess of loss reinsurances. Under this form of reinsurance the reinsurer agrees to pay the balance of a claim when the amount exceeds a certain stipulated figure. The claims covered by this form of reinsurance may relate to a single risk or to a number of losses arising out of one event or to an aggregation of losses. The stipulated figure, or retention of the reinsured, is based not so much on the potential exposure as represented by the sum insured, for example, but on the amount of a loss which the reinsured feels it can sustain for its own account. The reinsurance premium may be stipulated as a fixed monetary amount or as a percentage of the reinsured's premium income for the class of business being reinsured.

Chapter 5
The Facultative Method

The facultative method of reinsurance, though now to a large extent superseded by the treaty, was known and practised for many years before the first recorded treaty contract. It forms the basis upon which the structure of reinsurance has been erected and, though it is no longer so important as it once was, it is logical to deal with it first in a dissertation on the growth and development of reinsurance practice.

No record is available as to when the use of the word facultative first arose or how it came to be applied to this particular form of reinsurance. Its meaning in standard dictionaries is given simply as "optional" or as implying a faculty, that is "a facility or power to act according to a free choice." This gives the clue to the nature of facultative reinsurance. It is one in which each party to the transaction has an absolute free choice in arranging the matter; the reinsured may offer the reinsurance to any reinsurer that it may choose, while the reinsurer has an entirely unfettered discretion whether or not to accept any risk offered. It follows that each risk to be reinsured has to be dealt with separately and each facultative reinsurance forms a complete reinsurance contract in itself. This still remains an essential principle of facultative reinsurance, even though. as will be seen presently, some extension of the idea has been made under open covers and standing arrangements.

It is proposed to set out in some detail the method of working a facultative reinsurance, having primary reference to fire and accident business and with some explanation of the practice in marine business. Reference may first be made to a matter of terminology. In fire business facultative reinsurances were, for many years, dealt with through what was called the guarantee department, and facultative reinsurances were denoted by the term "guarantees." This expression arose through looking at the reinsurance transaction from a different aspect. The direct office which had accepted an insurance too large for it to retain was primarily concerned with finding another company to cover part of the risk or to "guarantee" that it would assume liability therefor. Hence the transaction was called a guarantee, though this again had a two-fold aspect, according to the point of view of each party to the transaction. The direct office, which had the risk to reinsure, was called the reinsuring company, and it described the reinsurance as a "guarantee obtained." The reinsurer was called the accepting company and to it the reinsurance was a "guarantee granted." The incidence of these terms is sufficiently obvious, though they were somewhat cumbersome and not easily to be understood by the uninitiated. The spread of the treaty has led to the introduction of simpler expressions, which more accurately describe the transaction. The direct office which has the risk to reinsure is called the reinsured and the company which accepts the reinsurance is called the reinsurer (where the surplus form of facultative reinsurance is employed the reinsured is often termed the "ceding company" and the actual risk reinsured is called the cession). These simpler terms have superseded the older forms and are used in the description of the business set out below. Reference should also be made to the form of the facultative reinsurance which may be placed. Facultative reinsurances may be structured on a surplus or an excess of loss basis in accordance with the needs of the reinsured. Thus, although the following description focusses mainly upon the placing and administration of facultative reinsurances in a surplus form, the description applies equally to facultative excess of loss.

The general procedure in placing a facultative reinsurance is as follows. A reinsurance slip is prepared by the reinsured, or its reinsurance intermediary if one is engaged by the reinsured, setting out brief details of the risk proposed to be reinsured. This slip will contain the name, address and description of the original insured, the nature of the trade carried on, the insured perils, the total sum insured, the form of reinsurance, the period of the reinsurance, the amount of reinsurance required and the retention of the reinsured, the rate of premium to be charged and the deductions therefrom. These are material facts upon which an intending reinsurer will be entitled to rely in exercising its judgment as to whether to accept the offer or reject it. The reinsurance slip is then taken out and shown to various offices known to write facultative business of a similar nature. Each reinsurer exercises its power of choice and if it accepts the offer will initial the slip, placing against its initial the proportion which it is prepared to take. It is important to note that the reinsurer's liability commences only from the time the slip is initialled. This must be so, since only then has it definitely exercised the power of choice which is inherent in the business. Without prejudice to their rights in this matter, however, facultative reinsurers will normally agree to date their cover back to any required date, provided they are satisfied that everything is in order. One of these requirements would be that there are no known losses under the cover at the time the offer is made.

Thereby the whole of the reinsurance on a particular risk runs for the same period. It follows that the reinsured cannot obtain its reinsurance cover, nor even be sure that is will obtain such cover at all, until the slip has been taken round and initialled by all the reinsurers required. This often means that the reinsurance arrangements have to be made before cover can be granted to the original insured. This in turn means that the slip has sometimes to be prepared before all the details of the risk are available. In such a case a reinsurer might make its acceptance subject to being satisfied as to the missing information when it comes to hand. Thus an acceptance might be marked "subject to survey" or "subject to rate" or otherwise as the case may be. This means that the reinsurer will hold covered and that its initial is binding in that respect, but that it has the right to reconsider the acceptance in the light of the required information when it becomes available and to terminate the reinsurance forthwith if that information proves not to be satisfactory.

When a substantial proportion of a risk has to be reinsured, this will entail taking the slip round to several offices and obtaining the initial of each for the amount it is prepared to accept. It often happens that this causes a great deal of labour and in the meantime the reinsured can not be sure of its ability to grant the required cover to its own insured. This feature illustrates one of the principal drawbacks to the facultative method and which became increasingly apparent as insurance business grew and the need to cover large amounts became more frequent. This disadvantage is to a large extent nullified by the introduction of the treaty method of reinsurance. As will presently appear the drawbacks of the facultative method largely disappear under the treaty method of reinsurance, with the consequent effect of correspondingly reducing the purposes for which the facultative method is used.

After a slip has been initialled, the next step is for the reinsured (or the intermediary) to issue a written request note (closing) to each of the accepting reinsurers. A form of the request note is set out in the Appendix. It is addressed to the reinsurer and sets out that the reinsured requests the reinsurance showing the date of commencement and termination, the business covered, the sum reinsured, the name of the original insured and the sum retained by the reinsured. If the request note relates to fire business and the reinsurance is made between members of the Fire Offices' Committee, the request note declares specifically that the transaction is subject to the rules adopted by the Fire Offices' Committee for the regulation of guarantee transactions. This declaration appears on all the documents—including take note and reinsurance policy—required for the completion of the reinsurance, and it has the effect of importing those rules into the contract, thereby giving certain rights to the reinsured in regard to the nature of the indemnity granted and the settlement of claims which it would not otherwise possess.

The request for reinsurance is for a uniform rateable share of the reinsured's risk. This may be for a share of the whole or part only of the coverage under the original insurance. In fire business it is quite frequent for certain items only of a policy to be reinsured, provided, however, each such item was a separate risk—separate that is to say from the items not reinsured. It would obviously be impossible to reinsure only a part of a policy if all the items formed one indistinguishable risk, though it is quite feasible to reinsure a building, but not the contents, for here the risks can be clearly distinguished. Alternatively certain specified perils may be reinsured out of a multi-peril policy. Thus a reinsured may seek reinsurance for the fire peril included in an engineering insurance issued to an insured. These practices are not necessarily universal, but are governed by technical considerations arising out of the nature of the business and the reinsured's methods of fixing its retentions.

On receipt of the request note the reinsurer issues its take note (see form in the Appendix). By this means the reinsurer puts into writing its formal acceptance of the reinsurance as set out in the request note. In the ordinary way that take note gives an unqualified acceptance of the reinsurer's share of the risk and is absolutely binding on the reinsurer, but dating from the time the slip was initialled unless otherwise agreed. But if some reservation was made on initialment of the slip, and the point reserved has not been disposed of when the take note is issued, the reinsurer will mark the same reservation on the take note, in which event the cover is not irrevocable unless and until the point reserved has been disposed of to the reinsurer's satisfaction.

The final stage in the completion of a facultative reinsurance is reached with the issue of the reinsurance policy. The usual form of this policy is given in the Appendix. Before the policy can be issued, the reinsured must send to the reinsurer either a copy of its policy, or, a specification setting out the particulars required, i.e., the name, address and occupation of the original insured, a description of the property insured, the insured perils, the period of the policy, the original policy premium and the proportionate share of the sum insured and of the premium allocated to the reinsurer. When the original perils insured are not standard or if there are unusual aspects of the risks or interest covered then a full copy of the policy and accompanying documentation, such as survey reports, would be required by the reinsurer. Such policy or specification would be incorporated by express reference in the reinsurance policy and would be the basis upon which the reinsurance contract rests.

It will be seen that this is a lengthy and cumbersome process. It has to be carried out separately in respect of every risk insured and for all the different reinsurers interested in any one risk. It adds greatly to the labour and expense involved and puts the administration cost of this kind of reinsurance at a fairly high level, one effect of which is the lower level of reinsurance commission which facultative reinsurance can command as compared with treaty business. However for various specific purposes the facultative method remains of great value.

Some development of method has been involved in recent years, with a view to reducing as much as possible the amount of clerical labour involved. Under one method the reinsurer will issue its take note and the parties agree to rely upon this document as if it were a policy. This eliminates one stage in the transaction. Another very common method reduces the work still further. After the slip has been initialled, the reinsured relies upon the cover thereby granted, without either party issuing either a request note or a take note. The terms and conditions of this "slip policy", as it is termed, will often contain a "Full Reinsurance Clause" along the lines of:—

> "being a Reinsurance of and warranted same gross rate, terms and conditions as and to follow the settlements of the Company and that the said Company retains during the currency of this Policy at least on the identical subject matter and risk and in identically the same proportion on each separate part thereof, but in the event of the retained line being less than as above, Reinsurers' lines to be proportionally reduced."

In this context, however, it should be noted that conflicts at law can arise between the application of the "follow the settlement" provision of this Clause and other terms or conditions as may have been incorporated in the reinsurance slip or policy. This topic is examined further in the discussion in Chapter 6 below on the "follow the fortunes" clause contained in surplus treaties.

Where the reinsured employs the services of a reinsurance broker, the reinsured will not be in possession of a copy of the signed slip and will therefore be supplied by the broker with a "Cover Note", signed by an authorised official of the broking firm, which confirms that the cover has been effected in accordance with the reinsured's instructions, summarises the cover so effected and list the names and shares of the reinsurers participating therein. At regular intervals, say weekly or monthly, all reinsured cases which have been completed during the period, are entered upon a bordereau, which sets out in abridged form the same particulars as are found on the specifications issued for policy purposes. One bordereau will include all the cases of the period and where required these can be duplicated when more than one reinsurer is concerned. Each such bordereau is issued in duplicate to the reinsurer, one copy being retained by the reinsurer for its records and the other copy returned to the reinsured duly attested by the reinsurer. The bordereau thus takes the place of the policy with the advantage that it includes in the one document all the reinsurances over a period. Considerable labour is thereby avoided and this abbreviated method of dealing with the business goes a long way to reducing its cost. In this context however, it must be recognised that many complications can arise out of a legal dispute over whether a risk is reinsured or not or over the amount of a loss, where the parties are forced to rely solely upon inadequate documentation in the form of summary bordereaux or broker's slips or Cover Notes.

It will be clear that much of the labour involved in the facultative method is connected with getting the necessary initials on the slip. In modern practice this can be largely avoided by the system of what may be called giving cover "in course of post"—though the term nowadays extends to the use of telex communications as much as to the mail. The reinsured will arrange facilities with a number of reinsurers, whereby it may issue request notes by post, for one or more lines of a risk to be reinsured, as may be agreed. The reinsurers will then hold covered each up to the amount of its agreed share and remains so bound, unless and until it has signified its declinature "in course of post". As a rule a limit is fixed, within which this must be notified say 48 hours after receipt, though sometimes this is extended up to as much as a fortnight to allow for possible delays in transmission. If no declinature is made within the period, the reinsurer is bound in the ordinary way. The system does save a great deal of work, and is much favoured by reinsureds accordingly. Yet it may be emphasized that it still remains facultative reinsurance, for the reinsurer is in no way deprived of its power to decline, even though it must accept responsibility in the meantime.

The period for which a reinsurance policy is issued corresponds in the usual way with that of the original insurance, except that the commencing date may not always be the same, for this depends upon the date the slip was initialled. If the original policy is itself renewable, the reinsurance may be renewable in like manner and the reinsurer will automatically remain on the risk as and from the renewal date, unless and until it is advised by the reinsured that the original insurance has not been renewed. This does not mean that both parties to the reinsurance transaction are bound to continue it as long as the original insurance subsists. The automatic renewal is merely for the purpose of protecting the reinsured until it knows whether or not its insurance has been renewed. Nevertheless, the reinsurance is an annual contract and may be terminated by either party at any renewal date, but in that case it is stipulated that thirty days' notice prior to the renewal date shall be given by the party desiring to terminate the contract. A clause to this effect would be included in the reinsurance policy. However the more usual modern practice is for the reinsurer to provide cover purely for the period of the original insurance so that the process of renewal requires a separate act of offer and acceptance.

But in the absence of any such notice or provision to terminate the reinsurance, it is continued as long as the original insurance remains in force, but no longer, since the reinsurance can only subsist as long as the original insurance subsists. Arrangements have, therefore, to be made to ascertain what reinsurance policies are renewed from time to time. This is done by means of periodical lists, issued monthly or quarterly as the case may be. These lists are prepared by the reinsurer from its records and include all the policies which fall due for renewal during the period. They are forwarded to the reinsured, who will in due course mark on the list against each policy "renewed" or "cancelled" as the case may be. This takes some little time in practice, especially if foreign risks be included, as the reinsured cannot complete the list until it has received the required information from its branches and agents. As soon as the list is complete it is returned to the reinsurer, who is then able to mark up its records in accordance therewith.

This clears the way for the rendering of accounts between the parties in regard to the facultative transactions. The practice in this matter has undergone some alteration in recent years. The original system, which still continues in many cases, was for the account to be prepared by the reinsurer and sent to the reinsured for confirmation. This account is made up quarterly or perhaps monthly. It embraces all the new reinsurance policies issued during the period, and all policies renewed as shown by the returned renewal list during the same period, and thus sets out the reinsurance premiums due. Since the introduction of the bordereaux system into facultative business, however, it has become the more common practice for the account to be prepared by the reinsured, or its reinsurance broker, and sent to the reinsurer for confirmation. In this respect the system resembles that in use for treaty business. In that event the reinsured decides what business falls into the period in question and under the bordereaux system this is more convenient. The point is one of detail only and as may be arranged between the parties.

The gross premiums as shown in the account may be subject to a deduction for reinsurance commission dependent upon the form of the facultative reinsurance which has been placed, though various other deductions such as premium and reinsurance taxes may also arise. The rate of commission on surplus facultative reinsurance is generally less than on treaty business, though the recent popularity of this method has to some extent narrowed the margin. The reinsurance commission is intended to reimburse the reinsured in respect of commission paid to agents and to make a contribution towards management expenses. The net balance as shown by the account is payable by the reinsured to the reinsurer. It is to be noted that the account does not in the ordinary way include claims, for facultative claims are payable as and when the original claim was settled in the same way as are cash losses under a treaty. This is not, however, universal. It is quite a common thing for smaller losses to be carried to account, in which case an item for claims will appear in the account. These are matters of procedure to be settled between the parties, according to their convenience and no point of principle is involved. Facultative reinsurance may or may not carry any profit commission, since this is a matter for negotiation.

A further item which may apply in the facultative account is in regard to alterations by endorsement. All endorsements which involve a material alteration in the risk or any alteration in the premium must be notified to the reinsurer for its approval, and unless such notification is made, the reinsurer would not be liable if it could show that a knowledge of the alteration would have affected its decision as to continuing its reinsurance. Alterations are usually advised by slip, the slip containing full particulars of the alteration and any additional or return premium. This endorsement slip would be initialled by the reinsurer by way of its acceptance of its share of the alteration. A summary of the additional premiums and return premiums is carried to the monthly or quarterly account.

Although the introduction of the treaty and the greater convenience which is obtained from that method led to a restriction in the use of facultative reinsurance, specific requirements still necessitate a facultative approach. Thus, facultative reinsurance is used to dispose of shares of particularly large risks which are beyond the compass of the treaty facilities. The same may arise with extra hazardous risks where the reinsured's retention has to be moderate. As will appear in a succeeding chapter, a reinsured can give off under its proportional treaty only a fixed multiple of its retention on any one risk. So that if the total sum insured exceeds the retention plus treaty lines, it is not possible to increase the amount ceded under the treaty, but the balance must be disposed of otherwise. It is here that the principal use of facultative reinsurance is found nowadays. It is also used sometimes in conjunction with a treaty, either for the exchange of risks among offices in certain localities abroad, or for the purpose of reducing the full allotment which might otherwise be made under a treaty if the interests of the parties seem to require it. This use of the facultative method is explained in greater detail in the chapter on treaties.

In life assurance the facultative method remains in common use in this country, though not to the same extent abroad. In this country the business is mainly shared between direct offices, and, with certain notable exceptions, British reinsurance offices do not write life business. Certain rules have been laid down for the transaction of life reassurance, under a Reassurance agreement to which most of the principal life offices are party. The available business is shared between those offices and to a considerable extent on a reciprocal basis. By the facultative method the accepting company takes a share of the assurance and, where necessary, a share of bonuses. The reassurance, like the original policy, is a permanent contract.

Apart from the life reassurance which is placed on a sharing basis, there is also another method known as the Risk Premium method, under which the reinsurer assumes liability only for its share of the risk of death during the ensuing year. This is therefore an annual and not necessarily a permanent contract, though it is generally renewed year after year until the policy becomes a claim. The annual premium payable to the reinsurer is actuarially computed as to the amount applicable to the death risk in the year of assurance to which the reassurance relates. It is not a uniform proportion of the original premium, but is at a low rate for young lives, gradually rising throughout the period of the policy. This type of reassurance, though it may be done facultatively, is very frequently provided for by a treaty.

In the marine department, facultative reinsurance is used to a considerable extent, even though the treaty method is firmly established. Marine usage has certain peculiarities of its own due to the nature of the business. The main principles are the same as in fire business, for the facultative reinsurer has the same power of choice and does not come on to the risk until a slip has been initialled. In order to comply with English law a reinsurance policy is always issued in the form prescribed by the Marine Insurance Act, 1906. To show the nature of this policy, it contains a clause to the following effect:—

> "The policy is declared to be a reinsurance of the Insurance Company and to be subject to the same clauses and conditions as the original policy or policies and to pay as may be paid hereon."

Such reinsurances are in all respects subject to the same requirements as to disclosure, good faith and the like as any other facultative reinsurance and in the usual way they carry the same rate of premium as the original policy. This would always be so where the reinsurance is effected at the commencement of the policy under a general arrangement by the reinsured to maintain its normal retentions.

Nevertheless there is a considerable volume of marine reinsurance done on different lines, where the reinsurer does not share in the original premium, but demands a higher rate according to circumstances. This occurs, for example, in what are called reinsurances in the overdue market. It may happen that a ship is overdue at its destination, in circumstances where it is feared that a loss has occurred, but this cannot be said with certainty. Here there is a contingency which the original reinsurer may properly require to reinsure. It is not, strictly speaking, the same contingency as that originally insured, for now the risk is specifically threatened with loss. Such reinsurances cannot be placed at the original rate, but only at such figure as may, in the opinion of the reinsurer, be commensurate with the risk as it now appears. That figure may in some circumstances be very high indeed. Although modern communications have sharply reduced the number of ships overdue without explanation, the concept of overdue reinsurance has been adapted to other risks. Thus, for example, reinsurances have been arranged on risks where a fire had occurred but where the amount of the liability claim for persons killed or injured was uncertain.

This feature of charging a different rate of premium may also occur when a very large risk has to be placed, in respect of which the market becomes very full. Then if one insurer desires to reinsure a part of its acceptance, it may only be able to do so at a higher rate of premium, even though there is no question of the risk being affected by loss. It is even possible, where a risk is one particularly sought after, for a reinsurance to be effected at a lower rate. Similarly facultative reinsurance may be used to reinsure part only of the original risks covered, as for example where a reinsurance is affected to cover total loss only or certain specified perils. It is clear that all such reinsurances such as these should only be dealt with by facultative means, since each case has to be dealt with on its merits, and no form of obligatory treaty could be devised to bring within its range all the various circumstances which will have a bearing on reinsurances of this nature.

The subject of facultative reinsurance will not be complete without some reference to the form of reinsurance called a "facultative obligatory" or "open cover", which is generally regarded as belonging to the facultative section of the business and is often so treated in the books of a reinsurer.

An open cover is a reinsurance arrangement under which the reinsured may at its option cede a share of certain defined risks, which share the reinsurer is bound obligatorily to accept. Such an arrangement thus partakes partly of the nature of a facultative reinsurance and partly of a treaty. To the reinsured it is facultative because cessions are optional at its discretion. It is not bound to cede insurances of the nature defined but can dispose of them as it thinks fit. To the reinsurer the open cover is more in the nature of a treaty. The obligation is an obligatory one and it applies not to an individual case but to all cases of a given class that may be ceded. No matter how the open cover may be regarded in a reinsurer's books, it is clear that it has none of the characteristics of a facultative reinsurance and in particular it lacks the fundamental feature, the power, inherent in a facultative reinsurer, to decline a risk if thought fit.

For reasons belonging to its nature, an open cover is not a particularly attractive form of reinsurance to a reinsurer, since the option reserved to the reinsured is likely to depreciate to some extent the quality of the portfolio ceded. This will depend upon the extent to which the reinsured may exercise its option against the cover. Since such covers are taken for a specific purpose it may be assumed that the reinsured will use them for that purpose and will not discriminate against the reinsurance in any haphazard way. Yet in practice the open cover has not the same solid virtues as a treaty and is not so keenly sought by reinsurers in consequence.

The open cover can be used in all classes of insurance but is most commonly found in fire and marine business, its main purpose being to provide for risks which are irregular in their incidence, or which for some reason may be set apart from the main bulk of the business. Thus, for example, in fire business an open cover will apply to particular classes or risk in given areas, where perhaps there are periodic sudden increases in sums insured at certain seasons of the year. It might apply to wool in warehouses in Australia, or to sugar risks in the West Indies, or otherwise as the facts may require. In marine business it may apply to certain trade routes or vessels in special trades, where heavy commitments may come from time to time. While there is no reason in principle why these risks should not be included in the ordinary treaty contract, it is convenient to deal with them through the open cover because of their sporadic nature. By keeping them separate they do not derange the balance of the treaty. They may even be of use as a supplement to the treaty, to deal with amounts remaining after the treaty is filled. It is in this way perhaps that in modern reinsurance practice the open cover can be most usefully operated.

Such covers require a form of contract not usually issued as a policy, but more like a treaty. Wordings are not standardised, but they will make provision as follows:—

(1) An exact definition of the nature of the risks which may be reinsured.
(2) The territorial area from which they may be derived, or the trade routes concerned as the case may be.
(3) The share to be allotted to the reinsurer and its relation to the reinsured's retention. Sometimes a reinsurer may accept several times the reinsured's retention, though generally with a fixed amount as the maximum liability. Following ordinary treaty methods, fire covers usually leave the retention on any one risk to the discretion of the reinsured, while marine covers give specified amounts on various classes of risk. However this may be, the amount which may be ceded under a cover bears a fixed relationship to the reinsured's retention.
(4) The rate of premium to be paid and the commission to be allowed by the reinsurer. Under fire covers original rates of premium are paid with reinsurance commission according to circumstances. Marine covers may or may not be at original net rates. If the original risk be reinsured, the rate will be as original, but if something less than the original risk be given off, as for total loss only, rates will be as may be agreed.
(5) The duration of the cover and the means whereby it may be brought to an end. Generally a cover runs for a year, with provision for continuance unless cancelled by proper notice. However, within this it would normally also be provided that no policy reinsured thereunder be issued for a period of greater than twelve months plus odd time in order to prevent the reinsurance of longterm contracts. It is possible, however, that the open cover may be for a short period corresponding to the needs of a seasonal trade. This is not very convenient for it involves taking out new covers every year, while the continous cover can just as well be adapted to seasonal risks as any other. In either form, the period of notice is usually a short one, say thirty days, in which respect there is a resemblance to facultative practice. It is to be expected from the nature of the business to be ceded that the results may sometimes be very uneven and the reinsurer will desire to reserve its right to revise the conditions at reasonably short notice if the results warrant it.
(6) Provision will invariably be made for the advice of all risks ceded under the cover, by means of bordereaux. In view of the reinsured's option is is absolutely essential since it would not be possible to leave any room for doubt as to whether a risk had been ceded or not. The issue of such bordereaux and the accounts which follow them, as well as the method of dealing

with claims recoverable under the cover, follow the general lines adopted in the working of a treaty.

For a number of reasons arising out of modern business practice, there has been a decided revival in the volume of business placed facultatively in recent years. The reasons include the greater aggregation of insurance risks arising out of major business organisations, the practice of "underwriting" treaty cessions and the improved methods of conducting facultative business already explained. In addition, there are various political and economic reasons which on occasion determine the demand for facultative reinsurance. Thus, governmental regulation in various parts of the world may restrict the placing of direct insurances overseas so that often this business would be placed in such overseas markets as a facultative reinsurance of a local insurance company. In addition, where treaty reinsurance capacity becomes restricted after a period of adverse reinsurance underwriting results, it will be found that business which previously might have been reinsured on a treaty basis is now reinsured facultatively.

Chapter 6
Reinsurance by Treaty
I—Surplus

Reference has already been made in a previous chapter to the development of reinsurance by treaty, and the purpose of this chapter is to analyse the nature and substance of the various kinds of reinsurance treaty and to elucidate the manner which they carry out their purpose.

Though, as previously pointed out, treaties have been used for a great number of years, so that it would not be strictly correct to describe them as a modern development of the business, yet it is true to say that the universal acceptance of the treaty as the recognised method of reinsurance is an attribute of modern times and represents the latest phase in the evolution of the business. The growth of the treaty method is undoubtedly due to the fact that it most conveniently and adequately provides the supply of reinsurance facilities which the tremendously increased demand makes necessary under present-day conditions of insurance business. The greatest stimulus to the development of any business is found in the insistent demand and there can be no doubt that this lies at the root of the extension of the treaty method.

The nature and purpose of a treaty may best be considered by reference to the various clauses which are found in the treaty wording. In this connection it must be remembered that there are different forms of treaty not only in regard to different classes of insurance but also in regard to the different forms of reinsuring. Moreover there is no standardised form of wording applicable even to treaties of the same kind, for reinsureds and reinsurers use such wording as is best adapted to their needs and this is not always the same, whether as between companies in the same country, or in different countries. Nevertheless since the main purpose of all treaties in a given class is the same, their terms are substantially alike even though differing in their wording, and it is possible to examine their fundamental characteristics and to analyse their meaning. To facilitate reference to what follows certain specimen forms of treaty are set out in the

Appendix, which do not necessarily represent the wordings used by any company, but in which an endeavour has been made to embody all the various features present in the most up-to-date forms of treaty, so as to give some description of every aspect of modern practice in the mattter. Before proceeding on a detailed examination of the treaty form of reinsurance, it must be emphasised, however, that a treaty wording represents the agreement in writing between the parties to a legal contract, i.e., the treaty reinsurance. Differences which might arise between reinsured and reinsurer are not always resolvable by negotiation or arbitration. In fact, in recent times there has been an increasing recourse to the Courts of Law by one or other party. In such circumstances the treaty wording becomes subject to close legal scrutiny in an effort to ascertain the true nature and scope of the parties' agreement. As such, therefore, it should set forth in clear detail the terms and conditions of the agreement, not only with regard to the scope and limits of the coverage granted by the reinsurer but also to such matters as the presentation of accounts etc.

Treaties may be divided into two broad classes—those which provide for the sharing of risks between reinsured and reinsurer, and those which provide for the reinsurer being responsible only for a loss which exceeds some agreed figure. Treaties in the first category are known as proportional reinsurances and include such forms as surplus or quota share treaties whilst those in the second category, known as non-proportional reinsurances, include the various kinds of treaties known as excess of loss covers. It will be necesary to examine each of these forms of treaty separately for they contain radical differences. The most common form of treaty is still the surplus treaty and it will be convenient to examine this first. The description which follows applies to the surplus treaty as used in fire and accident business, for though this form is also used in marine business, it then has certain characteristics peculiar to that branch of insurance and meriting separate treatment.

It will be gathered from what has been said that the treaty as a means of effecting reinsurance possesses certain advantages not found in the facultative method and which advantages make it particularly well adapted to modern insurance requirements. These advantages may best be brought out by a study of the first clause of the specimen surplus fire treaty which is commonly referred to as the operative clause (see Article No. 1 of the first surplus treaty wording contained in the Appendix).

In the first place this clause provides for an obligatory reinsurance between the parties, so that reinsured is bound to cede and the reinsurer is bound to accept the share of the risk to be reinsured as provided in the treaty (it is the usual practice in surplus reinsurance to refer to the reinsured as the "ceding company"). This is perhaps the most outstanding feature of the surplus treaty and the one in which it most vitally differs from other reinsurance methods. The surplus treaty is an obligatory contract providing for the cession of all risks falling within its purview on terms that the ceding company can exercise no option in withholding any particular cession from the reinsurer and the reinsurer foregoes all right to decline any reinsurance allotted to it. In this connection it should be noted, however, that although excess of loss forms of treaty share with proportional treaties the obligatory nature of the contract there is no cession or sharing of a risk under these forms of treaty. The excess of loss forms, rather, are contract of reinsurance to indemnify the reinsured against loss as defined within the terms of such reinsurance.

The vast difference which this obligatory nature makes in the practice of reinsurance becomes immediately apparent. The ceding company no longer has the right to offer its reinsurances to whom it will, to distribute its risks amongst various reinsurers with the complete freedom exercised under facultative methods. Once it has agreed the terms of a treaty with its reinsurer (or reinsurers) it must place under the treaty all its reinsurances falling within the scope thereof. Similarly the reinsurer must accept such reinsurances; it has no power of choice; it cannot accept one and decline another; its power of underwriting its acceptances is gone; it must take the good with the bad and can exercise but little control over the general character of the business coming to it. The treaty is thus an arrangement by means of which under one single contract a large volume of risks can be ceded. In facultative reinsurance each transaction forms a separate contract, each made on its own terms and having no connection with any other similar transaction. Under a treaty a large number of cessions must be made, all subject to the same terms and conditions and all connected with the one original transaction—the placing of the treaty. This has a necessary effect on the relations of the parties one to another. The ceding company is assured of a certain amount of reinsurance cover for its business and irrespective of the actual merits of the various risks, or of the views which the reinsurer might hold of them individually. The reinsurer has the certainty of receiving a steady and continous flow of business, sufficient to give a good average of risks throughout the year and productive of a sufficient volume of business to support the aggregate risks accepted.

Now obviously, an arrangement so far-reaching as this, must be limited and defined in such a manner as to set out beyond all doubt the intentions of the parties. The operative clause goes on to make provision in this respect as follows:—

(1) A certain fixed proportion of the surplus is to be reinsured.
(2) The class of business to which the treaty refers is defined.
(3) The territory from which the risks are derived is set out.
(4) The proportion which the amount ceded is to bear to the amount retained is agreed.

The surplus

This gives its name to the kind of treaty under review. The ceding company is not bound to cede every risk which it accepts from its original insureds, but is bound to cede only its surpluses. The "surplus" is the term applied to the amount of any risk over and above the amount retained by the ceding company for its own account. That surplus must be allotted to the treaty. The ordinary surplus treaty is called a first surplus, which means that the surplus must be allotted to the treaty, *first* and in priority to any other surplus reinsurance treaty. Whether the first surplus treaty operates in priority to any other form of reinsurance, whether facultative or treaty, is dependent upon the function which the treaty performs within the structure of the ceding company's overall reinsurance programme. Sometimes treaties are arranged as second surplus treaties, and these would receive a share of the surplus only after the first surplus treaty had received the full amount to which it was entitled. A second surplus treaty could be interested only in a risk where the original sum insured was larger than the amount of the ceding company's retention plus the amount to be allotted to the first surplus treaty.

Some explanation may here be made of the manner in which a surplus treaty is constructed. These remarks may be confined to the first surplus treaty since, except in the matter of priority, there is no difference in the operation of a first and a second surplus treaty. The reinsurer under the treaty is entitled to a certain share of the surplus and according to a later provision in the clause (vide No. 4 above) this must not exceed a fixed proportion of the original retention of the ceding company. Now in its essence a surplus treaty consists of a contract to dispose of the whole of the ceding company's surplus and though the ceding company will have a considerable number of reinsurers—and although each one of them enters into a separate contract with the ceding company; yet in effect, they are all participants, each for their own specified share, in one and the same contract. It is part of the spirit of the treaty method that all reinsurers participating in the treaty should be treated alike and, except only in regard to the share to be allotted to them, should be subject to identical terms and conditions. For various reasons to be hereafter explained, this may not always strictly adhered to, but it lies nevertheless at the root of the treaty system.

The structure of the whole treaty contract, being thus defined, supplies the clue to the manner in which it is constructed. The ceding company regarding its treaty as a whole, sets up a certain number of its own retentions to constitute the treaty. Those retentions are always called "lines". The number of lines which the treaty will be constructed to carry will be determined according to the normal requirements of the ceding company, bearing in mind its probable commitments to its agents and insureds and the maximum multiple of its ordinary retention which it will be called upon to insure in order to meet the demands which will be made upon it by its clients. Without laying down any strict rule, it may be said that the purpose of the first surplus treaty is to cover completely the normal needs of the ceding company and to leave nothing to be disposed of elsewhere. The second surplus treaty if required at all would be only for the occasional abnormally large case, or for special groups of risks in particular areas. So if the ceding company finds that normally its maximum reinsurance needs would not exceed, say, ten times the amount of its retention, it will construct its complete treaty accordingly, and this is called a ten-line treaty. This is perhaps the commonest form of surplus treaty and is well suited to the needs of large and well-established offices who must be ready to give ample facilities to their connections, but who are also able to retain substantial sums for their own account. Smaller offices may often need a large number of lines because, with their more limited resources, they are compelled to keep their own retentions on a low basis and must increase their treaty multiplier if they wish to be able to deal with reasonably large amounts of insurance. In such cases it is possible for a twenty-line treaty to be arranged or otherwise as the case may be.

Though there will often be occasions when a treaty containing a large number of lines is perfectly justified, it may be said as a matter of normal procedure that such an arrangement is not entirely desirable from the reinsurance point of view. It tends to reduce the ceding company's interest in the business and this tendency must increase in regard to the more hazardous risks. It makes it easy for the ceding company to accept sub-standard business because of its extended facilities to reinsure—and this sets up a temptation not always easy to resist. On the other hand, reinsurers will but seldom receive their full line on the good-class risks, since, with a large number of lines under the treaty, it will not be very often that the original policy will be large enough to fill the full capacity. Thus the general character of the treaty in such circumstances almost inevitably tends to deteriorate, even though that may far from the ceding company's intention. The tendency can be checked only when the position of the ceding company requires it to keep small lines even on the best-class risks, so as to give the treaty its fair share of these and when the commission terms are so arranged as not to give an unreasonable profit to the ceding company as against its original acquisition cost.

It will be obvious from what has been said that there must be always be a direct connection between the reinsurer's share of the surplus and its proportion of the ceding company's line. In a ten-line treaty, the ten lines will equal the whole surplus, and it follows that one line of such a treaty will equal one-tenth of the surplus. As each reinsurer's line is varied, so does its proportion of the surplus follow suit. A two-line reinsurer would have two-tenths or one-fifth of the surplus, a half-line reinsurer would have one-twentieth and so on. When all the different shares have been placed—and they may differ to any extent—the total number of lines and parts of lines must come to ten, and the corresponding fractions of the surplus must add up to exactly a whole number. This is a point of primary importance and is an integral part of the treaty system. Any lines or parts of lines of the treaty which have not been placed with reinsurers, due perhaps to market conditions prevailing at the time of placement, would revert to the account of the ceding company. However, for the purposes of making the necessary treaty computations this unplaced share would need to be included therein, i.e., as if the ceding company were the reinsurer for such share.

A concrete example will illustrate how the treaty is operated. Suppose a ceding company with a ten-line treaty has accepted a risk for £550,000 upon which it decides to retain £50,000. The surplus will be £500,000 and this must be allotted to the treaty in priority to any other reinsurers. As the "line" in this case is £50,000 the ten-line treaty will exactly absorb the surplus, giving each reinsurer its full line and leaving nothing undisposed of.

But suppose that the ceding company decides to keep £110,000; then the surplus is only £440,000. Again this must be divided among the treaty reinsurers so that each receives his due proportion and no more. So the one-line reinsurer will get only £44,000, even though the "line" is in this case £110,000. It would, however, be against the terms of the contract to give one reinsurer the full line at the expense of the others for all must be treated alike, according to the shares of the treaty which they have received.

If in the example given the ceding company decided to keep only £25,000, the surplus would be £525,000, but only £250,000, i.e. ten lines, could be ceded under the treaty, leaving £275,000, to be given off in some other way, either by second surplus treaty or facultatively.

In the early days of treaties a reinsurer sometimes accepted several lines of a treaty and seldom if ever less than one line. But modern practice has moved towards much greater sub-division, and it is now the exception rather than the rule for a big office to give as much as one line to a single reinsurer. Treaties are divided into half-lines, quarter-lines, and so on, and to facilitate the arrangements in that respect it is more usual to abandon the fractional system and to adopt the percentage method. This is much more flexible, as a ceding company can then allot to a reinsurer any percentage from 1 to 100 of its surplus, with the corresponding percentage of the line. In a ten-line treaty, ten per cent. of the surplus represents one-line and one per cent. of the surplus represents one-tenth of a line. This method enables a ceding company to distribute its surpluses over a wide range of reinsurers and thereby to increase the value of the cover afforded and minimise the chance of serious loss through the failure of reinsurers to meet their obligations. Under modern treaty developments, allotments may often be made of less than one per cent., even down to as little as a tenth of one per cent. This is done partly because the total surplus is sometimes is so large that even one per cent. is a substantial amount, and partly because of the need for a great subdivision, to meet the needs of reciprocity.

The next point deals with the class of business to which the treaty is to apply. A treaty may apply to fire business or to accident business, in the latter case generally to one or more branches of accident business such as burglary, personal accident, or as the case may be. Except in rare instances the same treaty would not cover both fire and accident, such as liability, business. There is nothing against it in principle; it is purely a matter of office methods in underwriting and accounting by the ceding company and/or the reinsurer. It sometimes happens that an accident treaty will apply to all classes of accident business, combining in the one contract a surplus treaty for some of the sections and an excess of loss treaty for others. This is occasionally done in this country, but is a practice not favoured abroad. It has perhaps the technical objection that a contract which embraces two quite different types of treaty must be cumbersome and complicated in wording, but a more real difficulty may arise when one section of the business runs badly and has to be supported, not by the proper alterations at the source, but by reliance upon other and more profitable sections. This is an objection to any kind of "omnibus" treaty arrangement whether in one contract or in more than one.

The class of business must be defined with some exactitude, so as to leave no doubt of what the ceding company must cede and the reinsurer must accept. In view of the open and obligatory nature of the cover, it is important that there should be no doubt on this point, so that nothing may be left out of the treaty which ought to be there and nothing be included which was not bargained for. This point is well understood in fire treaties, which are often required to cover risks other than fire. To meet this need it is not sufficient to make the treaty apply to fire insurance only, and the usual wording is enlarged to include any other perils of any nature which may be insured through the ceding company's fire department. The original purpose of such an extension was to bring in those various extra perils insured in conjunction with the fire risk under various forms of comprehensive cover. Nowadays it goes beyond that and enables cessions to be made of risks such as windstorm, hailstorm, earthquake, riot and civil commotion, etc., whether or not these are insured or reinsured in conjunction with the fire risk. The extension in this form is a wide one and can be considered as being necessary to enable ceding companies to deal with the many demands for cover which may be made upon them by the public. The reinsurance interest, however, requires that it should be interpreted reasonably so as to serve the real interests of the fire department and not be made the vehicle for disposing of the reinsurance of extraneous risks which perhaps could not be easily dealt with in any other way. Above all the interests of both ceding company and reinsurer require that the classes of risk and types of peril for which reinsurance is being sought be clearly identified at the time the contract is agreed. In recent years many disputes have arisen, after a loss has occurred, whether, for example, contingency and financial guarantee insurances were intended to be reinsured under a treaty covering "risks written in the property department" or what is the exact meaning of "risks written incidental thereto". One method of identifying more closely those risks and perils which are covered by the treaty is to list those which are excluded. A more extensive discussion of the role of the exclusion list in a treaty wording is contained in Chapter 7 below.

Otherwise it is reasonable to foresee that the effect of this broadening of the scope of fire treaties is likely to prove harmful to the character of fire treaties in general. To an extent it does include more than one kind of business in the one treaty, for many of the extra perils are quite unlike the fire risk. But since the experience of the treaty appears as a whole, the results of the individual parts thereof may be obscured, with a consequent delay in applying the proper remedies for any bad results. Nevertheless the system fills an obvious need and has undoubtedly come to stay. Any abuse of the facilities thereby afforded would eventually be checked by the fact that the value of the treaty would depreciate and jeopardise the continuance of the contract unless the methods of operating it were put right.

Next it is necessary to define the territorial area from which the business to be ceded is to be derived. This is done, not as a matter of any principle, but for convenience of working. There is nothing to prevent a ceding company including all its reinsurances under one treaty no matter from what part of the world them may come. But in practice this is seldom done. In this country both fire and accident business is divided into home and foreign business, and this division is followed in the arrangement of reinsurance treaties. The foreign business is further sub-divided into general foreign and United States, the general foreign being that derived from all countries in the foreign field other than the United States. Of the three sections of the business the United States is invariably placed under a separate treaty, but the home and general foreign may be placed together or separately. When placed together the treaty is described by the term—"worldwide (ex U.S.A)." The former practice was to place home treaties and general foreign treaties under separate contracts, and though this is still done by certain offices, the general practice tends now in the direction of world-wide treaties—always excluding the United States. Sometimes a world-wide treaty may exclude other specified areas, such as Canada or Australia, where the ceding company for reasons connected with its business methods desires to place these special areas separately.

Although the placing of its treaties by specified territorial areas is entirely a matter for the ceding company and must depend on its methods of working, there are certain arguments in favour of the world-wide treaty. Such a treaty automatically effects a wide distribution of the business and thereby is likely to produce results on a reasonably stable footing. The more a treaty is restricted in its area, the more its results are liable to vary, but as its area is extended so the good results of one country will help to counteract unfavourable results in another. This tendency has in the past been frequently illustrated by the experience of separate home and foreign treaties. It has often been found that when home treaties were passing through a bad phase, the foreign treaties would be extremely profitable, while after the lapse of a few years just the contrary would be the case, by the natural operation of that swing of the pendulum which is one of the few practical certainties of reinsurance results. It is clear that when such treaties are placed separately the reinsurers who may happen to be on the bad only, will constantly seek to obtain the good, and if this is not possible the market for the bad becomes disturbed and the facilities for that section of the reinsurance are in danger of becoming restricted. And since the bad of today may become the good of tomorrow, the whole position as between the ceding company and its separate series of reinsurers tends towards instability and uncertainty, a state of affairs, however, which is completely cured by an amalgamation of the two kinds of treaty, so that all the reinsurers obtain their fair share of each. The recognition of this fact has undoubtedly promoted the practice of placing treaties on a world-wide basis.

The operative clause is completed by a provision as to the proportion of the ceding company's retention, which may be ceded to the reinsurer, that is the share of the "line" which the reinsurer is to receive. The connection between the reinsurer's share of the surplus and its share of the line has already been explained.

It may be regarded as a material factor in the practice of surplus treaty business that the acceptance of the reinsurer bears a fixed and pre-arranged relationship with the retention of the ceding company, so that a one-line reinsurer cannot be interested for more than the ceding company itself on one and the same risk. The position is, however, affected by the present day practice, widely adopted by ceding companies, of taking out excess of loss covers to provide against catastrophe hazards. These covers are more fully explained in Chapter 8, but their effect on the ceding company's retention may here be noted. It may happen that such a cover will operate to reduce the amount to be paid by the ceding company below the amount which will fall to the cost of a one-line reinsurer and this might be held to break a material factor in the treaty. An American case, the North Western Mutual Fire v Union Mutual Fire which was heard in 1943, held that the ceding company owed to the reinsurer an obligation of the highest good faith to compute correctly its retention and to advise the reinsurer of all relevant factors bearing upon the said net retention. It followed that a reinsurer could adjust its liability if the ceding company had itself reduced its own liability by reason of an excess of loss cover. It is true that this case referred to the reinsurance of one specific risk and to an excess of loss reinsurance on one and the same risk. It did not refer to a proportional treaty arrangement under which risks of a whole range of business are ceded, nor to an excess of loss cover taken out over the whole business and not in relation to individual risks. It does not follow in any event that the English Courts would follow the decision in this case, but there seems no doubt that the existence of a catastrophe cover in regard to the business falling under the treaty is a material fact which ought to be disclosed. This has become universally recognised for most ceding companies do in fact disclose to their surplus reinsurers the existence of any excess of loss cover which they may have taken out, either by a letter to be attached to the contract, or sometimes by specially incorporating the necessary clause into the treaty. In a similar way facultative reinsurance slips may be stamped with a wording to show that the company has effected an excess of loss cover and that its stated retention should be read as subject thereto.

In regard to the ceding company's retention, a point of modern practice calls for comment. A feature of present-day insurance development has been the growth of amalgamations of insurance offices and the consequent aggregation of a number of companies under the control of one group. It frequently happens that a treaty will be negotiated to include the business of all the offices belonging to the group. In that event it is important to define what is meant by the ceding company's retention, whether it be an amount retained by the principal company alone or by all the companies in the group combined. Either method may be adopted, but it is a fact material to the treaty to disclose which it is to be. The system of group retentions is becoming more common, for this enables each member of the group to distribute its business among all the other members, according to the amount of the group retention, before interesting the surplus reinsurers. This is sometimes effected in another way. Where each member of a group places its own treaties apart from the other members, no question of a group retention can arise, but it may be stipulated that the ceding company shall have the right to interest its associated companies for specified shares of its retention in priority to its surplus reinsurers. Obviously the sharing of business among the group is one of the main purposes for which such groups are formed and no objection can be taken to it in principle. But it is equally obvious that it must tend to depreciate the value of the surplus treaty, by excluding a certain volume of the more desirable classes of business and reducing the amount available for cession on those risks which eventually reach the treaty. Where risks are ceded to associated companies in priority to the treaty, there ought not be discrimination in favour of the associates by ceding only the better-class risks and excluding them from the more hazardous, leaving those to fall fully on the treaty. This would be to depreciate the treaty at double speed, as it were, by reducing the volume of the good business but not of the bad, and this is a practice which would defeat its own object. The main point to be made here is that the wording of the contract should clearly define what method is to be followed, so that the parties may understand without any ambiguity what is intended.

Certain other powers are sometimes reserved to the ceding company in this part of the treaty. A right may be stipulated to the ceding company enabling it to reinsure locally a share of its business written by its foreign branches or agencies, and this will then take precedence over the obligation to cede under the treaty. The facility thus afforded to the ceding company enables it through its local representatives abroad to deal with its risks as may be required by local conditions and this facultative reinsurance will often act as a protection to the treaty. As most offices exercise the right to reinsure locally, the business is largely placed on reciprocal lines so that although a certain volume of reinsurance is diverted from the treaty some portion of the business received in exchange will be available for the treaty as part compensation. However, nowadays, there is also a tendency for insurance regulation in certain countries to require that insurers authorised to write business in such countries place with a local reinsurance company a priority reinsurance of at least part of the business written. A further encroachment on the prior rights of the first surplus treaty has grown up in recent years, which gives the ceding company the right to reinsure in priority to the treaty at any time when at its discretion this will be in the interests of the reinsurers. Since the priority attaching to a first surplus treaty is a vital and fundamental part of such a contract, it is of importance to examine in detail these departures from the rules to see how and to what extent they may be reconciled with the underlying principles of the business. It is clear that any general postponement of the rights of the treaty reinsurers, unless exercised with the greatest care and discretion, could not fail to be harmful to the treaty interests. The practice of reinsurance in front of the treaty arose at one of those periods in the past when fire reinsurance was passing through an unfavourable phase. It was felt that the bad experience was due to the fact that too large a proportion of hazardous risks was being ceded under the treaty and facultative reinsurances were effected with a view to remedying this state of affairs. What was sometimes done by the ceding company was to grade its risks into three or four broad classes according to the hazard involved and to cede reducing proportions to the treaty as the hazard increased. Thus, on risks in the non-hazardous class, the full ten lines would be ceded if such were available in the total sum insured. On the next hazardous class perhaps only eight lines might be given off, then for more hazardous risks, say, six lines, and for extra hazardous risks perhaps only five lines. This meant that each treaty reinsurer received less than the full allotment to which it was strictly entitled and if these reduced cessions did not exhaust the sum insured, the balance would be given off facultatively. Thus although the prior rights of the treaty were infringed the facultative reinsurance did not as a rule come in front of the treaty but ranked pari passu with it. Yet it might come actually in front of the treaty, for the ceding company if it regarded the risks as sufficiently hazardous might reinsure it all facultatively and give nothing to the treaty. When this practice first commenced it was not usually under any power reserved to the ceding company under the contract and it was thus strictly speaking contrary to its terms. Modern contracts have corrected this omission and specific stipulation is made in the treaty to that effect. Nevertheless, this derogation from one of the fundamental rules of the first surplus treaty requires to be carried out with considerable skill and underwriting knowledge. No doubt the reduction of cessions on hazardous risks must in the long run improve the treaty results, but much depends on the way the risks are graded for this purpose. Unless this is done very judiciously it would be quite possible merely to reduce the premiums ceded under the treaty without effecting a corresponding saving in claims, so that the last state of the treaty might be worse than the first. The development of this practice furnishes another illustration of the extent to which the reinsurer under a treaty must perforce entrust its interests to the care and skill and good faith of the ceding company.

The operative clause as above described is the fountain head of the treaty as it were, upon which and the operation of the reinsurance arrangement depends. The succeeding Articles of the treaty set out in detail the manner in which and the terms upon which the intentions of the parties are to be carried out. The numbers of the Articles which follow refer to the specimen fire surplus treaty set out in the Appendix.

Article No. 2 gives effect to what is a second outstanding advantage of the treaty when compared with the facultative method by providing that the liability of the reinsurer shall commence simultaneously with that of the ceding company, as soon as the retention of the latter is exceeded. This makes the protection afforded by the reinsurer automatic as well as obligatory, and makes certain that there shall be no time after the ceding company has accepted a risk when it may be left without reinsurance cover. It will be remembered that this was not so under the facultative method, where the reinsurer's liability did not commence until the slip had been initialled. The ceding company has the sole right to fix its retention on any one risk and to decide what constitutes one risk. As soon as that has been done, if there is a surplus the treaty comes immediately into operation. The ceding company undertakes to keep a reinsurance register in which all cessions made under the treaty will be entered. This provides the necessary evidence of the reinsurances effected and is necessary to enable the ceding company to make up the bordereaux or accounts to be issued under the treaty. But it should be emphasised that the liability of the reinsurer is in no way dependent upon an entry being made, for that liability commences as soon as the retention is in fact exceeded, even though the entry in the register may not be made until some time later. If, however, a loss should occur before it has been possible to make the entry in the register, the ceding company undertakes to retain an amount in accordance with its usual practice in regard to risks of the particular class in question. This is the only limitation placed on the absolute discretion of the ceding company in fixing its retention—a discretion be it remembered which operates not only when a risk is first accepted, but at any time during its currency, so that the ceding company may alter its retention at any time as it sees fit, subject always to the foregoing limitation in the event of a loss having occurred.

It may be noted that the form of this Article is not always the same, for sometimes a ceding company will construct a table of limits to form a part of the treaty under which maximum retentions are set down for various classes of risk. In that case the ceding company may retain less, but may not retain more than the amounts stipulated. This provision does not usually appear in the fire treaties of large offices, but it may be necessary for small companies, where the volume of premiums to be derived from the treaty is such as to require a limit to be set to the retentions. It is a point of importance to a reinsurer to consider the maximum liability of any one risk in its relation to the total premiums to be ceded under the treaty. If the maximum liability is anywhere near the total premium income, this means that conceivably one total loss might exhaust the whole of the annual premiums, and such a treaty would be ill-balanced and not likely to produce favourable results in the long run.

In the ordinary way however, the ceding company's discretion is absolute and it will not be affected by the fact that its branches or agencies have exceeded the limits laid down in their instructions. In that case the reinsurer is liable for its due share of such excess, provided that its proportion of the ceding company's line be not exceeded. The effect is that if a branch exceeds its authorised limit, the ceding company by enlarging its own retention can bring the insurance within the scope of the treaty if it so desires.

The calculation of the maximum amount which the ceding company is prepared to retain for its own account and the maximum amount of the risk to be ceded to the reinsurer or reinsurers is usually based upon the total of the sum insured. Thus on a 10 Line First Surplus treaty, where the ceding company retains £50,000 any one risk, the maximum underwriting capacity allowed by the treaty (including the retention) would be a sum insured of £550,000 any one risk. However many risks insured in the Property Insurance Department, for example, may be underwritten and reinsured on the basis of an EML (Estimated Maximum Loss) or PML (Probable Maximum Loss) basis. This means that the ceding company will estimate the maximum amount of damage that would be sustained in the event of the occurrence of a fire or other insured peril. The reasoning behind this is that certain risks, because of size or construction or spread over the location, would not be totally destroyed. Thus it could be estimated that a risk has a 10% EML, 20% EML or a 90% EML as the case may be. Assuming that there is a 10% EML on a risk which is insured for £5,000,000 the ceding company could retain an insured amount of £500,000 (i.e. £50,000 EML) for its own account, 9 lines of the First

Surplus treaty would be adequate for reinsuring the balance of the sum insured. The reinsurer's liability would then be expressed as a number of lines on an EML basis. The great advantage of this system is that it gives the ceding company a greater flexibility in the amount its surplus treaty can absorb. It can also provide the ceding company with an opportunity to increase its maximum retention on the more desirable risks which would tend to have a lower EML. The main disadvantage however is that only too frequently a loss occurs and it is found that the EML was underestimated. Thus, for example, a building on which there was a 10% EML, may be completely destroyed. In such event the ceding company and the reinsurer would lose more than they had expected. For this reason, a maximum monetary limit is often included in the treaty e.g. "Up to 10 Lines on an EML basis but in no case more than £1,000,000 any one risk". There would normally be nothing in the practice of the treaty to indicate whether cessions are being made on a sum insured or an EML basis. This is an aspect which needs to be fully explored during the negotiations leading up to agreement on the treaty contract.

Article No. 3 deals with a point of comparatively recent origin. It refers to insurances on goods or merchandise in docks, warehouses, wharves, bonded stores and similar locations where a company may insure many different interests, running for various periods, some annual and some for short periods, and constantly changing so that the total sum at risk may alter almost from week to week. The ceding company fixes its aggregate retention over the whole risk and usually also in respect of any one named insured. In the ordinary way, to maintain this retention, the ceding company would have to retain such a proportionate share of every separate insurance contained in the dock or warehouse in question, as would together make up the aggregate retention fixed. Then, whenever a new policy on the same risk was issued or an existing policy expired, it would be necessary to revise all the proportions retained on all the insurances remaining in force. This gave rise to a great deal of trouble and work, especially with the increasing complication of mercantile business in modern times. To avoid this, the Article of the treaty enables the ceding company to regard the risk as a whole irrespective of the separate interests involved. The retention by risk or by name is fixed on the first policies which may be issued and the surplus will be created out of any further policies as required. But in the event of loss, no matter under what policy it arises, the reinsurers are liable for their proportionate share according to their interest in the whole risk. This being so it is not necessary for the reinsurances to be constantly adjusted on all interests within the risk. The main retention remains unchanged and it is necessary only to adjust the reinsurances as the total sum at risk is varied.

Article No. 4 relates to another matter which has come into prominence in recent years and deals with insurances on the property in which the ceding company has an interest either solely or jointly with other parties. This will arise not only in regard to the ceding company's own buildings or property, but also to those numerous cases in which the ceding company having advanced money on property is interested therein as a mortgagee. It is customary in such cases for the company to insure such property with itself and it will naturally desire on occasion to reinsure. A difficulty then arises in this way. The reinsurer is liable for a due share of what the ceding company is itself liable for, but the ceding company cannot be under a legal liability towards itself. It would not be possible for the investment department of the company to sue its own fire department to recover a loss insured under a fire policy and in effect it may be said that a company insured with itself is not really insured at all. Yet the intention of such inter-departmental transactions is obvious and reasonable, so that it ought not to be impossible for a company to reinsure a portion of such risks under its treaty even though the essential character of the transaction be held to be that of direct insurance. To put the matter beyond dispute a clause is inserted in the treaty contract extending the agreement to include such insurances.

Article No. 5 as set out in the specimen form provides for the issue of the bordereaux. It has already been mentioned in previous chapter that the issue of bordereaux under treaties has been to quite a considerable extent dispensed with. Yet there are still certain contracts which provide for the issue of the bordereaux, so that it is proper to examine the manner in which this done. In its widest form the Article provides for issue of the bordereaux in three forms:—

(1) Preliminary
(2) Definite
(3) Alterations

Preliminary bordereaux are issued at fairly frequent intervals, very often every week. They give details of every cession made during the week as taken from the entries made in the reinsurance register as provided in Article No. 2. This kind of bordereau therefore contains many cessions which are not eventually completed since reinsurances often have to be made before a case has been settled on a permanent basis. The particulars given in the preliminary bordereaux are therefore of a brief and provisional nature. They give the preliminary cession number, name of the insured, description and situation of the property insured, sum insured, amount retained by the ceding company, and the amount reinsured as surplus under the treaty. The premium is not, however, shown and the sums insured and reinsured are to be regarded as provisional only.

Definite bordereaux are issued at rather longer intervals, generally once a quarter, as soon as practicable after the close of the quarter. They give final particulars of all cessions previously advised on preliminary bordereaux, which have been completed by the issue of a policy during the quarter. The definite bordereau gives the final cession number, the preliminary cession number, the policy number, name of the insured, description and situation of the property insured, sum insured, original premium, retention of ceding company, sum reinsured, and reinsurance premium. Thus the reinsurer obtains definite particulars of all cessions which are eventually completed under the treaty. The preliminary cession number is given to permit of the case being traced back to the preliminary bordereau, but it should be noted that where there is any difference between the particulars given on the preliminary and definite bordereaux respectively, the latter will be taken as correct. The definite bordereau brings in the reinsurance premium which enables the reinsurer to make its entries for accounting purposes. In practice, the bordereau in the reinsurance columns, gives the total sum reinsured and the corresponding premium for the whole surplus given off under the treaty. Thereby the bordereau can be duplicated and a copy sent to each reinsurer. The reinsurance premium is totalled for each month and the reinsurer's share is marked at the foot according to its share in the treaty. The totals of the monthly bordereaux are carried forward to the quarterly accounts in due course.

Alterations bordereaux serve a dual purpose. First they provide for the notification of all cessions on the preliminary bordereaux which are not eventually completed. In this way all preliminary cessions are eventually disposed of, either on definite bordereaux or on alterations bordereaux. Secondly, they provide a means of advising subsequent alterations made in risks reinsured, but only where these affect the amount of the premium. It is not necessary under a surplus treaty to advise any other alterations, no matter how they may affect the risk since the reinsurer's liablility is obligatory. In addition to the necessary particulars to identify the cession, the alterations bordereau contains two columns, one for additional premiums and one for return premiums and cancellations. These figures are likewise given for the whole surplus and the reinsurers' proportion is given at the foot.

Under a section of this clause the reinsurer is required to control the correctness of the numbering of the cessions as shown on the bordereaux, and to notify the ceding company of any break in the numerical order. If it should transpire that the missing number has been omitted inadvertently, it is expressly stipulated that the reinsurer shall be liable for its share of the cession which should have been made thereunder. This merely serves to make clear a point which is further provided for in the next Article of the treaty dealing with errors and omissions.

This Article, as drafted, provides for the rendering of the full series of bordereau, but in modern practice it is a frequent thing to dispense with the preliminary bordereau, the first intimation to the reinsurer being made on a definite bordereau. This obviates the need to advise cases which are not eventually completed and does something to save expense. This restricted system is generally sufficient for the reinsurer since it is advised of all cessions on which it eventually becomes liable and unless its system of indexing is very thorough, the preliminary bordereaux do not serve any real purpose. The alterations bordereaux will still be required under this system, as these refer to variations in entries on the definite bordereaux, but no entries will be necessary to cancel preliminary cessions not eventually completed.

Although, as already mentioned, the primary purpose of bordereaux is to give the reinsurer information as to the risks ceded and to allow it to index its business as required, they also serve a number of other purposes, even when indexing is not carried out. In the first place they enable a check to be kept on the proportion of risks reinsured to see that no greater amount is given off in relation to the ceding company's retention than is allowed under the contract. Secondly, a scrutiny of the bordereaux gives a useful insight into the methods of the ceding company. The classes of risk underwritten can be analysed, and the volume of the more hazardous noted in relation to the total. Information can be gained as to premium rating for various types of risks and some general idea can be gathered as to how the business may be located in various parts of the world, with an eye to the possibility of catastrophe hazard. Similarly it will be possible to see to what extent a fire treaty may contain cessions of other perils beyond the simple risk of fire. In general, the receipt of bordereaux under a treaty will enable a reinsurer to estimate the character and value of the treaty much more acurately than will be possible by a mere scrutiny of the annual trading results, and for this reason reinsurers, who attempt to conduct their business on scientific lines, will always wish to receive bordereaux, even though they do not intend to use them to the fullest possible extent.

Nevertheless, it must be emphasised that the trend of reinsurance in modern times, largely as a result of the two world wars, has gone a long way towards the complete abolition of bordereaux. The reinsurer must then depend entirely upon the good faith and accurate working of the ceding company, and this feature is not without influence on the mental outlook of those engaged in the administration of treaties. No treatise on the practice of reinsurance would however be complete without a description of the bordereaux system, which at one time was an integral part thereof.

Article No. 6 is the clause relating to errors and omissions. Its purpose is to make the contract watertight as it were, and to ensure that its purpose shall not be defeated by mere inadvertence. The general purpose of this clause is to protect the ceding company against any accidental omission, either to cede any share of a risk which could properly be ceded or to make the requisite entry in the reinsurance register, or to furnish the proper particulars by bordereaux, by providing that the reinsurer shall still remain liable for its due share of the risk affected by the omission. This enables the ceding company to repair the omission as soon as it is discovered and to date the cession back to the time at which it should have been made. This would be subject to the provisions of Article No. 2 requiring the ceding company to maintain its retention at its usual level if the risk has been affected by a loss. This proviso is important here, for the reason that accidental omissions are so frequently discovered because of the happening of a loss.

In treaty wordings for proportional forms of reinsurance this Article sometimes contains a provision that the reinsurer shall "follow the fortunes" of the ceding company. The exact import of these words is a little in doubt, though their intention is clear. This is a provision which belongs peculiarly to the proportional treaty and is not found in excess of loss treaties or facultative reinsurances. So far as is known the exact scope of these words has not been authoritatively laid down in the Courts, so that it is not easy to say with any certainty how far they would extend. In the opinion of the writer the intention is to set up a kind of community of interest in treaty matters, so that whatever fortune, good or bad, should befall the ceding company should be shared by the reinsurer and whatever the ceding company should decide to do in relation to any treaty matter should be equally binding on the reinsurer, even though it had not been consulted. This would clearly cover such things as mistakes or omissions in ceding, contesting of claims or making *ex gratia* payments and compromises of all kinds which the ceding company may see fit to make to its own insured. But wide as this power may be, it must be regarded as having certain limitations. It is submitted that it can only apply to the ceding company's fortunes in relation to matters properly falling under the treaty. It could not permit the ceding company to do something directly contrary to the terms of the contract. It could not be regarded as following the fortunes of the ceding company if the reinsurer were required to take a larger share of a loss than the proper treaty proportion or to accept a risk of a different category from that provided under the treaty. Whatever is to be done must be done within the four walls of the contract. Therein the ceding company is to have freedom to conduct the affairs of the treaty as it deems best, but not to stray outside them. It would not even give the power to make *ex gratia* payments so as to bind the reinsurer unless such a power were expressly reserved by the terms of the contract, as in fact it is, see Article No. 8. It is possible, however, for border-line cases to arise, when there will be a difference of opinion as to the powers of the ceding company or the responsibility of the reinsurer. Of these it can only be said that the matter would have to be determined by the facts of each case.

Some progress has recently been made in the English Courts towards a clarification of the meaning of the term "follow the fortunes". The first case, that of the Insurance Company of Africa v SCOR (U.K.) Reinsurance Company Ltd (and 11 following reinsurers), went through the Commercial Court and the Court of Appeals until finally decided in the House of Lords. A warehouse which had been leased to the Africa Trading Company by the Liberian Government was totally destroyed by fire on the 7th February 1982. At the time ATC held a fire insurance policy for $3,500,000 with the Insurance Company of Africa (ICA). A reinsurance had been placed with the SCOR as the leader, and the amount reinsured was 98.6% of the original sum insured. The reinsurance contained a "full reinsurance" clause (although in the subsequent litigation it was more usually referred to as a "follow settlements" clause) and a claims cooperation clause which provided as a condition precedent to liability that all claims be notified immediately to reinsurers, that the reinsured undertook to cooperate with the reinsurers in arriving at a settlement of a claim and that no settlement would be made without the approval of the reinsurers.

The loss was properly advised to the reinsurers. But soon thereafter, anonymous letters arrived from Liberia containing various allegations against the proprietor of ATC and an executive vice president of ICA (these allegations were later found to have originated from business rivals). SCOR told the brokers involved that the London market reinsurers were not prepared to make any payment in respect of the claim pending enquiries into information received. Investigators were sent, but as they turned up unannounced, did not clearly identify themselves and would not explain fully what they were investigating, ICA refused to cooperate with them. At the end of April 1982 ATC requested settlement of the loss under the terms of the proof of loss clause. Since the reinsurers would not approve settlement ICA had to resist ATC's claim in the Liberian Courts. Fraud could not be proved and not only were ATC awarded the amount of the loss of $3,500,000 but also general damages of $600,000.

SCOR relying upon the breach of the claims cooperation clause refused to pay their share of the loss and were sued in turn by ICA. Much of the legal argument centred around the conflicting application of the provisions of the "follow the fortunes" clause and of the "claims cooperation" clause. The judges ruled in favour of ICA deciding that where reinsurers agree to follow the settlements of the original underwriters a compromise, whether of liability or amount, between the insurer and the insured will bind the reinsurers unless they can prove that the compromise was dishonestly arrived at or that the insurer failed to take all proper and business-like steps to have the loss fairly and carefully ascertained. They also ruled that there is no breach of the claims cooperation clause whereby insurers undertake in arriving at the settlement of claims that they will cooperate with reinsurers if that non-cooperation is in respect of matters other than the settlement of the claim. The efficacy of the "follow the fortunes" clause was impaired by the existence of the claims cooperation clause only to the extent that the reinsurers were not obliged to indemnify the reinsured in respect of the damages and costs awarded by the Liberian Court. So ICA recovered its 98.6% of $3,500,000, but nothing of the $600,000 general damages.

The second case, Vesta v Butcher, 1985, involved a Norwegian fish farm which was insured by a Norwegian insurance policy and wholly reinsured on the same terms to London reinsurers. The reinsurance was subject to a "follow the settlements" clause as well as a "claims control" clause whereby no offer, payment or compromise of a claim would be made without the consent of the reinsurers (which would have been ineffective under Norwegian law). The question arose as to whether the contract of reinsurance ought to be interpreted in acordance with English or Norwegian law. The judge held that where a reinsurance contract is "back to back" with the original insurance the legal effect of the clauses defining the cover needs to be determined in accordance with Norwegian law. Thus, although the proper law of the reinsurance contract was English, the construction and effect of the clauses were to be determined in accordance with Norwegian law, in the same way as they were in the original contract.

These above cases show how the Courts view the "follow the fortunes" clause, and other forms of words which are intended to have a similar effect. It also shows that the other terms and conditions contained in the treaty contract need to be carefully drafted to avoid conflict with this provision.

By another paragraph of the same clause the reinsurer is given the right to inspect the books and documents of the ceding company so far as they relate to matters falling within the treaty. This right is reserved to an official or other duly authorised agent of the reinsurer and may be exercised by inspection at the offices of the ceding company at any reasonable time. This right to inspect books is useful in the case of accidental omissions, so that the parties to the treaty may be properly satisfied as to the facts, but its purpose goes much further, for the right may be exercised in regard to any matter falling within the scope of the contract. Where a reinsurer receives no bordereaux, as happens often in modern practice, the right of inspection becomes of greater significance, as it is the only means available to the reinsurer of ascertaining any details of what has been ceded under the treaty, or of the manner in which the treaty business generally has been operated. This right to inspect is indeed an important safeguard to the reinsurer. It may be sparingly used, and is not often called into operation as between companies of the first rank. But sometimes the need does arise, and to protect its interests the reinsurer may require to make the necessary inspection of books. It is doubtful whether this could be made as a matter of right unless the clause were included in the contract since this is not an implied condition of such an agreement as a reinsurance treaty. Where the need does arise, it may be necessary to examine the treaty affairs, not only to be satisfied as to how a cession has been made or how a loss has been charged, but also to investigate the circumstances in which the treaty was entered into and the nature of the information supplied by the ceding company and upon which the acceptance of the reinsurer was based. Upon the result of such an investigation may depend not only the procedure to be adopted in regard to a single cession or an individual claim, but also the fate of the whole treaty itself, involving possibly it being cancelled from inception and all entries made thereunder being written back. Such far-reaching investigations as these would be made as a rule by one or more professionally qualified persons, such as chartered accountants, lawyers, actuaries, etc., and would differ in degree from the mere inspection of an item in the books of the ceding company which could be made by an official of the reinsurer. The unsettled conditions of reinsurance affairs in recent years have led to a considerable increase in the number of full investigations, with results which have sometimes been a little disquieting but which emphasise the need for the clause in the treaty contract. Although, for certain classes of business, such audits of records are now commonplace as between insured and insurance company, the practice of reinsurance in this country has not yet reached that stage in certain other countries where reinsurers conduct regular audits of the records of the ceding company as a matter of course.

Article No. 7, in providing for the premium to be paid to the reinsurer, sets out in proper form the consideration which binds the contract. In the ordinary way the premium to be paid to the reinsurer is to be calculated at the same rate as that received by the ceding company on the original insurance. This is, in effect, the policy premium, i.e., the original rate less any discounts which may be allowed to the insured, and this follows the theory of proportional reinsurance whereby both parties share in the premium according to their respective shares of the risk. However, the matter does not stop there; for in regard to certain foreign business it has become the practice to stipulate that certain brokerages may be deducted from the premium before a share is allocated to the treaty. This practice gives rise to some difficulty, because it is not always easy to determine exactly what brokerages might be deducted. It clearly does not allow deduction of ordinary agents' commission, which, as will be seen presently, is taken care of in the reinsurance commission. The original intention was no doubt to apply the deduction only to local brokerages paid in certain localities, over and above the ordinary agents' commission. In that case it might be supposed that the rate of premium had been loaded to allow for the brokerage, so that the deduction merely removed the loading without depreciating the real premium applicable to the risk. There is justice in this argument and it is recognised by the usual wording of the clause, which permits deduction of only such brokerage as is paid by tariff regulation or local custom and to which reinsurers as a rule will raise no objection. But some treaty wordings are much wider and permit of deduction of any sub-agent's commission, or any kind of brokerage, without definition. This will permit of deductions where no tariff regulations or local customs exist; it will even permit of retrocession of treaty cessions with deduction of treaty commission. Various misunderstandings have arisen in the past as to the extent to which these deductions could legitimately be made and quite extraordinary differences in practice still exist between ceding companies. But where deductions are carried to excess, the reinsurers do not receive their proper share of premium and the inevitable result is to bring out a loss to the treaty, since the margin on reinsurance business is not large enough to withstand any such pressure. This state of affairs produces its own remedy, since if a treaty is consistently unfavourable steps will be taken to ascertain the cause and to apply the cure. For this reason the interpretation of this provision has tended to become stricter and to be confined to the deduction of brokerage allowed by tariff or local custom only, though it would perhaps be too much to say that there is even yet complete uniformity in the practice on the subject.

A further allowable deduction from the original gross premiums could arise in the form of the various types of premium tax imposed on insurance and reinsurance transactions. These can be many and varied and are to be distinguished from the corporate taxes charged on the results of the trading operations of the ceding company. Premium taxes of one kind or another, and this term should include all such costs as are imposed upon insurance policies by governmental authorities even when described as fire brigade charges and the like, can be found in many parts of the world. In addition to the taxes imposed on the original insurance transaction, there could be a tax imposed on the reinsurance cession itself. These reinsurance taxes are generally imposed on foreign "non-admitted" reinsurance. Great care should be exercised in identifying exactly how all these deductions are calculated, for example, whether the reinsurance tax is calculated on the gross premium after deduction of direct premium taxes and local brokerage or not. This point is of considerable importance in establishing the base premium on which the treaty commission is to be calculated.

There is another exception to the theory that the reinsurer receives a due share of what the original insured pays. This occurs in connection with the system of policy fees, which came into use on the continent of Europe from about 1920 onwards to meet conditions arising from the war of 1914–18. Although this system of policy fees was not revived to any appreciable extent in Europe after the end of the Second World War, it can on occasion be found in certain other parts of the world. Its purpose is to meet an exceptional rise in expenses of administration, by requiring the insured to make a contribution thereto in the shape of a policy fee. The usual argument is that as the reinsurer is not subject to these additional expenses, it is not entitled to any share of the policy fees. The idea is that the rise in expenses is of a temporary nature, not calling for a wholesale disturbance of premium rates, but conveniently to be met by the levying of a policy fee, which could be removed as easily as it was imposed once the emergency has passed away. The fallacy in this argument unfortunately is the fact that the rise in expense generally proves to be of a permanent rather than a temporary nature, which weakens the structure of the system. Another fatal disadvantage attaching to the system is that the real course of the trading experience is liable to be obscured by the policy fees, more especially when these become more or less permanent. It is not easy to see how far the policy fees may be supporting an additional expense, and how far an increased claim strain and if no part of the policy fees goes to reinsurers, the burden on the treaty will be the greater as the claims strain goes up. For this reason reinsurers hold strongly that the policy fee system is not suitable except to meet a purely temporary emergency. On permanent lines there is only one sound method, which is to construct the premium rating so as to support every charge on the business, claims, expenses, taxes, and so on; then to allot to the reinsurers their due share of such original rating and to cover the cost of acquisition within the calculation of the reinsurance commission. Reinsurers expect to pay their fair share under this heading, but see grave dangers in a system which leaves them entirely outside some part of the income derived from the original insured.

The second part of Article No. 7 makes the necessary provision in regard to the reinsurance commission. This is usually of two kinds, a flat commission computed on the premiums, less returns and cancellations, ceded under the treaty, and a further commission computed on the profits earned on the treaty. The purpose of the flat commission is to reimburse the ceding company the amount it has to pay in agents' commission together with a reasonable contribution towards its expenses of management. The ceding company has to incur considerable expense in obtaining its business, in surveying, in the issue of policies and in the adjustment of claims. The reinsurer gets the benefit of this and has itself to expend nothing under these particular heads. It is reasonable therefore that it should pay its share through the reinsurance commission. It is not possible to lay down any general rule as to the appropriate levels of reinsurance commission. To some extent the commission rate varies with the results of the treaty, in the sense that a treaty which can show consistently good claims ratios commands more favourable commission rates in consequence. This is perhaps a natural thing to expect, though not entirely logical. The treaty commission, as already stated, is a contribution towards the original acquisition cost and this is a factor which does not vary in any direct relationship with movements in the claims ratio. At the same time it is proper that the best treaties should obtain the best terms, but it is submitted that the logical way to ensure this is through the profit commission, for in this way the reinsurer's contribution is proportioned accurately to the results of the treaty. It may be admitted that some proportion of present-day expense ratios is due to action taken by insurers to improve the conditions governing the hazard and this in course of time should reflect itself in a reduced claims ratio, but even so, it is fairer to the reinsurer to contribute its share through the profit commission, rather than by too high a flat percentage of reinsurance commission, which presses with equal weight on the treaty in bad years as well as good.

After a period of bad underwriting results, reinsurers attempting to improve their results tend to give a high priority to reducing excessive reinsurance commissions. On such occasions they will try to relate the reinsurance commissions allowed more closely to the general levels of original commissions prevailing in the local market. Another approach is to allow premiums to be ceded to the treaty on a basis of premiums net of original commissions plus an overrider to defray part of the acquisition costs. Naturally in such event the levels of original commissions to be allowed should be clearly understood by both parties. In addition the method of calculation of the overriding commission needs to be clearly understood. The differences in calculation of the overrider on "net" premium after deduction of original commissions and on "gross" can be considerable. Thus, for example, on a premium ceded of say £5,000,000 and an original commission rate of 30%, an overrider of 5% calculated on "net" premiums would amount to £175,000 whereas if the overrider were to be calculated on "gross" then this amount would be £250,000.

These points are sometimes recognised by adopting a method of calculating reinsurance commission on what is called a "sliding scale" basis. Under this system the commission within specified limits bears a direct relationship to the claims ratio of the treaty. Briefly, a provisional rate of commission is fixed by the company, and allowable by the reinsurer on the premiums it receives for a fixed period, usually one year. At the end of the period the claims ratio is calculated and applied to the "sliding scale" table incorporated in the treaty, to determine the actual commission allowable by the reinsurer, e.g. in the undermentioned example a commission rate of 35% would be payable in respect of a loss ratio of 60%.

The actual rate of commission is applied to the premiums for the period and the difference between the amount of the commission arrived at and that provisionally allowed by the reinsurer is payable by the reinsurer to the company. It should be noted that the provisional commission is usually fixed at the lowest rate shown on the sliding scale table so that in no circumstances will commission be returned by the company to the reinsurer.

A draft of the "sliding scale" table is given as follows:—

"the Reinsurer shall allow to the Company a provisional commission of 32.5% (thirty two and one half per cent.) calculated on the reinsurance premiums payable to the Reinsurer under this Agreement and thereafter at the 31st December in any year in which the Agreement is in force the provisional rate of commission shall be adjusted in accordance with the following scale:—

Rate of commission		42.5%	if claims ratio is		less than 46%
,,	,,	42%	,,	,,	46% but less than 47%
,,	,,	41.5%	,,	,,	47% but less than 48%
,,	,,	41%	,,	,,	48% but less than 49%
,,	,,	40.5%	,,	,,	49% but less than 50%
,,	,,	40%	,,	,,	50% but less than 51%

Rate of commission	39.5%	if claims ratio is	51%	but less than 52%
,, ,,	39%	,, ,,	52%	but less than 53%
,, ,,	38.5%	,, ,,	53%	but less than 54%
,, ,,	38%	,, ,,	54%	but less than 55%
,, ,,	37.5%	,, ,,	55%	but less than 56%
,, ,,	37%	,, ,,	56%	but less than 57%
,, ,,	36.5%	,, ,,	57%	but less than 58%
,, ,,	36%	,, ,,	58%	but less than 59%
,, ,,	35.5%	,, ,,	59%	but less than 60%
,, ,,	35%	,, ,,	60%	but less than 61%
,, ,,	34.5%	,, ,,	61%	but less than 62%
,, ,,	34%	,, ,,	62%	but less than 63%
,, ,,	33.5%	,, ,,	63%	but less than 64%
,, ,,	33%	,, ,,	64%	but less than 65%
Rate of commission	32.5%	if claims ratio is	65%	or over

The 'claims ratio' shall be arrived at by dividing:—

(a) The reinsurance premiums for the period to the 31st December less the unearned premium reserve for that period plus the unearned premium reserve brought forward from the preceding period into

(b) The claims paid for the period to the 31st December plus the reserve for outstanding claims at that date less the reserve for outstanding claims brought forward from the preceding period."

This clause is drafted on the basis that the treaty is operated on a "clean cut" basis whereby all outstanding liabilities, whether by way of unexpired insurance exposures or unsettled losses, are withdrawn from the reinsurer at the 31st December of each year. The unearned premium reserves and outstanding claims reserves representing such unexpired insurance exposures and unsettled losses, are credited to the reinsurer(s) participating in the treaty for the following year. However, where the reinsurer participates on a "pure" underwriting year basis there is no assumption or withdrawal of premium or loss portfolios, so that it remains liable until all liability has expired or has been liquidated. In such event it may be necessary to make a number of adjustments to commissions calculated on a sliding scale of commission as and when the outstanding losses come to be settled.

It can be seen that the operation of this method under a treaty will tend to stabilise the results; reducing the profit to reinsurers in good years and similarly reducing the loss in the bad years. However it must be clearly understood that this method is subject to fixed limits, both as regards the rate of commission and the loss ratio, and thus in a year when the loss ratio is extremely high, the commission will not be reduced accordingly but only to the minimum specified in the sliding scale table, e.g., with reference to the above table the rate of commission will never be lower than 32.5% whether the loss ratio is 65% or even 80%. In the same way, the maximum rate of commission will never exceeded, no matter how low the losses may fall. Thus it is important for the parties to negotiate at inception of the treaty an appropriate sliding scale for the anticipated range of loss ratios.

Profit commission is often payable on surplus treaties. The idea of this is that the profit which is earned on the business passing under the treaty is due to the skill and care with which the ceding company conducts its business and that some part of that profit should therefore be returned to the ceding company as a reward therefor. Yet this is a theory which calls for a careful adjustment if the interests of both parties are to be served. It should be in no sense a penal clause, designed to keep the reinsurer's profit permanently at too low a figure, for unless the reinsurer is able to earn and keep for itself good profits in good years, it cannot possibly accumulate the reserves which will be necessary to meet the deficits of bad years, deficits which may on occasion be very heavy. The whole purpose of reinsurance commission, whether flat commission or profit commission, is to recoup to the ceding company a due share of its acquisition cost, and the fact that a treaty produces good profits over a period of years is not in itself a good reason for increasing the total commission payable beyond the requisite level for that purpose.

As the wording of this Article shows, the profit on a treaty is to be computed on an earned basis, i.e., after making the necessary adjustments in the reserves set up for unexpired risks and outstanding losses. However there is an increasing tendency to compute this profit on a "pure" underwriting year basis, as this more likely to give a "truer" result unaffected by estimation errors in computing the values of the reserves set up for unexpired risks and outstanding losses. In many parts of the world, the unexpired risk reserve is generally taken as being 40% of the year's gross written premiums. This calculation arises from a very simple estimation of the premiums written in each quarterly period. Thus, assuming that insurances are written equally during such quarter, then all insurances written in the First Quarter of the year may be assumed as having been written on or about the middle of that quarter. Therefore some 12.5% of the premium written should be allocated towards the unexpired liability which might arise in the following year. For subsequent Quarters the precentages would be 37.5%, 62.5% and 87.5% respectively. The average thereof would be 50% which, after deduction of an assumed rate of reinsurance commission of 30%, equates with the figure of 35%, which is then grossed up to 40% to be safe. Various other methods may be used to estimate a proper and adequate premium allocation for that liability unexpired at the end of the year of account. Thus, for example, there are the "twenty-fourths" system (based upon the mid-point of monthly estimations of premiums) and the "actual days expired" system which is based upon an exact estimation, for each policy, of the unexpired premium relating thereto. With modern electronic methods this latter avoids the problems arising from the necessity to make a different provision for special classes of risk or of business. Nonetheless, if the original premium rates are inadequate then it might be necessary to establish a higher unearned premium reserve than that calculable from one date to another. Therefore, the method to be adopted should always be clearly set out in this clause of that treaty. In addition to the ordinary trading items—premiums, claims, commissions, taxes, etc., it is often provided that the reinsurer is entitled to debit to the account a percentage of the premiums ceded—often 5%.—for the account of its management expenses. This is not necessarily, however, a universal practice though there is this reason in support of it that the reinsurer's profit on the business must necessarily be diminished by its own expenses of management. The profit commission statement does not normally include on the debit side the amount of any profit commission paid during the year of account, whether on that year or on a pervious year, as this is generally considered as being obviously no part of the trading results of the business. This aspect will be considered more fully below in the discussion on the carry forward of deficits.

The percentage of profit which is paid as profit commission varies according to the circumstances, but in the normal way it would not be less than ten per cent., nor more than twenty per cent., though this statement is made broadly speaking, for the parties will make such terms as they think proper in the matter. Differences in practice exist as to the exact method of computation. The profit may be made up on an annual basis, each year being entirely self-contained and the profit commission payable on the result thereof. This is however, rare, and is only possible under treaties producing exceptionally even results. It is in the nature of treaty business that its results are subject to considerable fluctuation, so that a good profit on one year may be succeeded by a heavy loss on the next. If profit commission is payable on each separate year's results, it might well happen that over a period of four or five consecutive years the reinsurer would have paid profit commission on two or three of them, while the loss incurred in the remaining years had more than wiped out the profits earned. The reinsurer would have suffered a loss in the aggregate over the period, but would still have paid some profit commission.

The unfairness of this is readily recognised and it is obviated by a system of equalising results. This is done in two ways, by a three years' average or by carrying losses forward.

Under the three years' average system, the profit of the year, as ascertained according to the trading statement contained in the treaty, is averaged with the profit similarly ascertained during the two preceding years, and the commission is payable only on the average of the three years. Special provision is made for the earlier years of the treaty. In the first year, commission is payable on the profit of that year; in the second year on half the aggregate profits of the first and second years; in the third year on one-third of the aggregate profits of the first, second and third years; and thereafter, as each new year's result is brought in, the earliest of the old years drops out.

The second method, adopted in most treaties containing profit commission provisions, is to carry any loss disclosed in one year's profit statement to the debit of the next year. The effect is thereby to diminish any profit which the next might show, or to increase any loss. As long as the profit statement by this method shows a deficit, that is carried forward to the next year, so that, in reality, no profit commission can be payable until all previous losses have been extinguished. Modern practice limits the extent to which a deficit can be carried forward so that rather than "losses carried forward to extinction" it will be found that treaties often contain a provision that losses are carried forward for three or four or five years, as may be negotiated. Thus, if a loss were not fully absorbed by profits in, say, the three following years, any deficit remaining would thereafter be omitted from the computation. Obviously, the longer periods of carry forward of losses are more beneficial to the reinsurer. The method of carrying losses forward is more favourable to the reinsurer than the three years' average system, since it might often happen that a heavy loss in one year would not be completely extinguished by profits in the two following years, but in the third following year that loss would nevertheless drop out of the account. However, there is seldom any provision for reimbursement of profit commission previously paid as may arise where the initial one or more years of a treaty shows a profit, but are then followed by consistent losses.

Special provision may need to be made for the computation of the profit for the last year of the treaty following upon a termination of the contract. This problem does not so much affect profit commission calculated on a pure underwriting year basis, since adjustments would continue to be made until all liabilities have been liquidated. However, it will be realised that, where the profit commission is calculated on an accounting year basis, the trading statement contains reserves which are estimated figures to take care of future liabilities.

While the treaty continues in force, these are carried forward from one year to the next, so that it is not material whether or not they exactly meet their relative obligations. They will automatically adjust themselves as the years proceed. But in the final year of the treaty the running account comes to an end and it then becomes important to ascertain whether or not the reserves set up are adequate to run off the outstanding risks and to settle the outstanding claims. Here again there are two methods in vogue. One is to make up the profit statement in the usual way at the end of the final year and then to carry the reserves forward to a final account against which all further claims are charged as they are settled and which account is not completely made up until all liabilities have been entirely disposed of. The other is to delay the profit commission statement in respect of the final year until it is possible to ascertain all the liabilities on a settled basis. This is merely a matter of procedure and the eventual result is the same in either case. Whichever method be adopted the final account is brought into average with the two preceding accounts or includes any loss due to be brought forward from prior years as the case may be.

Here it is of interest to consider a further development appearing in certain surplus treaties which provides for the Profit Commission to be payable by the reinsurer on a sliding scale basis. A draft of an extract from an Article incorporating this method is given, as follows:—

"In addition the Reinsurer will also pay to the Company a profit commission calculated on the average profits derived from this Agreement in accordance with the following scale:—
14% if net profit does not exceed 5% of gross premiums for the current year.
15% if net profit exceeds 5% but does not exceed 6% of premiums.
16% if net profit exceeds 6% but does not exceed 7% of premiums.
17% if net profit exceeds 7% but does not exceed 8% of premiums.
18% if net profit exceeds 8% but does not exceed 9% of premiums.
19% if net profit exceeds 9% but does not exceed 10% of premiums.
20% if net profit does exceed 10% of gross premiums".

It can be seen from an examination of the above Article that the rate of profit commission is variable and bears a direct relationship to the profit of the treaty, e.g., if the treaty profit is 10% then the profit commission rate will be 19% thereof. The scale given is a specimen only and is not, of course, the only one possible.

It should be noted that this method in no way affects the calculation of the treaty profit which, as previously mentioned, may be either on a three years' average or losses carried forward basis.

To a large extent this method of computing profit commission fulfils the same purpose as a sliding scale of ceding commission. For this reason it would be unusual to use both methods in the same treaty, as in good years that would reduce the reinsurer's margin below a reasonable level.

Article No. 8 deals with the procedure in the event of losses and a number of points arise here having particularly to do with treaty methods.

In the first place the ceding company reserves to itself the sole right to dispose of losses in anyway it thinks fit, either by ordinary settlement, or by way of compromise or by ex gratia payment or otherwise at its discretion. Further it has the right to contest any claim by litigation or to institute any action in relation to a claim. In whatever way the claim is disposed of the reinsurer is reponsible for its proportionate share of the claim and also for any expenses of litigation or otherwise incurred in the settlement of the claim. This is intended to refer only to expenses which can be earmarked as specifically incurred in connection with the claim, such as litigation costs, assessors' fees and the like, but not to salaries paid to the ceding company's staff or any share of general management expenses. The point is generally made clear in the treaty wording.

This provision of the contract disposes of any difficulty which might otherwise arise as to the ceding company's control of its claims, or as to the reinsurer's right to be consulted in regard to disputed claims which exists in facultative reinsurance. The intention is that all such matters should be left to the ceding company and a special provision is necessary to give effect thereto. Nevertheless it would not be reasonable that the reinsurer should be left completely in the dark as to what claims have been incurred, and provision is accordingly made for notice to be given by the ceding company immediately it itself is notified of a claim which will affect the treaty.

This does not apply to all claims, since a great many of these will be for quite small amounts and to notify them all would involve the ceding company in a great deal of labour without giving any real advantage to the reinsurer. Notice has, therefore, to be given only of claims which will involve the whole treaty in a total estimated amount exceeding an agreed figure. For a ten-line treaty this figure might be put at £5,000 though this is a matter of agreement between the parties. This system, by advising the reinsurer of the larger claims as soon as they occur, will not only enable it to keep a note of the current experience of the treaty, but also furnish it with the information to pass on to its reinsurers.

It should be noted that these provisions as to claims apply only to surplus treaties and not to excess of loss treaties, under which the reinsurer usually reserves for itself certain rights to be consulted in regard to claims. The point is more fully discussed in Chapter 7 below.

In regard to the payment of claims by the reinsurer, when settled, the treaty provides a two-fold method. In view of the many risks reinsured under a treaty it would not be practicable for every claim to be paid in cash, for this would mean constant remittances often for quite trifling amounts. It is, therefore, stipulated that claims where the reinsurer's share is less than an agreed figure shall be carried to the quarterly accounts and this system applies nowadays to both treaty and facultative reinsurance. All claims above that agreed figure would be payable within ten days (or as may be agreed) after written demand has been made by the ceding company. These are commonly called "cash losses" and a usual provision is that any claim of which the share of the whole treaty is (say) £50,000 or more shall be a cash loss. The need for some such provision is obvious for although the ceding company may conveniently carry small losses to the quarterly account, seeing that it holds the reinsurance premiums as a cover, yet for the larger claims it is proper that the reinsurers should pay their share at the same time as the ceding company has to make its payment to its own insured. Under a ten-line treaty, the usual cash loss limit would be (say) £5,000 a line, which may be regarded as a reasonable figure. The greater sub-division of lines, which is a feature of modern treaty practice, can result, of course, in reducing this figure considerably, for where a reinsurer has only one-tenth of a line of the treaty, its cash loss limit would be reduced to £500. This cannot very well be avoided, since the cost to the whole treaty remains at £50,000 and the ceding company has the same need to collect cash from its reinsurers irrespective of what amount each may be called upon to contribute. Yet it is sometimes felt to be a hardship to a reinsurer to have to pay a cash loss at so low a figure as £500 or lower, and the point may be met by the ceding company increasing the limit to a minimum of say £1,000 for its smaller reinsurers. This is not very convenient, however, as the one-line reinsurers would pay a cash loss which totalled £50,000 while a tenth of a line reinsurer would pay only if the loss reached £100,000, so that the same loss might be recoverable in cash from some reinsurers but not from others, This leads to complication and possiblity of error in the office of the ceding company, and is therefore to be avoided as far as possible.

Article No. 9 lays down the procedure to be followed for the rendering of the treaty account. At one time the system of rendering accounts on a quarterly basis was universal for surplus treaties, following no doubt the long-established quarter-day system in fire insurance. Subsequently, the period for the rendering of accounts extended to half-yearly and, even, annually. However, the quarterly basis is a convenient interval for the purpose of the submission of accounts as not giving the ceding company too much clerical work nor requiring the reinsurer to wait too long for its account. The quarterly account is normally made up on a calender year basis to the last day of the quarter months, i.e., 31st March, 30th June, 30th September, and 31st December, and these quarters in reinsurance parlance are designated first, second, third and fourth quarters respectively. With certain ceding companies or in parts of the world, where either the accounting or the fiscal period is different, the last day of each quarter, and, indeed, the whole accounting year may be calculable on a different basis. The actual form of the account depends to some extent upon the practice of the ceding company, but the account should contain details of the premiums ceded during the quarter, and the commission and claim settlements to be charged, due allowance being made for any cash losses having been paid. Sometimes it is necessary to adjust the amounts of the premium and loss reserve deposits and to credit interest thereon. This aspect is more fully dealt with in a succeeding Article in the treaty. In short, the purpose of the account is to summarise all the transactions falling under the treaty during the quarter and so to arrive at the balance in favour of one party or the other. Where a treaty provides for the issue of bordereaux, the premiums shown in the account can be checked against the bordereaux supplied, but under a non-bordereau treaty the reinsurer can only accept the figures supplied by the ceding company. A list of all losses is generally supplied, so as to give the reinsurer details of this item including all the smaller losses which had not been notified under Article No. 8. Commission is, of course, computed at the rate stipulated in the treaty on the premiums ceded thereunder. A separate item may be necessary for premium taxes or fire brigade charges or any other charges for which the reinsurer is responsible.

For the information of the student a specimen form of a quarterly reinsurance account is given in the Appendix.

Reinsurance accounts cannot be rendered immediately after the close of the quarter to which they relate. It is to be noted that under a treaty the account is always prepared by the ceding company, for the reason that the ceding company alone possesses the information which has to be included. Much of this has to be obtained by the ceding company from its agents, and if the treaty is a world-wide one, this may take some considerable time. It is generally reckoned that three months at least will be necessary to settle the various items, renewals, etc., which fall within the quarter, so that at least that time must elapse before the treaty account can be issued. Some definite provision needs to be made on this point and it is a common thing to stipulate that accounts shall be rendered within three months after the close of the quarter, though there is no uniformity in the matter. In some cases this period has been extended up to as much as six months. An alternative has been not to give any definite period, but to stipulate that accounts shall be rendered "as soon as practicable" after the end of the quarter. This would give a considerable latitude to the ceding company, though under this clause the period would seldom be considered as exceeding six months at the most. Whilst it must be admitted that some delay in rendering accounts is a necessary incident of treaty business, it will likewide be allowed that undue procrastination works to the detriment of the reinsurer. It postpones the payment of the premium due although in some cases losses are brought into account up to a short time before the account is issued. As a result the reinsurer may be prejudiced by the loss of interest on what is, after all, its money and there can be no doubt that as much promptitude as may be reasonably possible in the rendering of treaty accounts is to be desired in the interests of all the parties concerned. The account has to be confirmed by the reinsurer and a definite period is allowed for this, say within fifteen days after the account has been received by the reinsurer. The period cannot be conveniently run from the day the account is issued, for the many accounts issued under the same treaty have often to be sent to all parts of the world, with a consequent considerable variation in the dates they are received. Provision is then made for payment of the balance due by the debtor party within a fixed period, say another fifteen days after confirmation. If the balance is payable by the ceding company, this period must run from the day upon which the confirmation is received in the ceding company's office, but if the balance is payable by the reinsurer, payment must be despatched within fifteen days after the date the confirmation was given.

The practice of constructing treaties on a world-wide basis, makes it necessary to provide some method of dealing with the different currencies in which the business is transacted. When cessions are made under a treaty relating to risks in various countries of the world, the original premiums and claims will be dealt with in the local currencies, and the cessions will in the first instance be made in the same currency. The question then arises how these are to be dealt with in the quarterly accounts. Two different systems are in use. The first of these is to convert all the figures in the account—premiums, commission, claims and so on—into the currency of the ceding company. Thus, in this country domestic treaties and British world-wide treaties would be rendered in sterling. This is a practice coming down from the days prior to the Second World War when rates of exchange were stable, moving only within a narrow range of values, so that the question presented no particular problems. The erratic course of exchange rates which has been a distinguishing feature of modern times has, however, made it necessary to make some specific provision as to the rates at which the conversion should be made, for to work on par values would often cause a very great deal of prejudice to one party or another. Whilst the practice in this matter is not uniform, the usual stipulation provides that foreign currencies shall be converted at the same rates of exchange as those at which they were remitted to or paid by the ceding company, or, failing this, at the rates of exchange ruling on the last day of the month or quarter in which the account was made up at the ceding company's foreign branch or agency. A variation of this latter provision might provide for the rate to be deemed to be the average of the rates of exchange ruling during the quarter. The operation of the provision depends upon the methods adopted by the ceding company in handling its currencies. Where the premiums are repatriated and converted into (say) sterling that rate of conversion applies equally to the share of the premiums reinsured, while when it is necessary to purchase out of sterling funds a draft in currency to pay claims, the share of the reinsurer must likewise be paid at the rate of exchange applicable to the draft. But when, as frequently happens, the currency is not repatriated, but is kept in the country of origin, then premiums are received and claims are paid in the original currency and no conversion ever takes place. It is to provide for such currencies as these that provision is made for conversion in the reinsurer's accounts at the rates ruling on some specified date.

Under an alternative system of trying to limit the effect of sharp fluctuations in exchange values, separate accounts are kept under the treaty for every different currency involved, segregating all the various items—premiums, commissions, claims, etc., and thus arriving at a number of balances each in its own currency. These are then settled in the original currency and no question of conversion arises. The same would apply to any cash loss which had to be paid outside the quarterly accounts. This system can add very greatly to the bookkeeping work involved in the offices both of ceding company and reinsurer and the system of accounting must be constructed accordingly. Where a range of currencies are involved, with only minor volumes of premiums or claims arising in respect of certain currencies, any benefits could be rapidly negated. Thus, it will often be found that the accounts are maintained in two or three major currencies, with the minor currencies converted into one of these major currencies at an agreed basis of currency conversion. Nonetheless this system has the advantage of keeping the currency trading items under the treaty independent of any variations in exchange values, since the whole business will be ascertained in its original currency and when it has to be converted for balance sheet purposes, it is open to the reinsurer to adopt what rates of exchange it thinks proper. The balances of such accounts received or paid by the reinsurer will be converted at the rates ruling at the date of the remittance. Many reinsurers, however, eliminate some of the uncertainty thereby caused, by keeping accounts in the principal world currencies, into which receipts are paid and out of which remittances are made, and only the balances of such accounts need to be converted at the end of each year for inclusion in the balance sheet, this being of course a book entry only, not involving any actual transfer of the currency. The idea behind this is to maintain a balance in currency sufficient to act as a buffer against the effect either of depreciation or appreciation in the value of a currency when measured in terms of the reinsurer's own currency. The currency balance is in effect an asset set against certain corresponding liabilities in the form of unexpired risks and outstanding losses, and any variation in the value of the one will be compensated by a similar variation in the value of the other. This eliminates both the risk of incurring a loss, and the chance of gaining a profit out of movements in currency values and it may be said as it were to remove any element of gambling from this aspect of the reinsurance transaction. It may very well be argued that taking chances on currency fluctuations is no part of a reinsurer's business, and that it is a good thing to do everything possible to avoid it. Those who take a contrary view argue that they are bound to have more faith in their own currency than in any other, being more closely acquainted with the factors with regulate its value. In this regard the many currency difficulties of the past twenty years, characterised by sharp fluctuations in exchange values, tend to gainsay this approach. However, these are matters for the indidvidual decision of each reinsurer. The important point is that the treaty should define clearly the method to be adopted in the accounts in relation to foreign currency transactions.

All these considerations, which arise out of the basic principles of reinsurance, may be and often are affected by currency regulations, i.e, restrictions imposed by a State on the transfer of its currency to countries outside its borders. These restrictions have become increasingly common over the past twenty years and insofar as they prevent the free transfer of currency, reinsurers must perforce maintain banking accounts in each such currency. No conversion would then take place, except as a matter of accounting for balance sheet purposes. All such restrictions are inimical to the true interests of reinsurance, a fact which fortunately tends to be well recognised in many States where, whenever any relaxation of currency restrictions becomes possible, reinsurance is among the first industries to which those relaxations are applied.

Article No. 10 provides for the retention by the ceding company of a certain proportion of the premiums payable to the reinsurer, as a premium reserve deposit. This is a comparatively modern—and controversial—introduction into the practice of reinsurance. The necessity for some such provision became apparent at the time of the First World War, when so many reinsurance relationships came to an abrupt end. It was further underlined by the many failures amongst reinsurance companies which was a feature of the difficult years succeeding the termination of that war. The purpose of a premium reserve deposit is to provide the ceding company with a collateral security for the due performance of the obligations of the reinsurer under the treaty. When treaties are brought to a sudden termination, either because the reinsurer has gone out of business by liquidation or because the contract can no longer legally continue, the position is that the ceding company has paid to the reinsurer a considerable volume of premiums for which there is a continuing risk exposure running for varying periods into the future. That risk exposure is then no longer covered, and even though the ceding company may be entitled to a return of premiums corresponding to the unexpired term of each cession, that right by itself is not of great value. The ceding company must at once incur the cost of replacing the unexpired cessions with another reinsurer, while having to take its chance of what it may recover against the defaulting reinsurer either in a liquidation or at the close of a war or otherwise as the case may be. This state of affairs was obviously unsatisfactory and the system of premium reserve deposits grew up to remedy it. At first it was applied only in cases where some reasonable doubt might exist as to the future course of the treaty relationship, but its advantages to the ceding company quickly became so manifest that its use soon became universal. Thus it was found in practically all proportional treaties and was applied alike to all reinsurers as a purely business precaution and implying no reflection whatever on the standing and security of the reinsurer. When it was first introduced it met with considerable opposition from the reinsurers, especially from old and well-established offices whose professional pride was perhaps piqued and who saw in this innovation a reflection on their stability. An objection of more substance was the adverse effect which such a system was bound to have first on the reinsurer's liquid cash position and secondly on its interest earnings. The withholding of balances due to a reinsurer naturally restricts its available working cash, while the interest credited to the cash deposits retained by the ceding company is inevitably less—and often much less—than can be obtained on securities or investments. The system nevertheless came to stay. However, the recent long period of adverse reinsurance underwriting results have led reinsurers to adopt many measures for the improvement of these results. Among these has been the reluctance to allow the ceding company to retain premium reserve deposits unless there is a local statutory requirement to that effect. There is also a considerable reluctance to allow the retention of cash deposits rather than alternative forms of security, such as the deposit of securities or the lodging of Letters of Credit issued by a major international bank.

The amount of the premium reserve deposit is always a fixed percentage, as may be mutually agreed, of the premiums ceded and in the majority of cases it is fixed at 40% of the premium ceded to the reinsurer during the preceding twelve months. Under a new treaty the reinsurer is not required to constitute this reserve all at once, in advance, for that would impose too great a financial burden. The reserve is built up by the ceding company retaining forty per cent. of the premiums shown in each quarter's account, so that by the end of the year the full amount has been accumulated. In succeeding years the reserve deposit is maintained each quarter at the proper level by withholding the reserve on the new quarter's premiums and releasing the reserve for the corresponding quarter of the previous year. When, however, a new treaty is accepted with a portfolio assumption, i.e., where the reinsurer assumes liability for the unexpired portion of risks already in force at the commencement of the treaty, the premiums to be ceded to the reinsurer in consideration thereof form a ready made premium reserve deposit, which can be retained by the ceding company at the commencement of the treaty without any burden on the reinsurer. In that case the usual practice is to charge the necessary percentage of premiums as reserve in each quarter during the first year and to release one-fourth part of the portfolio premiums.

The reason for fixing the premium reserve at 40% of the premium is clear. In effect it is supposed to represent the value of the unexpired risks, and this is what the ceding company requires to safeguard itself if anything untoward occurs. As has previously been explained, the system of calculating reserves for unexpired premiums on the eighths method—estimating unearned premiums on the basis of the mid point of the quarter in which such premium was written—approximates to 40%.

Although the premium reserve deposit is, of course, the property of the reinsurer it is completely controlled by the ceding company and interest as accordingly stipulated is credited thereto. This may be at a fixed rate which would be fixed very roughly with regard to the local interest rates available at the time. Alternatively it may be based upon a fluctuating rate, say 1% below the London market interbank rate or some such local equivalent. The traditional rates of interest still allowable at the level of say 3 or 4% per annum no doubt reflects these criteria from an age when such was the level of the market rate.

In the general way it is inevitable that cash retained as a premium reserve must carry a lower rate of interest than that which could be earned if the funds were invested in securities. However, investment earnings are of primary importance to a reinsurer as constituting a substantial part of its eventual trading surplus. This point is recognised by the increasing degree whereby premium reserve deposits, where they are still maintained, are substituted by the reinsurer making a deposit of approved securities in lieu of a cash deposit or supplying a Letter of Credit issued by a major international bank.

Where the practice of lodging securities is followed, such securities must be deposited in the name of the ceding company—although the use of an escrow account whereby the securities are held in the joint names of the ceding company and the reinsurer is becoming more widespread—and are put up for the required amount at the commencement of the treaty, with a provision that if by reason of an increase in treaty premiums or a decrease in the market value of securities, the amount deposited falls below 40% of the previous year's premiums, an additional deposit of securities shall be made to bring the amount of the premium reserve deposit up to the proper level. If no such additional deposit is made the ceding company retains the right to retain cash for the difference. When such securities are deposited in lieu of cash, the dividends thereon would be paid to the reinsurer as they become due. Where there is a cash deposit the interest is credited in the treaty accounts, either quarterly, half-yearly or annually as may be agreed, though in this matter the practice is not uniform. The interest is generally payable less taxation levied at the local rate and the reserve deposit commences to bear interest from the date at which the amounts are credited to the premium reserve deposit fund. There may be some difference of opinion as to what the date should be. The account, and the reserve, may be made up at the end of the first quarter, say the 31st march, but may not be actually ascertained and prepared until the date the first quarter's account is issued, which may be some time in the following July or August. It seems to be the practice that the date the account is issued fixes the time from which the interest is to be credited.

If and when a treaty is cancelled, it is necessary to determine what is to happen to the premium reserve deposit. The usual stipulation is that the ceding company must retain the whole of the premium reserve deposit held at the termination date of the treaty date whether or not the unexpired risks are cancelled by a withdrawal of the premium portfolio, but outstanding losses, as and when settled, are to be charged against the retained reserve deposit as long as the amount remaining is sufficient for the purpose. No part of the balance of the reserve deposit, if any, would be returned to the reinsurer until all liabilities under the treaty have been finally disposed of, and if the amount of the reserve deposit proves to be insufficient to meet those liabilities, the reinsurer would be bound to make the deficiency good. This is to provide the ceding company with the necessary security. In actual practice what tends to be done, when a treaty is cancelled with return of portfolio, is for the ceding company to estimate the amount of the claims outstanding, and to add to it a margin for contingencies. Then, since the return of the premium portfolio would extinguish any liability for the unexpired risks, it would be possible to release that part of the premium reserve deposit not required for outstanding losses, and this will often be done if the treaty had been terminated in the ordinary way of business, though not, of course, in the event of a liquidation of the reinsurer or other extraordinary cause of termination.

As already shown, the intended purpose of the premium reserve deposit is to give the ceding company something in the way of extra security, and this would most often be required were the reinsurer to go into liquidation. If then the premium reserve deposit is to serve its purpose, the ceding company must be able to retain it against any claim by a liquidator, until all the obligations under the treaty have been discharged. In this, however, some difficulty may arise. It must be remembered that the premium reserve deposit is the property of the reinsurer and forms part of its assets. It is the duty of the liquidator to collect the assets and the question arises as to what extent a ceding company could set off any sums due to it under a treaty as against a claim by the liquidator for the return of the premium reserve deposit in full. It would seem that any ascertained balance of account including any return premium due on cancellation of the portfolio could be so set off, but not, in the absence of agreement to the contrary, any amounts not ascertained, such as reserves for outstanding claims. So far as these were concerned, the ceding company would, it is submitted, be bound to return the premium reserve deposit and prove in liquidation for outstanding claims as and when settled. This would give the ceding company only such dividend on its claim as the liquidation might allow, while the premium reserve deposit so returned would go to the benefit of the general body of creditors. To that extent the purpose of the premium reserve deposit would be defeated and to obviate this a clause is inserted in this Article stating that "if and insofar as it may be necessary to secure the ceding company in the event of the liquidation either voluntary or compulsory of the reinsurer, the ceding company shall have a prior charge and lien on the said premium reserve deposit and also upon any further monies which may be credited to the reinsurer under the Agreement and the ceding company shall be a secured creditor to that extent." The effect of this clause is to give the ceding company a contractual right over the premium reserve deposit and any further monies credited, which would avail against a liquidator until the liabilities under the treaty had been met. When a treaty provides for the retention of loss reserve deposits in addition to premium reserve deposits, this clause would need to be amended so as to give the ceding company the same rights in regard to both forms of reserve deposit.

At this point it is of interest to consider the provision of loss reserve deposits under reinsurance treaties. The purpose of a loss reserve deposit, like a premium reserve, is to provide the ceding company with a further security for the due performance of the reinsurer's obligation. The growth of the practice of retaining loss reserve deposits is attributable in no small measure to the currency difficulties experienced by many countries in the years after the end of the Second World War, with the subsequent inclusion in the legislation in certain countries of terms which, in many instances, require the provision of loss reserve deposits under reinsurance treaties. Thus, it will often be found that there is greater legal justification for the inclusion of a loss reserve deposit requirement in a treaty than the more commonly encountered provision for a premium reserve deposit.

The applicable legislation may be sub-divided into two distinct classes as follows:—

(1) that which compels the insurance company domiciled in the territory governed by such legislation, i.e, the ceding company, to make provision for loss reserve deposits under their reinsurance treaties, and
(2) that which compels the foreign insurance companies, i.e., the reinsurers, to make provision for loss reserve deposits in respect of treaties accepted from territories governed by the relevant legislation.

Generally speaking reinsurance companies are averse to the provision of loss reserve deposits under treaties for reasons similar to those previously outlined on the subject of premium reserve deposits. However, when as in (1) above the existing legislation requires the provision of loss reserve deposits by the ceding company it is inequitable for the reinsurers to expect such companies to cede their treaties without the provision of loss reserve deposits whilst having to comply with the regulation by setting up such reserve deposits out of their own pocket. Therefore, in many instances, if the circumstances warrant it, the reinsurers usually agree to the provision of loss reserves.

Similarly in (2) above if the terms of the legislation require the provision of loss reserve deposits by reinsurers and they wish to continue accepting reinsurance treaties from the territories concerned then they have no option but to comply with the terms of such legislation.

It should be noted, however, that should such treaties be the subject of a reciprocal arrangement it is often required that the provision of loss reserve deposits be likewise reciprocal. The loss reserve deposit is usually calculated at a rate of 100% of the losses outstanding under the treaty in question and may be adjusted either annually or quarterly, bearing interest at the same rate as the premium reserve deposit.

It is not usual for this reserve deposit to be utilised by the ceding company for the payment of losses during the currency of the treaty, such losses being paid separately by the reinsurer. However, upon termination of the treaty the loss reserve deposit may be retained by the ceding company and utilised for the settlement of the reinsurer's share of the then outstanding losses. Such reserve deposit will be adjusted annually in accordance with the settlements effected until all the liability of the reinsurer in respect of outstanding losses has been finally disposed of when the balance of the reserve deposit, if any, will be returned to the reinsurer. It should be noted, however, that as with the premium reserve deposit should the amount of the loss reserve deposit prove to be insufficient to meet the liability the reinsurer is bound to make good the deficiency.

In recent years the practice has developed of the reinsurer supplying a Letter of Credit as an alternative to the depositing of cash or securities. Originally this practice developed in the United States of America and Canada as a means of resolving the problem of the disallowance by the authorities of credit for non-admitted reinsurances. However, the practice has now spread to many other parts of the world, including the United Kingdom. The Letter of Credit is issued to the ceding company by a major bank for a specified period, corresponding to the treaty requirements, in a form which is "clean, irrevocable and payable on sight." This means that at any time prior to the expiry date the holder, the ceding company, can draw on the Letter of Credit any sum or sums up to the stated limit. Thus, the ceding company has the security under the treaty with all the benefits as if it had retained cash deposits. The disadvantage is that the ceding company does not have the use of funds which would otherwise have been withheld, nor the benefit of the difference in interest between that credited to the reserve deposits and that earned. The benefit to the reinsurer is that funds which would otherwise have been retained by the ceding company are now under its own control and the investment income thereon would undoubtedly be greater than the amount of interest which would have been credited by a ceding company. Among the disadvantages are the annual charge made by the bank for the issuing of a Letter of Credit (calculated upon the full limit of the credit) and the invariable requirement that the Letter of Credit be collateralised by the deposit of adequate cash or securities with the bank, thus reducing the investment flexibility available to the reinsurer. The greatest disadvantage to the reinsurer, however, arises from the danger that as the Letter of Credit is "clean, irrevocable and payable on sight" the ceding company could make drawings without justification. The only remedy therefor would then lie in an action at law. It may be found that the ceding company and/or the local regulatory authority would require that the Credit be established with a specified bank or a bank registered in the territory concerned. In such event it may be necessary for the reinsurer's own local bank to confirm the Credit to the issuing bank.

Article No. 11 is that which defines the period of the treaty and the manner in which it may be brought to an end. In the usual way the treaty takes effect for all cessions made in respect of insurances issued or renewed on or after an agreed date and thereafter runs for an indefinite period. This is to say it will run year after year without any need for special renewal, and will not come to an end unless definite steps are taken to terminate it. However, nothing prevents the parties from agreeing a fixed term to the period of the treaty, should they so wish. The period of the treaty is in no way concerned with the periods of the insurances ceded under it, for in theory the treaty could continue in force even though all the cessions made under it had expired, and it would still be available for any new cession as and when required. In practice this does not happen but there is nothing in the nature of the contract to prevent it.

It will be obvious that an agreement of so far-reaching a nature as a treaty, once entered into, is not to be lightly cancelled, and detailed stipulations are made in all treaties as to how they are terminated. Cancellation of a treaty arises in two different ways, either by the free action of one or other of the parties, or from some extraneous cause.

Either party has the right to cancel the treaty by giving a period of notice of its desire to do so. No fixed rule can be laid down as to what this period of notice shall be, but it is seldom less than three months or more than six months. It is true to say that nowadays the period of notice tends to be three months, or the equivalent of ninety days, though there are exceptions to accord with specific requirements. The use of longer periods of notice has tended to decline if only for the reason that, for a treaty having a year-end expiry date, the reinsurer will be in a better position to determine the results at the end of September rather than at the end of June. The notice must be given in writing and, usually, sent by registered letter, so that there may be no room for doubt as to whether the notice has been given or received. Nowadays, the use of more modern forms of communication, such as telexes, is becoming increasingly common. There is also some difference in practice as to the time at which notice must be given. Originally it was the rule that notice could be given at any time, but this is not very convenient to either party. A ceding company might find itself with notices on its hands expiring at various dates, necessitating replacement of the cancelled shares at inconvenient times. The reinsurer, having secured a treaty, would never be sure how long it would be able to keep it. Therefore free notice at any time is seldom provided in modern treaties, but a stipulation is made requiring the period of notice to be given so as to expire on a fixed date. This is most often the 31st December, though sometimes it may be the last day of any quarterly period. The advantage of requiring notices to expire at the 31st December is that all alterations will take place at the close of the ceding company's business year, thus facilitating the work in the office which is always involved by a change in the treaty reinsurers. Although the annual period of most treaties tends to coincide with the ceding company's business year, i.e. from the 1st January to the 31st December, there are certain exceptions. Thus, in countries such as Australia, the annual period of treaties tends to coincide with the local ceding companies' business year, which extends from the 1st July to the following 30th June. In addition, an increasing number of ceding companies prefer to have their treaties' expiry date to be other than the 31st December since they feel they can obtain more considered attention from reinsurers than might be available in the busy time at the year end.

Cancellation imposed on the treaty by extraneous causes arises in two ways. Because of the provision for immediate termination of the treaty in the event of the occurrence of certain contingencies, the Article appearing in the treaty tends to be referred to as the "sudden death" clause. The first of these is covered by the war clause, which came into use some time after the end of the First World War. Under this clause the treaty is automatically brought to an end if war breaks out between the country of the ceding company and that in which the reinsurer resides or carries on business or is incorporated, whether war be actually declared or not. The last phrase was added owing to the manner in which the Second World War developed, when so many countries became involved without any formal declaration of war. By a further addition, also made necessary through the experience of the

Second World War, the clause is made to apply to a country which is in the effective occupation of an enemy. Within the terms of this clause it is further provided that all liability of the reinsurer in respect of current cessions shall cease as from the date of the outbreak of war. To some extent this clause is merely declaratory of a state of affairs which would arise in any event, since the outbreak of war makes all contracts with enemy nationals illegal and so brings these contracts ipso facto to an end. The position in that event in regard to current cessions would not, however, be clear, but the clause puts it beyond dispute that these are immediately terminated.

The legal effect mentioned refers to the position under English law, and it does not follow that the laws of other countries would make the same provisions in regard to their own nationals. So it might happen that one party to a treaty would have to regard it as having been cancelled, while the other would consider as still being in force. This provides another reasons why a "war cancellation" clause is desirable, for this, being part of the contract, is binding upon both parties, irrespective of what their laws may provide on the subject.

A further clause in this Article used to give the ceding company the right to terminate the treaty forthwith if at any time the reinsurer should:—

(1) lose the whole or any part of its paid-up capital, or
(2) go into liquidation or have a receiver appointed, or
(3) cease underwriting new or renewal business by order of an insurance department or other competent authority, or
(4) be acquired or controlled by any other company.

Nowadays this clause tends to give both ceding company and reinsurer the right to apply this clause if any of these conditions applies to the other party. Thus, in the event of either party suffering the occurrence of any of these contingencies then the other party may put the terminaton in force immediately.

It will be observed that the circumstances in which this clause may be put into operation involves the financial position of the other party, whether it be the ceding company or the reinsurer, and its position in the insurance world. Thus, if a reinsurer were to suffer the events described in paragraphs (1) to (3) above it would be in actual, and probably severe, financial difficulties, while paragraph (4) has as its basis the fact that the treaty is a contract of a personal or quasi-personal nature, made with a particular reinsurer. If that reinsurer amalgamates with another company, its identity may be lost, and the ceding company may find its contract in effect transferred to another company with which perhaps it would not wish to do business. Similar considerations would also apply to the reinsurer should the ceding company suffer the occurrence of any of these contingencies, and therefore, in equity, the clause nowadays should apply equally to either party.

It is clear, therefore, that if any of the contingencies described above were to occur, then it would not meet the situation that the party possibly suffering prejudice thereby should merely have the right to issue notice of cancellation within the terms of the contract, for, except in the case of liquidation, this would entail the making of cessions during a period of notice to or from a party whose position may not be satisfactory. The fears of the ceding company would naturally arise from the apprehension that neither the premiums paid by way of cession nor claims arising on such cessions would be recoverable. However, the reinsurer could be subject to equally adverse apprehensions such as their being liable for claims recoveries on cessions on which they would probably receive no premium. But the greatest fear of the reinsurer must be to be brought into a direct relationship with the original insured (as is tending to happen in certain jurisdictions) when an insolvent ceding company is unable to settle a claim. The right to give immediate notice of cancellation is clearly vital to the other party to take prompt measures to safeguard its position. To assist to this end it is often provided, in the event of liquidation, that notice may be given if a petition is presented for the winding-up of the other party, or a resolution is passed for voluntary liquidation, so that thereby the treaty is terminated at the earliest possible moment.

Some treaties add to this clause a further paragraph giving the right to the other party to terminate the treaty forthwith in the event of any law being passed or regulation becoming operative so as to prohibit or render illegal any part of the business falling under the treaty, but in that case the right to terminate applies only to the particular locality concerned. This resembles the war section of the clause and merely sets out what is in fact enjoined on the parties by law.

Political and economic upheavals since the end of the Second World War have from time to time given rise to further additions to the clause. Thus, one such variation attempts to provide for the monetary upheavals which have been such a feature of this century. This provision runs somewhat in the following terms:—

"In the event of the currency or currencies of (country of the ceding company) or of (country of the reinsurer) being

(1) devalued

(2) subjected to government decree forbidding the export of such currency which decree would thereby prevent the debtor party from paying to the creditor party any balance or balances due,

then the party domiciled in the country not subject to such devaluation or government decree shall have the right to terminate this Agreement as from the last day of the quarter immediately preceding the date when such devaluation or government decree shall have taken effect.
For the purpose of this provision a currency shall be deemed to have been devalued when the official rate of exchange falls by 20% or more below the following assumed standard values namely: (here follows the respective relation between the two currencies)."

The object of this provision, as its terms imply, is to prevent either party being prejudiced by a devaluation in a currency or by restrictions on its export, the idea being that the conditions under which the treaty was entered into have so radically changed that the party prejudiced thereby ought not to be held to its contract. This provision, though useful, has not been adopted for general use in treaties and is for that reason not included in the specimen wordings given in the Appendix. It is possible that, had this provision been in general use over the past twenty years, the severe fluctuations in rates of exchange which have affected most currencies would have given rise to extreme volatility in treaty relationships. Although both parties, having suffered considerable adverse effects due, often, to quite arbitrary authoritarian action, might feel that they ought to be able to limit the adverse effects devolving upon themselves through factors connected only remotely with reinsurance considerations, it is doubtful whether an abrupt rupture of the treaty relationship would solve such problems.

Having stipulated how and when a treaty may be cancelled, it is desirable to lay down definite provisions for the manner of dealing with the unexpired portion of the cessions current at the time of cancellation. This is a matter in which treaty practice developed somewhat slowly and surplus treaties did not always lay down the position very clearly. Modern treaties tend to be more clearly drafted in this respect. This is provided for in Article No. 12. Even though notice to determine the treaty has been given, the reinsurer is entitled to receive its share of all the cessions made while the period of notice is running. This follows from the fact that until the notice has actually expired the treaty remains in full force with all its rights and obligations. Now the period of each cession follows the period of the original policy, so that on the date on which the treaty expires there will be in force a large number of cessions with various periods of unexpired time to run. In the ordinary way, without express provision to the contrary, the reinsurer will remain liable for its share of all cessions until their natural expiry, even though the contract under which they were made is, apparently, no longer in force. The reinsurer has received premium for the full period of each cession and its liability continues accordingly. In their early days surplus treaties were generally drawn up in this way, but the increasing complication of insurance business, coupled with some frequent changes in treaty arrangements, made it necessary to devise a method whereby the liability might be cut off short as it were and a fresh start made with a new treaty. It will be realised that when a treaty is transferred from one reinsurer to another, if the previous reinsurer is to remain liable for all its cessions until expiry, this adds considerably to the work of the ceding company. In the years following the change, all losses will have to be categorised according to the year in which the policy was issued and the cession made, so as to be sure that each loss is charged to the proper reinsurer. Two or three or more years may well elapse before all the losses relating to any given year's cessions are finally disposed of, and since it is quite a common thing for treaty changes to be made every year, the ceding company will be obliged to keep a number of treaty series in being, each overlapping one another, adding greatly to the work involved and very liable to lead to error. Such a system is not impossible but it is certainly very inconvenient. A practice has accordingly grown up whereby all the unexpired risks at the termination of the treaty are withdrawn from the old reinsurer and transferred to the new. This leads to a consideration of the portfolio system. The term "portfolio" may in one sense be used to mean the whole volume of business ceded under a treaty and this is no doubt its strictly accurate meaning. In reinsurance usage, however, it has been narrowed to denote the proportion of the business which is in fact unexpired at the end of any given period. When a treaty is cancelled at the end of a year (or at any other time) the volume of business unexpired is represented by a certain proportion of the premiums which have been ceded during that year, and by debiting the reinsurer with that amount by way of return premiums, it is possible to release that reinsurer from any liability in respect of the running off of those risks. This is what is known as "withdrawing the portfolio" and is a very common practice under modern conditions. But obviously the ceding company does not desire itself to assume the liability so released, for that would derange its system of limits. It will therefore arrange to pay the premium recovered from the old reinsurer over to a new reinsurer, who will thereupon assume liability for all claims arising in the new year on the running off of the old cessions. This is what is called "taking over (or assuming) the portfolio" and it usually follows as a necessary sequel to a withdrawal of portfolio. Some reference has already been made to this question of portfolio in the remarks on a previous page with regard to premium reserve deposit.

The Article now under review provides a method of operating the portfolio.

In the most modern development of the surplus treaty a distinction is drawn between a cancellation made with the prescribed period of notice and a cancellation without notice under the special clauses of Article No. 11. Where a treaty is cancelled by due notice, the ceding company reserves to itself the option either to hold the reinsurer liable under current cessions until their expiry, or to withdraw the portfolio, according as the circumstances at the time may dictate. This option is necessary for the ceding company's protection. If the treaty is cancelled either because it is desired to transfer it to another reinsurer or because the ceding company is for some reason not entirely satisfied with its reinsurer, then it would be natural and convenient for the portfolio to be withdrawn. But if the cancellation is made because the ceding company has discontinued that particular treaty and does not desire a new reinsurer, or because, owing to an unfavourable run of the business, it would be difficult to replace the portfolio, then it would be proper to require the reinsurer to complete its obligations and not to withdraw the portfolio. Since the position at some cancellation date in the future cannot be foreseen in advance, the option which the ceding company reserves is a very necessary precaution.

If the treaty is cancelled without notice, then if this is done under the war clause, or because the business has become illegal, no option can be excercised. The business comes to an abrupt end and the portfolio must be withdrawn. Under the "sudden death" clause, where the reinsurer's status is in question, the ceding company's option is generally reserved, with this proviso that in practice the portfolio is much more often withdrawn than otherwise. If it is a case of the reinsurer being in liquidation, it will certainly have to be withdrawn, and if there is a loss of the paid-up capital, it will generally be safer to withdraw the portfolio, though this part of the clause is operated with discretion and would not be put in force for some temporary impairment of capital of a trifling nature due to some exceptional bad fortune. Where the reinsurer amalgamates with another company and immediate notice is given, the ceding company might exercise its option either way according to the circumstances.

When a portfolio is to be withdrawn it is necessary to determine how it is valued. It is clear that what is at stake is the proportion of the reinsurance premiums unexpired at the time of cancellation, and there is only one strictly accurate way of computing these. That is to work out the pro rata unexpired premium under each individual cession, thus arriving at a total representing the gross value of the portfolio. But since the reinsurer will have paid commission on the total premiums ceded, this total must be reduced by the same rate of commission in order to arrive at the amount of premium to be returned, i.e., the net value portfolio. This is a long and costly business, for the number of cessions made under a treaty during a year may run into many thousands, though modern electronic methods of data storage can make it possible to calculate a true value of the unexpired premium on an "actual days" basis. In the absence of these facilities, certain empirical methods have been devised to short-circuit this work. The commonest of these is to assess the value of the portfolio at a percentage of the total premiums ceded during the previous year. This is the method usually adopted in this country, and an amount of 40% of the premiums is perhaps most often adopted though sometimes the figure is taken at 35% if the portfolio of business contains a significant proportion of policies with periods of less than twelve months. However, if the portfolio contains a volume of long-term business, i.e. policies issued for periods greater than twelve months, as is often the case in Canadian treaties, the percentage may be increased to 45% or 47.5%, or possibly even more. Whatever percentage be adopted, it is taken as a net valuation and no commission is to be deducted. A 40% portfolio follows the usual practice of computing the reserve for unexpired risks under an ordinary direct insurance account, and this no doubt accounts for its frequent use. The assumption is that there is an even flow of new business and renewals throughout the year so that at least 50% of the premiums will be unexpired at the end of a year. Where there is a considerable volume of business of premiums written in a particular quarter, either through custom or legal regulation requiring common renewal dates, this proportion could be very different. If a treaty commission were to be deducted from 50% of the premiums, this would bring out the net value of the portfolio to 35%, so that in fixing the value of the portfolio at 40% due allowance is made for a larger proportion of unearned premiums in the hope that the figure may perhaps err on the safe side. In the event, unless the calculation is based upon an "actual days expired" basis, there is no strictly accurate mathematical basis to the computation, since the assumptions upon which it proceeds are so variable and may be affected from one year to the next by alterations in the composition of the business, by long-term business, by short-period business, by sudden accretions of business in the early months of the year and so on. This has been recognised by attempts which have from time to time been made to arrive at some method of computation which would be more exact without going to the length of working out every cession pro rata. Two of such methods may be instanced by way of illustration. One is known as the "eighths" system and one as the "twenty-fourths" system, both of which are found in use by various ceding companies in different parts of the world.

Under the "eighth" system the premiums ceded during the preceding year are dissected into four parts according to the quarter in which they were given off. It is then assumed that on the average each quarter's premium will expire at the middle of the quarter. Thus the premiums ceded during the first quarter of the year will expire halfway through the first quarter of the next year, or say the 15th February. So at the 31st December these premiums still have half a quarter to run, and therefore one-eighth is unexpired. Similarly the premiums of the second quarter have a quarter and a half-quarter to run, i.e., three-eighths; those of the third quarter have five-eighths and those of the fourth quarter seven-eights still to run. A simple sum in arithmetic will thus give the value of the unexpired premiums, which of course is a gross figure and must be reduced by the rate of the treaty commission. This method, though still depending on assumptions which are only approximate and still liable to be deranged by long-term and short-term policies, does at least introduce some mathematical calculation into the matter. The "twenty-fourth" system proceeds on similar lines and is an attempt to narrow the margin of error still further. Under this system the premiums are dissected according to the months in which they are ceded, and each month's premiums are assumed to expire half-way through the month. So, at the end of the year, the January premiums have half a month, or one twenty-fourth part to run, the February premiums a month and a half or three twenty-fourths, the March premiums five twenty-fourths, and so on in increasing proportions month by month throughout the year up to the December premiums with twenty-three twenty-fourths unexpired. The resultant figures are totalled and reduced by commission in the same way as under the "eighth" system, bringing out a portfolio value which, for a normal business, will be as accurate as is necessary for the purpose, though even then it may be necessary to provide specially for long-term insurances if these represent a substantial item in the account.

The taking over and withdrawal of portfolios has become a recognised and widely adopted adjunct to treaty business, and a word may be said here of its effects on the reinsurer's accounts. The system gives rise to a number of minor problems which hinge on the question of whether the portfolio consideration is to be regarded as premium. The point to be remembered is that the portfolio consists of risks accepted in the previous year and running to maturity in the year of account. So if a reinsurer takes over a portfolio at the 1st January, 1987, this will refer entirely to risks commencing in 1986 and having completely expired before the 31st December, 1987. So if the reinsurer adds this portfolio consideration to its premiums it will thereby inflate its premium revenue and will at the end of 1987 put up a reserve for unexpired risks thereon, although in fact there is no unexpired risk to provide for. If on the other hand a portfolio is withdrawn from a reinsurer, by the same reckoning it will deduct this from its premium income, thereby reducing this below the true level of its current premiums, and making its normal calculation of unexpired risk reserve insufficient. Of course, where a reinsurer has a substantial account it may rely upon its portfolios coming in to balance more or less against its portfolios going out, so that the effect on its accounts is cancelled out. Or, although crediting or debiting its portfolios to premiums, it may make the proper allowance for these when computing its unexpired risk reserve. Neither of these is very satisfactory and the practice of dealing with portfolios as part of the premium income has undoubtedly certain disadvantages. For one thing the portfolio consideration is not the real premium, but has been reduced by commission and, in theory at all events, it ought to be written up to gross figures if it is to be added to the premium income. But its disturbing effect on the constitution of the reserve for unexpired risks at the end of the year is the principal objection. Varying opinions are held as to the best method of dealing with the matter. The most logical seems to be to treat the portfolio consideration as a reserve and to operate it in the accounts as an adjustment of the insurance fund. Thus, if a portfolio be taken over at the 1st January, the consideration received would be added to the fund brought forward from the previous year. By taking the portfolio the reinsurer is assuming liability for the running off of the risks which commenced in the previous year and to take care of such risks is exactly the function of the fund. Similarly, if a portfolio is withdrawn, the amount which the reinsurer has to return would be deducted from the fund, since a certain portion of the liability covered by the fund is thereby released. From every point of view this method seems best to meet the logic of the situation.

Portfolio consideration is usually based upon the premiums ceded under the treaty in the previous four quarters' accounts. This is done for convenience, though those premiums may not always represent the premium belonging to the previous year. For various reasons there is some unavoidable delay in ceding premiums, so that, at the end of a treaty, there are sometimes premiums belonging to that year which are not then ascertained and have, therefore, to be carried forward into the next year's account. Thus under a running treaty the first quarter's account contains premiums belonging to the previous year, while the fourth quarter's account is short of premiums which really attach to it. In the long run this factor is self-compensating and, although the premiums shown in the accounts are slightly out of alignment, the total is not materially affected on a normal treaty. It would cause unnecessary trouble to adjust the quarters' accounts to an exact basis in order to calculate the portfolio consideration. But since the past four quarters' premiums represent substantially a year's premium income, it follows that a return portfolio calculated thereon represents the whole consideration for the release of the unexpired liability and no further return can be required from the reinsurer. It follows that any belated premiums which may be due to the outgoing reinsurer must be credited in full and no further deduction could be made to pay for the portfolio return. This is a point of practice which is not always understood

As previously mentioned, upon the cancellation of a treaty the ceding company may withdraw the portfolio from the reinsurer and retain a reserve deposit until all outstanding liability under the treaty at the date of such cancellation has been settled. As some time may elapse before all the outstanding losses have been settled a large amount of work will have to be undertaken by the ceding company on the preparation of the periodical accounts giving details of the settlement of losses and the subsequent reduction of the reserve held. Further, the reinsurer has the disadvantage of having to leave a large amount of reserve with the ceding company for an indeterminate period after the cancellation of the treaty.

With these conditions in mind some ceding companies have adopted a system whereby in the event of cancellation of a treaty the liability of the reinsurer in respect of losses outstanding is settled by the payment of a lump sum in similar manner to the cancellation of the unexpired liability in respect of cessions by the withdrawal of portfolio.

The amount paid to the ceding company by the reinsurer in respect of losses outstanding is termed the "loss portfolio".

In the event of the cancellation of a treaty providing for the payment of a loss portfolio at cancellation the ceding company will withdraw the premium portfolio in respect of the unexpired liability together with the portfolio in respect of outstanding losses and return any premium reserve deposit to the reinsurer, thereby terminating the interest of the reinsurer completely.

The loss portfolio is usually fixed at a certain percentage of the outstanding losses, to be determined between the parties in accordance with the class of business involved, and such percentage may vary between 90% and 100% although in some instances it may reach a figure of 110%. It will be understood that if the outstanding losses tend to be overestimated by the ceding company then a payment by the reinsurer of an amount of 90% of such losses would in all probability be equitable, whilst conversely if such outstanding losses are underestimated then a percentage of over 100% would not be inequitable. This is a matter for negotiation between the parties in the light of the information available and most treaties usually provide for a loss portfolio calculated between 95% and 100% of the amount of the outstanding losses. However in certain instances the ceding company reserves to itself the right to review the position and adust the percentage of loss portfolio should it appear at a later date that such percentage is inequitable.

A further extension of this method termed the "clean cut system" has been adopted by many companies in an endeavour further to reduce the administrative work under treaties. At the inception of the treaty the reinsurer is credited in the treaty account for the 1st Quarter with a portfolio for cessions unexpired at the date of inception together with the portfolio in respect of losses outstanding at such date. Thus the reinsurer will be liable for losses occurring under all cessions expired at the date of inception and for all outstanding losses existing at such date. Usually in the same account the premium portfolio is debited to the reinsurer to form a premium reserve deposit in the hands of the ceding company.

During the currency of the treaty the reinsurance accounts are rendered in the normal manner until cancellation or alteration of the interest of the reinsurer is contemplated.

In the account for the 4th Quarter preceding the date of termination or alteration of the interests of the reinsurer, the reinsurer is debited with the portfolio in respect of cessions unexpired at the end of the 4th Quarter together with the portfolio in respect of outstanding losses at such date. Further, the premium reserve deposit held by the ceding company will be released and credited to the reinsurer.

In the account for the 1st Quarter of the following year the new reinsurer, if such is the case, will be credited with amounts debited to the old reinsurer in the account for the 4th Quarter in respect of premium and loss portfolio. However, if there has been an alteration in the interest of the reinsurer then the reinsurer will be credited with the amount of premium and loss portfolio calculated on the altered share.

Article No. 13 makes provision for any alterations which may be made in the terms of the treaty during its currency. Such alterations may be made by addendum, which would be drawn up in a formal way and signed in the same way as the treaty itself. The main purpose of this Article is to provide for alterations of a less formal character. These may be made by an exchange of letters, provided that these are signed by a responsible official of each of the parties. Sometimes the official is specially designated. Such letters are then to be regarded as an integral part of the contract and equally binding on the parties.

Article No. 13 is also an appropriate location for two further general provisions which practice, in recent years, has led towards being expressed in the formal treaty wording. Treaty documentation can become quite complicated with various attachments, amendments and the like becoming included as part of the basic treaty agreement. Some formal statement is therefore required to emphasise the basic legal position that all such attachments shall be interpreted as part of a whole and that there be consistency in the meanings of the words, technical terms and expressions used in the documentation.

In addition it is necessary to identify the legal system which applies to the treaty contract (ref. Vesta v Butcher above). In the distant past it was assumed almost automatically that English law would govern the terms of reinsurances. Since that time other reinsurance centres have developed and many countries have produced comprehensive legislation governing insurances and reinsurances. Thus many legal systems can be applied as the proper law of the contract, but the system used should be specified to minimise the problems arising from possible conflicts of jurisdiction and law. The rule is that, all things being equal, the legal system of the ceding company shall be applied as the proper law of the contract.

Article No. 14—The Confidentiality Clause is another result of modern developments. Although proper practice between the parties would naturally assume that transactions would remain private, errors of carelessness do sometimes arise. It is therefore necessary to make explicit that which should be implicit in the nature of the contract. However, it is doubtful whether the existence of such a confidentiality requirement would provide an adequate defence against any authority seeking evidence of illegal transactions!

Article No. 15 makes the necessary provision for the sending of any notices or communications which may be necessary under the treaty. The domicile of the reinsurer is given and the address to which it is agreed any notice shall be sent. Any such notice or communication is to be deemed to have been received in the ordinary course of post, if sent by prepaid letter properly addressed. The wording of the Article appearing in the specimen surplus treaty wording contained in the Appendix relates to direct communication between the ceding company and the reinsurer. However, nowadays many reinsurance treaties are placed through the intermediary of a reinsurance broker. Thus communications and settlements between the parties would normally be made through the broker. In such circumstances the Intermediary Clause, which is a little different to the Communications Clause, is used. A copy of this Clause appears as Article No. 13 of the specimen excess of loss treaty wording contained in the Appendix.

Such communications may consist of bordereaux or accounts, notices of default, notices of cancellation and the like. Since the sending of these is part of the obligations under the treaty, and the time factor is often of the essence of the matter, it is necessary to have a definite understanding as to how they are to be sent and when they are assumed to have been received. A point may arise as to the giving of notices of cancellation. The terms of Article No. 11 provide that either party may terminate the treaty by giving three months' notice. But some interval may elapse between the time such notice leaves the offices of the ceding company and the time at which it is received by the reinsurer in the course of the post. If the reinsurer is at the other end of the world there may be a considerable interval. On the strict wording of the Article it would seem that the ceding company will be in order if it gives three months' notice on the 30th September to expire on the 31st December, even though the reinsurer could not possibly receive that notice until some time in October or later. But to avoid disputes it is usual to give the notice so that it may be actually in the reinsurer's hands by the 30th September.

In the past the treaty wording also contained an arbitration clause laying down the procedure to be adopted for the settlement of disputes. It is the invariable rule in fire and accident treaties to provide that disputes shall be settled by arbitration, and although there are minor differences in the form of the arbitration clause used in various wordings, all of them are intended to mean substantially the same thing. However, there is now an increasing practice for the wording of the Arbitration Clause to be signed by the parties as a separate agreement. This practice arises from the extension of the use of the Arbitration Clause from not only dealing with disputes arising out of the reinsurance contract but also the disputes regarding its very validity and existence. In such latter circumstances reliance upon an arbitration clause contained in a contract which itself might be void from inception would be somewhat illogical. In addition, there is an increasing systematisation of the arbitration wordings in use. The Arbitration Agreement 1985 has been agreed by the British Insurance Brokers Association and the Reinsurance Offices Association and this wording appears in the Appendix. It is intended to be used in conjunction with the specimen treaty wordings.

The arbitration procedure as previously used in reinsurance treaty business has certain special characteristics which may best be explained since not all treaty wordings follow the form of the new arbitration clause.

The court of arbitration is to be composed of two arbitrators, one to be appointed by each party, and of an umpire to be appointed by the arbitrators before entering on the reference. The decision is to be made by the arbitrators, if they were able to agree, and the umpire is only called upon to make an award if the arbitrators are unable to come to an agreement.

The arbitrators and umpire are to be executive officials of fire insurance or reinsurance companies. If either party fails to appoint its arbitrator within four weeks of being required to do so, or if the arbitrators fail to appoint an umpire within four weeks of their nomination, the required appointment shall, at the request of either party, be made some independent person nominated in the treaty wording. It will commonly be found that such nominator will often be either the Chairman of the Reinsurance Offices Association or the Chairman of Lloyd's. The purpose is to secure an appointment by some responsible neutral person, who may be relied upon not to be prejudiced in favour of either party. It is obvious that this provision imposes no obligation on the person designated to make the appointment, since he is not a party to the contract, and he acts accordingly only as a matter of courtesy. It is in fact very seldom that his services are called upon.

The arbitration is to take place in London, or some other place as may be specified. It is usual always to fix the venue of the proceedings and this is generally the city in which the offices of the ceding company are situated. At one time it was invariably the practice to apply English law to the contract, but with the international expansion of the business many other jurisdictions could be involved.

The claimant in the dispute is to formulate its claim within one month of the appointment of the court of arbitration, and the respondent is to make its reply within one month of the receipt of the claim. These periods may be varied in some treaties, but it is customary to set down some specified periods so as to avoid any undue delay in bringing the matter before the court of arbitration. The arbitration tribunal has full power to fix all procedural rules and act upon all evidence, whether oral or written, strictly admissable or not, as it shall in its discretion think fit. This is a significant feature of the treaty arbitration clause. It provides a reason why the arbitrators are to be chosen from insurance officials. The intention is that every factor bearing on a dispute shall be taken into account, such as the customs and practice of the business. The real intentions of the parties are to prevail and are not to be invalidated by some technical defect. To give effect to these considerations, it is necessary that the arbitrators should be men well versed in insurance business, able to appraise the weight of the evidence and to make a decision in accordance with the merits of the case even though that decision may not be in accordance with the strict legal terms of the contract.

The proceedings may be carried on, if thought fit, in a quite informal manner, at the discretion of the arbitrators. In practice there are two ways of conducting arbitration proceedings under a treaty. Under one of these the parties may be represented by counsel, witnesses may be called and examined on oath, and proceedings may partake of much of the formality of a court of law. By the other method the arbitrators may meet together and consider the various documents submitted to them, discuss the points which may arise, and come to a decision without the need to call any witnesses or to hear counsel on behalf of the parties. It is possible that the proceedings may consist of a combination of the two methods. Without laying down any fixed rule, it may be said that the majority of treaty arbitrations are decided with the minimum of formality by men who are well acquainted with the practice of the business. The decision of the arbitrators or umpire is intended to be final and not subject to appeal. This is a natural consequence of the equitable nature of the proceedings, for if the parties agree to abide to a decision made on equitable grounds, it should not logically be open to either of them to impugn it upon any pretext that it was not in their favour. But although it is in the nature of any arbitration award that it should be final, there are certain grounds recognised by law upon which the Court will set it aside. It is also possible for one of the parties to apply to a court of law for enforcement of an award made against the other party should such other party default.

The costs of the arbitration and award are to be paid as the arbitrators or umpire may direct.

Although the provision of two arbitrators and an umpire is almost universal in treaty arbitration clauses there is much in favour of the appointment of a single arbitrator. In practice each arbitrator tends to uphold the view of the party appointing him, with the result that the arbitrators are seldom able to agree and the dispute has to be settled by the umpire. This comes to the same thing as a single arbitrator, but adds unnecessary complication and delay to the proceedings. Perhaps the objection to a single arbitrator is that the parties might find difficulty in agreeing on an arbitrator acceptable to them both.

The provisions of the Arbitration Agreement 1985 as agreed by the British Insurance Brokers Association and the Reinsurance Offices Association are similar to the description of the procedures outlined above. There are, however, two significant differences. Firstly the distinction between two arbitrators and the umpire is eliminated. The arbitration tribunal consists of three arbitrators and awards are made by majority decision. Secondly, as the arbitration agreement is intended to apply internationally and it is possible that London would not be the seat of arbitration, the appointor becomes the Secretary General for the time being of the Court of Arbitration of the International Chamber of Commerce.

The treaty wording is concluded by an Attestation clause, which usually provides that the treaty has been signed in duplicate by and on behalf of each party, each party to receive one copy thereof. Although treaties were at one time frequently completed under seal, it is now the more usual practice to complete them under hand, this being equally binding and sufficiently formal for the purpose, unless there was anything to the contrary in the articles of association of either of the companies which are party to the contract.

Some remarks may here be offered as to the application of the treaty to marine reinsurance. This subject is dealt with in an excellent specialist monograph by Messrs Robert H. Brown and Peter B. Reed, published by Witherby & Co. Ltd in 1981, and the reader is referred to that book for a fuller exposition on the subject.

The general methods of reinsurance already described may all be used in marine reinsurance as and when required, but subject to certain qualifications due to the nature of marine business. Quota share treaties, surplus treaties and excess of loss covers are all found. Certain variations have however to be noted. Thus, it is a very usual thing for marine treaties to be placed separately for hull and cargo respectively, though sometimes the contract may apply to both. Or, again, treaties may be placed to cover only specified risks such as total loss only. These are matters of practice necessary to comply with the varying needs of marine underwriters.

The surplus method is in common use in marine business, but in marine parlance, such a treaty was for a long time called an "excess cover". This must be carefully distinguished from an "excess of loss cover". Such a marine excess treaty is in all essentials a surplus arrangement, and the term excess has an identical meaning when used in this connection. The reinsurer is only interested in risks which exceed the ceding company's retention and when the reinsurer is allotted an interest in the "excess", it is liable for its proportionate share of the whole risk and receives its same share of the premium. This is essentially a feature of the surplus method of reinsurance and is equally essentially not an ingredient of the "excess of loss" method. Though perhaps the term "surplus" is a better one, as being less liable to misunderstanding, and is now in more common use there is nothing inaccurate in the term "excess."

The provisions of a marine surplus cover have much the same effect as those of a fire surplus treaty. There are, however, certain differences in procedure which have evolved out of the different practice of marine business. One of the main differences is to be found in the method of constructing the treaty as set out in the operative clause. In the first place the ceding company does not reserve an absolute discretion to fix its own retentions on any risk, nor does it have the very large number of different retentions which are common in fire insurance. Instead, the different risks which may be underwritten are graded according to the class of vessel insured and the whole business may be divided into about six grades or a little more. These grades often refer to gross registered tonnage, the limit increasing as the tonnage goes upward or grades may be constructed according to the class or use of vessel. The ceding company's maximum retention is then fixed for each grade, at reducing amounts according to the hazard of the classification, but at the same amount for all vessels within one grade. The grades and retentions so fixed are included as part of the treaty and cannot therefore be exceeded, but there is generally a clause in the treaty permitting these limits to be increased in certain circumstances.

The marine ceding company does not then place its surplus in lines, with each reinsurer taking an agreed percentage of the total amount reinsured at a fixed proportion of the line. Throughout the marine surplus cover is worked on amounts not on lines, even though the ultimate effect may be the same. Having determined the amounts of its retention, the ceding company will invite an intending reinsurer to say what amount of the surplus it is prepared to accept, and will offer varying amounts to different reinsurers until the total thus arrived at amounts to a figure sufficient for the ceding company's requirements. In this matter the marine department has developed a specialised practice. That is to over-place the reinsurance, and then on completing the case, to reduce each reinsurer's acceptance, proportionately so as to arrive at the required amount. Thus if a cover of £1,000,000 is being arranged it is quite usual for amounts to placed totalling say £1,200,000, and when the reinsurance is closed each reinsurer would receive 10/12ths of the amount which it had initialled on the slip. The system adds to the detail work involved, but it is well established in this section of reinsurance. The effect is that the reinsurer cannot be allotted more on any one risk than the amount which it has signified its willingness to undertake, but it may on occasion be allotted less. An example may make this clear. Suppose a ceding company retains £100,000 on a risk and has in mind to place a cover for £1,000,000. The reinsurers may take any reasonable amount they wish so that one or more may write £100,000, others £90,000 or £50,000 or £25,000 or as the case may be, until the full figure of £1,000,000 is made up. In that event, as soon as a risk is insured which exceeds the ceding company's retention the surplus is divided amongst the reinsurers, each taking the proportion which the amount of its acceptance bears to the total amount of the cover. This the true first surplus idea, and prevents any one reinsurer being favoured at the expense of the others. So a £100,000 reinsurer would receive 1/9th of the surplus, a

£90,000 reinsurer 1/10th, a £25,000 reinsurer 1/36th and so on, thus dividing the surplus (i.e. the excess of line) exactly between all the reinsurers, but so that no one of them received more than its maximum. There is a certain flexibility about this arrangement, for if for some reason the ceding company does not place its cover for the full £1,000,000 this will not affect the amounts which can be placed with each reinsurer; it will merely vary their respective proportions of each surplus. Thus suppose the cover is completed at a total of £900,000, the £100,000 reinsurer would then have 10/90ths, the £900,000 reinsurer 9/90ths and so on, thus arriving at the same result, with a reduction in the gross acceptances which the ceding company could accept.

Provision is made as a rule for the reinsurer to be liable for any amount beyond the maximum which the ceding company may have inadvertently accepted, provided that all the parties, i.e., ceding company and all the reinsurers, share the extra amount between them. Such extra amount when discovered would have to be reinsured outside the treaty, but the treaty reinsurers would be responsible for their share of any loss which might occur in the meantime.

Marine treaties generally run from the 1st January to 31st December, and continue from year to year unless cancelled by due notice—say three months to expire at the end of the year. The liability of the reinsurer is to attach as long as the liability under the original reinsurances. This may apply to all risks accepted by the ceding company during the year or to all vessels sailing during the year, even though declarations may not be made until after the end of the year. The marine system of accountancy provides for the separate recording of each year's business until completely run off and this applies with equal force to reinsurance treaties. It is necesary to keep separate series for each year's accounts under the treaties and the system of transferring portfolios is not used. This adds something to the detail work involved, but it does not present the same difficulty as it would in fire insurance because the system of marine book-keeping is designed to meet it.

The reinsurance premium payable on marine surplus treaties is a share of the original premium, but worked on a net basis, i.e., after deduction of original brokerages, discounts and agency commission. This again follows the system in vogue in direct marine business. As the premium is ceded net, the reinsurance commission is not heavy, and may vary from 2.5% to 10% on the net premiums according to the character of the business. In addition a profit commission will be payable on the results of the treaty, varying between 10% and 20% or possibly more. The profit commission is generally computed at the end of the third year after the close of each year's accounts and it payable on the year's results as then ascertained.

Provision is sometimes made for the retention by the ceding company of a premium reserve deposit to be accumulated out of the balances due to the reinsurer and to bear interest at an agreed rate. This premium reserve deposit represents the value of the unexpired risks and also the outstanding claims in most cases. It is not therefore computed on a flat 40% of the preceding year's premiums as is customary in fire business. It follows, naturally, marine methods and is computed on a three-year basis with varying proportions on each year's account still open. One method is to retain a sum equivalent to 70% of the premiums of the current year then ending, 30% of the premiums of the previous year and 10% of the premiums of the year before that. This is perhaps rather an exacting standard and many ceding companies might be content with something less as may be agreed when the treaty is drawn up.

The marine surplus treaty wording contains various other clauses, which provide for the procedure to be followed in operating the cover, and these are in substance the same as those which have already been described under the fire surplus treaty.

Chapter 7
Reinsurance by Treaty
II—Liability Excess of Loss

The method of reinsuring on what is known as an "excess of loss" basis is a distinct system of reinsurance which, though of much more modern origin than the surplus method, has very greatly extended its use in recent years. The system is considered to have certain definite advantages, which have no doubt stimulated its growth. It can be used in a variety of ways to provide for contingencies not suitable for a surplus treaty; it is economical in working and involves the minimum of labour, and it extends a special kind of protection to the account of the reinsured.

The fundamental difference between the excess of loss form of reinsurance and the surplus form is that there is no proportionate sharing of risks and the consequent claims arising thereunder between the reinsured and the reinsurer. Thus there is no cession of any individual risk (though this statement does not preclude the excess of loss form being used to reinsure a specific risk facultatively). The treaty arrangement applies to a specific branch of the reinsured's business and it ranges over the whole of that business without particular reference to any of the separate policies which make it up. It does not, however, apply to every claim which may arise, but as its name implies only to such claims as may exceed a certain agreed figure. This may be done in a number of ways. The figure at which the excess of loss cover is to commence to operate may be a certain fixed amount, say £10,000, or £100,000, or £1,000,000, or as the case may be. That amount is called the "underlying retention" or perhaps more commonly in modern practice the "priority" or the "deductible". The reinsurer has no interest at all in any claim below that amount, and for claims above that amount it is responsible for the whole of the excess, subject of course to the terms of the contract. This is completely different from the sharing forms of contract, where reinsured and reinsurer share in every claim in accordance with the share of the risk which had been ceded. This is the commonest form of the excess of loss treaty. It may however be fixed at a certain loss ratio computed annually on the business, so that the excess operates only when that loss ratio is exceeded. This is called "excess of loss ratio" reinsurance or "stop loss" reinsurance or sometimes "aggregate excess of loss" reinsurance, the idea being that the reinsured stops its loss at a certain ratio. In fact the expression "stop loss" is mainly used today. Or again the excess may apply only to a certain kind of hazard arising within the orbit of a given branch of insurance. A common example of this is a reinsurance of the excess of a certain number of fatal claims arising from one accident under workmen's compensation business. These special covers will be dealt with separately, but the main fabric of excess of loss reinsurance is best dealt with by reference to the excess of a fixed amount.

A treaty of this nature may operate in a number of ways. As applied to certain classes of business, notably motor and other forms of liability insurances it may be used as the sole method of reinsurance. The underlying retention is then fixed at a figure corresponding to the maximum amount which the reinsured considers its account can stand, and the purpose is to limit the loss in respect of any one claim to that figure. Reinsurers would normally expect a number of losses to arise on such a reinsurance and the premium therefor would be calculated accordingly. As applied to other classes of business, as for example fire insurance, the cover may operate as a pure catastrophe cover—or conflagration cover. Its purpose would then be not to limit each and every loss to a given figure, but to stand behind the surplus treaties and to protect the reinsured against disaster because of an aggregation of net loss limits by reason of one fire or conflagration.

At one time the application of excess of loss reinsurance to the various classes of insurance business was quite clear, and it was felt that a sharp distinction ought to be maintained between the two contrasting functions of reinsuring by excess of loss. In those classes of business to which it was traditionally applicable as the sole means of cover, it was felt that the claims arise from circumstances which are largely similar in character, no matter what the nature of the risk may be. For, though risks may, and do, vary in hazard, this would affect the frequency rather than the cost of claims. It would therefore be logical to determine a figure as the underlying retention applicable to all classes of risk alike, the higher risks being taken care of by the reinsurance rate. If however, such a method of fixed underlying retentions were applied to business such as fire insurance, conditions would be quite otherwise. The circumstances likely to give rise to a claim vary very widely and hazardous risks possess not only a greater chance of claim but also a much greater potential cost. Therefore to apply the excess of loss method as the sole means of reinsuring fire business would be to impose a uniform retention over the whole range of a business to which by its very nature such a retention would be quite unsuitable and which would very greatly restrict the reinsured's opportunities to underwrite its business on sound lines. As a conflagration cover used in addition to the surplus treaties and meant to apply only to the reinsured's net retentions, it was considered to be quite a suitable means of reinsuring, so as to set up a safeguard against the accidental accumulation of risk which, even with the most careful system of net limits, it is not always possible to avoid. To reinforce this point of view it was considered that the sum insured under an insurance policy covering property was normally a measure of the actual value at risk, whereas the sum insured in respect of a liability insurance was merely the limit of indemnity which the insured was prepared to purchase. For a long period the limit of indemnity far exceeded the general level of claims. However the escalation of losses under liability insurances, often far beyond the insured limit of indemnity, and the methods of estimating maximum possible losses under property insurances have considerably reduced the former distinctions between the different classes.

Therefore, the use of this form of reinsurance has become so extended that, nowadays, in many instances it becomes the sole form of reinsurance even for all the various classes of property insurance. The sheer variety of the uses to which the principles of excess of loss reinsurance can be adapted often leads to considerable confusion of exposition and of comprehension. It may therefore, at this stage, be of value to identify the major areas which require particular care and attention. These areas concern:—

(1) Definition of the circumstances under which a claim may arise under the reinsurance. Under proportional reinsurances this problem is not of such importance since the reinsurer shares in the reinsured's original loss in the same proportion as it shares in the original sum insured and the premium. Under an excess of loss contract a loss, or even a series of losses, sustained by the reinsured may not involve the reinsurer.

(2) Calculation of the reinsurer's liability. Under excess of loss reinsurance the limit of the reinsurer's liability is not based on the proportion of the original sum insured which has been ceded to it as the limit of reinsurance purchased.The amount of the liability itself may be modified by various factors.

(3) Calculation of the premium under the contract. Under proportional reinsurances the reinsurer shares in the original premium as set by the reinsured and its only freedom arises in negotiation on the deductions and the ceding commission. Under an excess of loss contract the reinsurance premium need have little or no relation to the original premium.

It will often be found that in order to secure a full measure of coverage of its exposures it will be necessary for the reinsured to place a number of excess of loss treaties. This is done by constructing excess of loss treaties in layers one above the other so that in total a large indemnity is secured. For example, a treaty might be placed for, say, £200,000 in excess of £50,000 thereby providing cover up to £250,000. The second layer might be for £250,000 in excess of £250,000 to provide cover up to £500,000. The third layer might be for £500,000 in excess of the first £500,000 thus providing for a major loss costing up to £1,000,000. Then there might follow a further layer of, say, £1,000,000 in excess of £1,000,000 and so on up to the amount required. This enables the reinsurance to be spread amongst a large number of reinsurers without imposing too heavy a burden on any one. It also provides reinsurers with an opportunity to choose the level at which they wish to become involved. Thus certain reinsurers may wish to participate in the lower layers where premium levels are higher, although there is of course the concomitant higher incidence of losses under the treaty. Other reinsurers prefer to participate in the higher layers where, although there may be a lower volume of premium, the risk of a claim arising on the reinsurance is also, hopefully, very much lower.

The modern accumulation of risks together with the depreciation in the value of money have led to the limits of retention and indemnity under treaties being very considerably increased. Contracts which relate to a mixed account may run up to several millions of pounds, and a top layer may well be constructed to cover, say, £100,000,000 in excess of £100,000,000. These are matters of negotiation and the availability of reinsurance capacity. The principle remains the same no matter how large the amount of the cover, but the practice shows how the reinsurance market responds to the demands upon it.

Where excess of loss reinsurance represents the reinsured's sole method of protection the function of these "layers" of coverage will therefore tend to range from "working" to "catastrophe". These terms may require some elucidation. The term "working excess of loss" is usually applied to that layer of excess of loss reinsurance where it is expected that a number of losses will arise in each year. The premium for such a reinsurance will often be related to the loss experience. The term "catastrophe" can be very confusing since it is used in two distinct meanings. Firstly it can refer to the excess of loss reinsurance designed to protect the reinsured's retained account. Thus in the event of a fire destroying several insured properties, each already subject to reinsurance, the excess of loss treaty would limit the accumulation of retained losses. The nature of the "catastrophe" arises not so much from the size of the potential loss but from the uncertain extent of the accumulation. The term can also be used to refer to a very large loss on a single policy or risk which could involve the upper layers of the excess of loss treaty programme. These upper layers are usually referred to as the "catastrophe" layers.

Of these two forms of excess cover, although the catastrophe cover has increased in use under modern conditions, the fixed excess limit as applied to motor and third party business is still the more common and may be taken to represent the standard form, or that in commonest use. For this reason it has been taken as the specimen form for the purpose of illustrating this chapter. There is, however, a much wider difference in practice in the forms of excess of loss reinsurance as applied to the motor and third party classes of insurance and as applied to the property classes. This chapter therefore concentrates on motor and third party excess of loss. Chapter 8 covers property excess of loss reinsurance. The functions of the excess of loss treaty may conveniently be considered by reference to a specimen form of contract, a copy of which will be found in the Appendix. This specimen form of contract is based upon a treaty covering motor business. Where property business is to be reinsured a number of changes would need to be made to various Articles contained in the contract wording. The significant changes which would be required are discussed in the following chapter. As certain Articles and clauses used in the excess of loss treaty wording are identical to those appearing in the surplus treaty wording, the explanation of such clauses has not been duplicated here and the reader is directed to the appropriate section of the previous chapter.

It will be seen that the operative clause does not provide for the cession of any given proportion of risks, since that is not the purpose of the agreement, thus:—

> "The Reinsurer shall pay to the Company by way of excess of loss reinsurance the amount of its ultimate net loss (as hereinafter defined) in excess of £ arising out of any one claim or series of claims due to the same cause."

This is the crux of the matter. The reinsured must pay the whole of every claim which does not exceed that figure, the reinsurer pays the difference between the agreed underlying retention and the total cost of the claim. The underlying retention must be borne by the reinsured in respect of each and every claim, but for this purpose all the different claims which may arise out of one and the same proximate cause are to be deemed to constitute only one claim. The one cause is taken as the unit as it were and the reinsured thereby limits its cost of any such series of claims to the amount of its retention. In view of the many different claims which may arise out of one motor accident or an incident involving death or injury to third parties this is a necessary provision of the contract.

Some observations may here usefully be made on what is meant by the term "any one event", which is also used in excess of loss treaty wordings, as from time to time practical difficulties have been encountered in deciding its exact effect. Treaties differ in their actual words though the intention is the same in all cases, i.e., to provide an excess cover in respect of one loss. The wordings used in contracts include "event", "occurrence", "disaster", "series of events arising out of the same cause", "all losses due to one event", or "each and every loss".

It has always been felt that as it is impossible to foresee all the possible sets of circumstances which might be brought into the expression "any one event", no contractual definition is possible. Furthermore, to include by definition certain types of circumstances, would by inference exclude any other types not specifically mentioned. The intention of the parties is to exclude nothing which can reasonably be included, and an exact definition might well defeat this object, but this does not imply that the phrase can be stretched beyond its normal and natural meaning. We have therefore to look for the intention of the parties, and what ideas were in their minds when they first constructed this type of reinsurance contract. Some historical reflections may help to discover this intention.

In the early days of Excess Loss covers there is no doubt the development of motor insurance was a strong factor, because this was a type of policy covering many risks of a differing nature—damage, third party liability, personal accident, etc. There was no single limit to the sum insured upon which a retention could be based so as to permit of a proportionate reinsurance. To overcome this difficulty the excess of loss method was devised, under which all the different losses arising under a policy could be aggregated, so that the insurer could bear its share as agreed in advance, and the reinsurer took the excess.

There can be little doubt that in its earliest days this applied to the insurance of a single motor vehicle and the "event" was the accident to that vehicle only. By subsequent practice this original idea was extended. First it was found that occasionally two cars might be in collision, both insured with the same insurer. Secondly, it was found that injury or damage flowed beyond the actual loss caused by the accident without any break in the chain of causation.

When two cars are in collision, this is prima facie two events, and when the cars are insured with two different companies, clearly each company must bear its own underlying retention. When both cars are insured with one office, however, it soon becomes obvious that only one priority should be borne and this led to the introduction of the amended wording—any one event or series of events due to the same cause. This wording would apply also to the spread of damage or loss beyond the original accident, as where a passer-by is injured, or the car collides with an adjacent shop or sets fire to a building. The resultant damage would fall under the third party section of the policy. In the early days of the excess treaty these were regarded as separate events, but being due to one and the same cause their cost was aggregated for the purpose of allocating the reinsurer's share.

It is submitted that an event must be a single definite occurrence altering the status quo ante and this would be so, whether the occurrence has one single result, or a number of results happening without any intervening cause. That is to say a series of events arising from one and the same cause.

By the same reasoning the word "disaster", sometimes used in contracts, means only an occurrence giving rise to a series of events a widespread and costly nature.

In this connection it is of interest to note that the Oxford Dictionary describes a disaster as a "sudden" event, and whilst this is not necessarily conclusive it does seem to show that in the mind of the ordinary person an event is limited both as to time and space, no matter whether its results are trivial or widespread.

The development of insurance business in course of time brought risks which went beyond this original concept and produced losses arising from a continuing state of affairs, not always of long duration but nevertheless spreading over both time and space. The commonest example is found in hail insurance, whilst another is in third party insurance against loss from defective products, i.e. products liability. It was soon recognised that in such classes it was impossible to say by definition, what constituted one and the same event. Who could say with precision what was the effect of one particular hailstorm? Where did it begin and end? The sharp limits of the one single sudden happening became blurred and it was apparent that an excess of loss treaty in its original simple form would require some qualification. This was done by creating for the purpose of the contract, an artificial event, as it were, by imposing a limit on the area in which damage by hail was sustained, and the time during which it occurred. With the development of storm, tempest and other natural perils insurances, the same qualification was naturally imposed.

In Products Liability, the same difficulty arises. If, say, a manufacturing chemist negligently issues a deleterious product, the results will be spread far and wide throughout the country, and will occur at many different times. Though by strict definition these may be a series of events arising out of the same cause, yet in practice they are reinsured on a separate aggregate basis of the stop-loss kind, with a method of calculating reinsurance premium appropriate to the retention in each case.

These types of reinsurances are more fully referred to on a later page. The main difficulty turns on the distinction between an event which is sudden and determinate and one constituting a continuing state of affairs.

It seems clear from a consideration of the facts set out that no hard and fast rules can be laid down, available to settle all possible questions, but there can be little doubt of the original intention of those who framed the early excess of loss treaties.

However, although the treaty wording is intended to give expression to the intentions of the parties to the contract, circumstances may arise some time in the future where it is not possible to ascertain clearly the original intention of the parties to the contract. Or the very looseness or flexibility of the terms used may allow an interpretation which imposes an added burden of liability on one or other of the parties which may not have been part of such original intention. Thus, it must be remembered that the treaty wording is also a legal contract subject to interpretation by the Courts and extreme care should be exercised in the drafting thereof.

The example of the problems which have arisen recently in connection with third party bodily injury arising from the use of asbestos is relevant in this connection. Many thousands of people have suffered serious lung damage through the constant inhalation of asbestos in the course of their employment. This has led to widespread disputes, particularly in the United States of America, about the liability for such "latent" injury the effects of which may only manifest themselves years later. Thus a dispute arose from the considered inadequacies in the definition of "loss occurrence" in the insurance conditions (i.e., in specifying the time when the loss took place).

The normal intention would be to cover losses occurring during the period of the insurance. However, decisions in U.S. Courts have given rise to three separate interpretations of this intention. In the first significant ruling in 1980, Insurance Company of North America v Forty-Eight Installations Inc., the Sixth Circuit Court of Appeals decided that the time of the actual damage was based on the exposure theory, stating that "Bodily injury should be construed to include the tissue damage which takes place upon initial inhalation of asbestos." The insurance cover must therefore apply at each time the injured party inhales asbestos, and the insured therefore is covered under all the policies in force during the entire application period.

In the case of Eagle-Picher Industries v Liberty Mutual Insurance Company, the First Circuit Court of Appeals adopted the manifestation theory which recognises the date when the disease became reasonably capable of medical diagnosis.

In Keene Corp. v Insurance Company of North America, the District of Columbia Court of Appeal extended the exposure and manifestation theories and held that all insurers on the risk between exposure to asbestos and manifestation of the disease were liable for indemnity and expense costs. According to this view, the entire period from the first harmful exposure to the manifestation of the disease forms part of the loss occurrence for legal insurance purposes. This theory to determine the date of the loss occurrence is known as the "triple trigger" theory from the three elements forming the basis of the occurrence, i.e. the exposure, the manifestation of the disease and the latent interval in between. All three elements give a right to coverage under all the policies in force during this period.

Although the above involves cases decided under United States law and applies to direct insurances, there are profound consequences for reinsurers, not the least being the need to reactivate excess of loss treaties which had been thought to be long expired and the accumulation problems which arise as between different treaty years. In addition, despite the extreme difficulties which are inherent in attempting an adequate contractual definition, it seems that some further effort will need to be made to clarify both the extent of the exposure of the excess of loss treaty to certain types of liability and the timing of the loss event so covered.

Except in rare instances the reinsurer does not accept liability for the whole cost of a claim in excess of the underlying retention without any limit. A definite figure is thus set down as the maximum amount for which the reinsurer will become liable in respect of any one occurrence. This may be £50,000 or £500,000 or £5,000,000, or as may be agreed, but some limit is almost invariable with the result that if a claim arose greater in amount than the figure covered by the excess of loss treaty the balance would revert to the reinsured's own charge. It is possible to enlarge the cover by taking out a second excess to operate above the limit of the first excess and a third or fourth excess above that. This is commonly known as reinsuring layers, and it is a method of securing a large cover for the reinsured without imposing too great a burden on any one reinsurer. In this way a cover can be built up sufficiently large to meet all reasonable requirements. It is true that under certain types of compulsory third party insurance, such as motor, the liability insured is unlimited in amount, so that on occasions even an unlimited reinsurance cover can be obtained though most old fashioned reinsurers hesitate to regard this as sound practice.

The class of business is next defined and the point here is that the cover applies to all the policies issued in that class (subject to the exceptions made later) without distinction of size or hazard. Thus in a motor treaty all the motor business must be included, though it is possible to allocate it separately by territorial areas. In fact it is common to place home business in one treaty and perhaps foreign business in another. The United States business would always be separately placed. This is quite legitimate, as the home and foreign motor business is quite distinct, but there must be no discrimination against the reinsurer by excluding, for example, certain non-hazardous classes of business within either of the two sections. This would be against the interests of the reinsured since the costly claims are as likely to happen in any category of risk, so that the reinsurer for its part must also accept the business as a whole or not at all. However, it is quite legitimate for the reinsured to make separate reinsurance arrangements for certain hazardous classes of risk in order to protect the treaty. It may be noted that a home motor treaty would have to extend to cover any foreign extension granted under a home policy. It is sufficient if the policy is issued at home; the reinsurer must then follow its scope wherever that may go.

Where a treaty refers to foreign business, some special provision may be necessary to meet the fact that the original business is written in foreign currency, whereas the excess of loss contract may deal in sterling figures. If, for example, the general terms of the operative clause provide for an excess of £50,000, it is important in regard to foreign business that there should be no doubt as to what is intended. In the absence of any express provision on the point, the actual cost of a claim paid in currency would have to be arrived at in sterling by using the rate used by the reinsured in acquiring that currency. But since the reinsured will often maintain acounts in currency, and make all payments without any conversion from sterling, no such rate might be available, and it is therefore usual to make express provision on the point to avoid any misunderstanding. The methods of conversion of premiums and claims are dealt with in a later clause of the treaty. The point of importance in the operative clause is the manner in which the reinsured's underlying retention is to be determined, and this point has been emphasised by the changing conditions of exchange values which have been such a feature of recent years. The intention of the reinsured is of course to limit its loss to a certain figure, as measured in its own currency, which is the currency of its accounts, and for this reason the underlying retention will usually be worked out in the same way as the premiums and claims as later provided in the appropriate clause of the contract. But circumstances will arise in which this may work some hardship to the reinsurer, and this has plainly been seen at each time when this country was subject to the currency devaluations which have occurred at intervals since the end of the Second World

War. These were not a gradual variation in currency value, but had the effect at a stroke of enhancing the value of all foreign currencies when measured in terms of sterling. The effect was a little complicated on excess of loss treaties designed to operate in sterling. The reinsurer received its due share of currency premiums and these produced a larger amount in sterling than before. Against this the cost of paying in currency was also increased in relation to sterling and it may be said that these two factors more or less offset one another. But the effect on the underlying retention, if this was to be calculated at current rates of exchange, was more far-reaching. Suppose, for example, a British reinsured had in force a treaty covering the excess of £50,000, and under this certain French business was included. This, prior to the devaluation, would be, say, an excess of French Francs 600,000, whereas, after the devaluation, it had become an excess of Frs 500,000. But it is clear that the cost of settling claims in France will bear no relationship whatever to the value of French currency as expressed in terms of sterling and the chances of a claim exceeding Frs 600,000 would be exactly as they had been before. So in effect the reinsurer found itself made liable for all claims between Frs 500,000 and Frs 600,000, which previously it would have escaped. These figures are of course not intended to reflect any actual relationships between Sterling and French Francs, but are quoted purely for the purposes of illustration. The principle is not, however, affected. Nor does this affect the underlying principles upon which excess of loss treaties are constructed, though it may emphasise the need to consider the effect of the uncertainty as to the future of exchange values on the system of premium rating.

The remedy for this increased exposure as a result of the fluctuation in exchange rates was originally sought in an adjustment of the premium rate intended to apply only to treaties current at the time, for treaties made subsequently would be entered into with due regard to the conditions then existing. Nevertheless it is not convenient to have to make continual variations in rates, either up or down, to meet exceptional movements in currency values. Furthermore, the effect of a currency fluctuation may not necessarily increase the reinsurer's exposure, but may rather impose this burden upon the reinsured. For this reason sterling treaties covering foreign business sometimes stipulate the rates of exchange to be used for the purpose of computing the amount of the underlying retention, though generally this follows from the provisions for converting currency losses into sterling. Alternatively, where possible, the problem would be minimised by expressing both the retention of the reinsured and the limit of liability of the reinsurer in the original currencies in which the reinsured does business. However, this may not always be practicable.

Therefore, in order to share more equitably the exchange risk under excess of loss treaties most reinsurers have adopted a method whereby the liability of the reinsurer is adjusted to correspond with changes in the rate of exchange. A "Currency Fluctuation" clause used in excess of loss treaties to give effect to this method is as follows:—

"In respect of losses in a currency other than that in which the monetary limits of the Agreement are stated, the liability of the Reinsurer shall be calculated as follows:—

(i) The retention of the Company and the liability of the Reinsurer as expressed in this Agreement shall be converted into the currency concerned at the rate of exchange ruling on the Commencement Date of this Agreement in accordance with the attached Currency List

and

(ii) The balance of any loss payment in excess of the Company's retention shall be converted from the currency in which the loss was settled into the main currency stated in this Agreement at the rate or average rates of exchange as used by the Company and ruling on the date or dates of settlement of the loss by the Company."

An example of the operation of this clause may be given as follows:—

The excess of loss treaty is placed for a limit of £100,000 in excess of an underlying retention of £50,000 and the exchange rate applying at the commencement of the treaty is £1 = Frs 12. A loss occurs and is settled for an amount of Frs 1,000,000. Due to a recent devaluation the rate of exchange rate is now £1 = Frs 10. Thus:—

(1) If the fluctuation had not occurred, the retention of the reinsured would have been calculated as Frs 600,000 (£50,000 converted at £1 = Frs 12), while the balance of Frs 400,000 would, converted at this same rate, give rise to a loss of £33,333 to the reinsurer.

(2) If the Currency Fluctuation Clause had not been applicable, the retention of the reinsured would have been calculated as Frs 500,000 (£50,000 converted at the new rate of 10 to the £), while the balance of Frs 500,000 would, converted at this same new rate, give rise to a loss of £50,000 to the reinsurer.

(3) By application of the Currency Fluctuation clause the underlying retention would be calculated as Frs 600,000 (£50,000 converted at the previous rate of 12 to the £) and the reinsurer's liability would amount to £40,000 (Frs 400,000 converted at the new rate of 10 to the £).

Contrariwise if the movement in the exchange rate had gone against the reinsured, say from £1 = Frs 12 to £1 = Frs 14, then in the absence of such a clause the retention would have been converted to Frs 700,000 and the reinsurer's liability would have been £21,428. The effect of such a clause on the loss to the reinsured would be to maintain the retention at the original equivalent of Frs 600,000 so that the recovery becomes £28,571 (Frs 400,000 converted at the new rate of £1 = 14).

There is of course no problem of this nature under a treaty between a British reinsurer and a foreign reinsured, where the business is written in the reinsured's currency only, since no question of exchange value then arises.

A further point of practice in the working of excess of loss covers arising out of modern conditions may here be mentioned. This is embodied in what is known as the "cost of living" clause, which is designed to secure that where higher awards are made in actions for damages, because of an increase in the rate of inflation, the whole burden thereof shall not fall on the reinsurer.

When an excess of loss treaty is being entered into, the rate or premiun charged for a given underlying retention is based upon certain factors then existing, from which the reinsurer can estimate the general level of awards of business at the particular time. This may be called the "incidence of loss" which in settled economic conditions is a fairly constant factor.

But when a country encounters conditions such as those which have widely prevailed throughout a large part of this century, with a steadily rising rate of inflation, there is an immediate effect on this constant factor, since the general levels of damages awarded will rise in association with inflation. Therefore, without an alteration in the character of the business, the excess of loss reinsurer, if the underlying retention remains unaltered, will inevitably be faced with a greatly increased claim strain. Or, in reinsurance language, the technical equilibrium of the treaty is radically upset.

To counteract the effect of this increase in the incidence of losses under excess of loss treaties most reinsurers, when reinsuring classes of business which cover third party liabilities, have adopted a method whereby the underlying is, in certain circumstances, adjusted to correspond therewith. Because the effect of inflation, as described above, tends to be more clearly reflected in the size of the award for bodily injuries, the method of adjustment tends to be applied only to the third party bodily injury part of a claim. It must be pointed out here that this method is designed solely to minimise the effect of inflation, i.e. increases in prices and their impact on claims awards, on the reinsurer's liability. The method is not intended to cope with increases in the "incidence of loss" such as may arise from changing social and legal conditions.

A draft of the "cost of living" clause, more generally known as the "Index" or "Stability" clause, which is incorporated in excess of loss treaties to give effect to this method is as follows:—

> "It is agreed that the retention of the Company and the liability of the Reinsurer as set out in this Agreement shall retain the relative values existing at the date of commencement of the Agreement.
>
> Any change in relative monetary value shall be ascertained from the latest published index of average earnings of all employees: whole economy (not seasonally adjusted) issued by the Department of Employment and published monthly in the Employment Gazette by Her Majesty's Stationery Office.
>
> On payment of any claim the retention of the Company and the liability of the Reinsurer shall be increased or decreased in proportion to the increase or decrease in the above index from the date of commencement of the Agreement to the time of payment of the claim.
>
> The time of payment of any claim for the purpose of this Agreement shall be deemed to be as follows:—
>
> (1) Where no award is made by the Courts the actual date upon which payment is made by the Company.
> (2) The date an award is made by the Court (if no appeal is made).
> (3) The date an award is made on final appeal. However, if such an appeal is made with the consent of the Reinsurer then the operative date will be the date of the original award.
> (4) Notwithstanding anything to the contrary contained herein it is understood that in the event of a loss being settled by more than one payment, all advance payments in respect of any one claimant shall be added to the final payment to that claimant and the index used at the time of the final payment shall be that used to calculate the retention of the Company and the Reinsurer's liability hereunder in respect of such payments."

It can be seen from the aforementioned clause that the factor used for the calculation of the adjustment to both the deductible and the reinsurer's limit of liability is a form of Cost of Living Index. These are statistics prepared and issued periodically by various organisations which show the cost of living in relation to various economic factors, e.g. wages. In the above instance the figures issued by official sources relating to salaries have been used as a basis, for the reason that the salary scale of the individual concerned is one of the main factors employed to determine the amount of the award. Thus awards will bear a direct relationship to salaries and therefore a general trend towards an increase in salaries will be followed by an increase in the amounts of awards.

An example of the operation of the above clause may be given as follows:—

The excess of loss reinsurance is placed for an amount of £100,000 in excess of an underlying retention of £100,000 and the wages index used is at 100 at the inception of the treaty. In the absence of any form of Index Clause, a loss settled in the amount of £200,000 would be covered to the extent of £100,000 by the reinsurer in excess of the reinsured's retention of £100,000. However, in the event of an Index Clause being applicable and such a loss arising then the underlying retention and the reinsurer's liability would be increased in accordance with the increase in the index as at the date of settlement of the loss. Thus if the loss were to be settled for the amount of £200,000, and the index stood at 160, the underlying retention would increase to £160,000 (£100,000 × 160/100) and the reinsurer's liability would amount to £40,000.

But complications do arise where a series of payments are made and a different index figure applies at the date of each such payment. Thus, assume that the total loss settlement is £230,000 with the following payments being made:—

1st Settlement— £30,000 with index at that date being 108
2nd Settlement— £50,000 with index at that date being 150
3rd Settlement— £150,000 with index at that date being 200

In this instance, likewise, if no Stability Clause had been applicable the liability of the reinsurer would have been calculated as £100,000 by the simple subtraction of the retention of £100,000 from the total amount of the loss. The balance of the £30,000 remaining would have been covered by the reinsurer on the second layer of excess of loss reinsurance (or revert to the reinsured if it had not purchased such further layer).

But, where an Index clause is applicable, and a series of payments is made over a period of time in respect of one loss, the first stage in calculating the liability of the reinsurer needs to be the development of a composite index. Such a composite index needs to be produced because not only does the underlying retention need to be indexed but so does the reinsurer's limit of liability.

Therefore, firstly, the values of the settlements are adjusted back to the value, as represented by the level of the wages index, existing at the inception of the treaty:—

1st Settlement—	£30,000 adjusted by (100/108)	£ 27,777
2nd Settlement—	£50,000 adjusted by (100/150)	£ 33,333
3rd Settlement—	£150,000 adjusted by (100/200)	£ 75,000
	TOTAL	£136,110

Thus the eventual settlement of £230,000 would have been equivalent to a loss settlement valued at £136,110 at inception of the Agreement. This produces a composite index of 169 (£230,000 divided by £136,110). Within the terms of this example, the retention would be increased to £169,000 (£100,000 × 169/100) and the reinsurer's limit of liability likewise increased to £169,000 (£100,000 × 169/100). Therefore the amount of the loss to be borne by the reinsurer beomes £61,000 (£230,000 – £169,000) and there is no balance which needs to be incurred by any reinsurer on the second layer, if any.

In earlier editions, it was stated in connection with this Clause that "It has been adopted for some overseas treaties but not, so far as is known, by any reinsured in the United Kingdom. Although the cost of living in most countries still shows a steady upward trend, this clause has never been widely adopted, and is not much in use at the time of writing. If the position between the parties became seriously out of balance it would be rectified by either an increase in the reinsurance rate or an uplifting of the priority."

Unfortunately, since that time inflation has become a feature which is not merely inflicted upon various economies from time to time but is prevalent in even the most advanced societies. Furthermore, it is now recognised that sudden and short spurts of an excessive inflation rate in particular year are nowhere near as damaging as a constant annual inflation rate of, say, 10% to reinsurers of excess of loss treaties covering third party bodily injury business where losses, due to various factors, do take quite a few years to settle.

Although the method of calculation may appear to be complicated, it will be seen that the purpose is clear. However, many variations on the above approach will be encountered. The most common of these may be summarised as follows:—

(1) Since the effects of inflation tend to be more apparent on the bodily injury part of third party losses, the normal wording of the Clause given above should be restricted purely to indexation of bodily injury losses. Undoubtedly inflation would also affect the replacement values of property damaged or destroyed, but the index applying thereto would be very different. In addition, the reference to "bodily injury" should not be held to include losses arising under personal accident or certain forms

of workmen's compensation where settlement on a loss is based not upon indemnity (which could be affected by inflation) but upon a schedule of benefits.

(2) On a point of negotiation as between the reinsured and the reinsurer, it will often be agreed that a "Severe Inflation Clause" will apply. This variation is intended to reduce the workload of adjustments to be made to settlements where the effect of inflation had not yet been significant. Thus a "15 per cent. Severe Inflation Clause" would mean that, in the calculation of the composite index as described above, those loss settlements where the increase in the index has not exceeded 15 per cent. would be included in the calculation at the level of the index ruling at the inception of the Agreement. In the example used above, the first settlement (where the index had increased to 108 and therefore by less than 15 per cent.) would not have been adjusted, so that the figures would have shown:—

1st Settlement–	£30,000 not adjusted	£ 30,000
2nd Settlement–	£50,000 adjusted by (100/150)	£ 33,333
3rd Settlement–	£150,000 adjusted by (100/200)	£ 75,000
TOTAL		£138,333

This, in its turn results in an index factor of 166 (£230,000 divided by £138,333) so that the underlying retention of the reinsured becomes £166,000 and the reinsurer's liability is increased to £64,000. Variations would include a "20 per cent." and a "25 per cent. Severe Inflation Clause."

(3) Approximations which were intended to decrease the burden of calculation and which used to be encountered included (i) a substitute for the "Severe Inflation Clause" whereby loss settlements made within, say, three years of inception of the treaty would not be subject to indexation and (ii) indexing loss settlements at a fixed rate irrespective of the actual wage indices applicable, so that a loss settlement made after 1 year after inception would be subject to an index of (say) 105, a loss settlement made after 2 years after inception would be subject to an index of (say) 110, a loss settlement made after 3 years after inception would be subject to an index of (say) 115, etc. Such attempts tend to be of a more arbitrary nature than even the effects of inflation, and move a long way away from the intention to preserve the monetary values applying at the date of the inception of the Agreement. Variations of this nature are becoming, deservedly, more rare.

(4) One of the more complicated variations of the "Stability Clause" is necessary to deal with the problem of "indexed annuities" whereby the award to a claimant is made in the form of an "annuity"—a periodic payment made during the lifespan of the claimant. Where the amount of such annuity is increased in accordance with the rate of inflation, the "Stability Clause" needs to be adapted accordingly.

The effect of inflation upon loss settlements as described above should not be confused with the effect of the periodic increase, in certain territories, of the schedule of benefits applying under state controlled forms of insurance such as workmen's compensation. Although the intention on the part of the authorities is, no doubt, to maintain the value of such benefits in accordance with the depredations of inflation, the spasmodic nature of such adjustments and the, often, retroactive aspect of the increases, tend to impose upon the reinsurer purely arbitrary alterations in its liability. Thus, such circumstances would be more suitably covered, not by the application of a "Stability Clause" but rather something in the nature of a "Change of Law Clause" whereby, in the event of such an alteration being made which increases the liability of the reinsurer, the terms of the contract are re-negotiated between the parties to reflect the changed circumstances or an "Acts in Force Clause" whereby the indemnity granted under the treaty is related to the benefits payable at inception of the contract and any subsequent revisions are ignored. The wording of these clauses would be along the lines of the following:—

Change of Law Clause

"In the event of any change in the law affecting any business covered by this Agreement by which the Reinsurer's liability is materially increased the parties hereto agree to take up for immediate discussion a suitable revision in terms of the Agreement. In the event of failure to agree a suitable revision this Agreement shall operate from the effective date of the change of law as if the change had not occurred."

Acts in Force Clause

"The provisions of this Agreement are based upon the benefits payable and the terms as provided for under the various Workmen's Compensation Acts and/or Laws in force as at . Any Act or amendment enacted or made after that date granting increased benefits shall be disregarded and the Reinsurer shall be liable only for such amounts as would have been payable had the Act and/or Law not been amended."

The operative clause concludes with a statement of the reinsurer's limit of liability. This is usually limited to a fixed amount, i.e. £50,000 or £100,000 or £1,000,000 etc., dependent on the form of reinsurance cover negotiated. Reinsurances unlimited in amount are rare, and tend to be encountered only where reinsureds are required by law to issue insurances which are themselves unlimited in amount, e.g., compulsory motor policies covering third party liability for bodily injury.

Although there are no absolute rules for computation of a proper and adequate relationship, it will normally be found that the limit of the reinsurer's liability represents a certain multiple of the deductible under the treaty. The rationale underlying this approach arises from the quite understandable attempt to structure layers of coverage which are homogeneous in nature. Statistical models of claims tend to show a common pattern whereby the frequency of the smaller losses is large and the frequency is reduced as the larger losses are encountered. Thus the extent of the layer of cover provided needs to be confined within an identifiable degree of frequency. In the not so distant past, a single excess of loss treaty for (say) £19,000 in excess of £1,000 might have been totally adequate for the needs of the reinsured. However, assuming that the figures need to be increased a hundredfold due to inflation, etc., the placing of a single layer of coverage for £1,900,000 in excess of £100,000 becomes less obviously acceptable, because:—

(1) For the reinsured the principle of homogeneity is breached in that losses of a lesser frequency (though of greater impact if and when they do occur) impinge upon the losses of a greater frequency. Not only is this reflected adversely in the level of the reinsurance premium rate charged, but also in the restriction on the ability of the reinsured to place specific layers of reinsurance with reinsurers who prefer to participate in certain layers rather than in others.
(2) These considerations apply with equal force to the reinsurer but with the added factor that a limited layer of exposure also quantifies for the reinsurer the level of acceptable exposure for both its own account as well as for its retrocessionaires.

The general rule of thumb applying hereto uses a multiple in the region of 3 to 5. Thus, for example, on a layer where the retention of the reinsured amounts to £10,000 any one event the limit of the reinsurer's liability may be £40,000—a multiple of 4. From such a basis the layering of an excess of loss reinsurance programme would be structured, viz:—

FIRST LAYER: Up to £40,000 in excess of £10,000 any one event.
SECOND LAYER: Up to £200,000 in excess of £50,000 any one event.
THIRD LAYER: Up to £750,000 in excess of £250,000 any one event.
FOURTH LAYER: Up to £4,000,000 in excess of £1,000,000 any one event.

The specimen treaty form being used by way of example is based upon the reinsurer being liable for amounts in excess of the reinsured's retention on its ultimate net loss arising out of any one claim or series of claims arising out of any one occurrence. The limit of the reinsurer's liability would be expressed in like manner. However, the manner in which a liability arises to the reinsurer can be expressed in different forms, as can the methods of expressing the limit of that liability. Thus among the more common variations may be found:—

(1) The retention of the reinsured and the limit of liability of the reinsurer in respect of any claim can be expressed in terms of any one risk rather than of any one event or occurrence, i.e., any series of claims arising out of one cause. Such a cover is termed a "risk" excess and may be placed facultatively or as a treaty. Such a treaty would be considered as being of the nature of the "working" excess referred to above, in that a reinsurer would anticipate that a number of losses would arise thereon in each year. Risk excess of loss reinsurance protects individual risks and is therefore used as an alternative to surplus reinsurance. It is a form of reinsurance extensively used for property insurances and is therefore described in greater detail in the following Chaper 8.
(2) Under the "any one event" or "occurrence" form of excess of loss reinsurance there is normally no limit to the number of loss occurrences covered during the period of the treaty. The payment of the full limit of indemnity in respect of a loss would not therefore exhaust the cover in the same way that a total loss does under a direct insurance policy. Thus there is an individual, not an aggregate, limit to the reinsurer's liability. However, there are instances of excess of loss treaties of this type which provide for a limit for any one occurrence and a separate (and sometimes larger) aggregate limit for any one year. This approach is often found in treaties covering U.S. Casualty business and catastrophe excess of loss reinsurances covering business such as fire and marine which provide for a single limit for any one occurrence and for any one year, but allow for

reinstatement of the cover upon payment of an additional premium. Such catastrophe covers are explained in greater detail in the following chapter. However it should be noted that limitations of this nature are beginning to be found even in excess of loss treaties where, traditionally, the coverage provides what are in effect "unlimited free reinstatements".

(3) The retention of the reinsured is usually expressed as a single underlying deductible applicable to any one risk or to any one occurrence or however the circumstances of the reinsurer's liability may be defined. But the retention of the reinsured may be expressed as both a deductible applicable to any one such risk or loss occurrence and a separate deductible in the aggregate. In such circumstance the reinsurer would not become liable until the reinsured had borne for its own account both the amount of the deductible applicable to any one risk or loss occurrence plus a number of losses which would otherwise have been recoverable under the treaty but which in total did not exceed the amount of the aggregate deductible. By way of example, a treaty may provide thus:—

> "The Reinsurer shall pay to the Company the amount of its ultimate net loss in excess of £50,000 arising out of any one claim or series of claims arising out of any one occurrence up to a further £100,000 each such ultimate net loss but only where losses otherwise recoverable hereunder exceed £200,000 in the aggregate."

Such a formulation, termed a "buffer layer", is intended to eliminate an expected normal level of losses from the treaty so that the coverage under the treaty would apply only to the fluctuations beyond that level. By way of example, losses of £130,000, £140,000 and £90,000 would normally have exposed the reinsurer to losses of £80,000, £90,000 and £40,000 respectively, i.e. a total of £210,000. The operation of the aggregate deductible provision would result in the reinsurer being exposed only to the final £10,000 of the third loss; but subsequently it would be involved on all future losses as soon as these exceeded the deductible of £50,000 any one claim. This reduction in the expected number of losses under the treaty would be reflected in the premium rate to be charged, which would otherwise be inflated by the element of "currency swapping" which would have occurred.

(4) Normally the liability of the reinsurer is related to the whole of the layer placed in excess of the stated deductible, or the reinsurer's share thereof where the coverage is placed with a

number of reinsurers. Thus, for example the reinsurer may accept 55% of a layer for £40,000 in excess of £10,000 any one event,.i.e. a limit to such reinsurer of £22,000 any one event. However, there are instances where reinsurers insist upon a measure of "co-insurance" by the reinsured. This provision is normally found in the "stop loss" forms of excess of loss reinsurance as described in more detail in Chapter 9 below. But its application also has a long history in the "any one event" form of excess of loss reinsurance, particularly after a period of adverse underwriting results. The intention is to ensure that the reinsured preserves an interest in the control and minimisation of losses even where these may have exceeded the amount of the deductible. Under the normal terms of a 100% placement of a layer of excess of loss reinsurance there could be a lack of concern on the part of the reinsured once the total amount of the loss had exceeded the amount of the deductible. Thus reinsurers may be prepared to cover only 90% of a layer for £40,000 in excess of £10,000 any one event subject to the reinsured retaining the balance of 10% for its own account.

(5) In certain forms of excess of loss treaties, both the underlying retention of the reinsured and the limit of liability of the reinsurer are expressed purely in aggregate terms, either as monetary limits or as percentages. Such forms are also explained in greater detail in the subsequent Chapter 9.

Article No. 2 of the treaty specifies the risks which are excluded from the scope of the contract. These exclusions differ according to the class of business which is to be covered. The form of excess of loss reinsurance here under discussion refers to motor and third party business, and the following exclusions are those commonly found in treaties covering those two classes of insurance:—

Motor:—

(1) Vehicles other than those running on terra firma.
(2) Vehicles running on rails.
(3) Charabancs, coaches, buses, taxicabs, self-drive hire cars or any vehicle plying for public hire.
(4) Vehicles engaged in racing or speed trials.
(5) Vehicles engaged in the carriage of explosives or inflammable liquids or gases in bulk.
(6) Workmen's Compensation or Employers' Liability risks.
(7) Personal Accident benefits, other than those granted under the standard form of policy without extra charge.
(8) Goods in transit insurances other than those arranged as an extension of motor vehicle policies.

(9) Excess of Loss Insurance and/or Reinsurances and policies with a self-insured deductible exceeding £250.
(10) Obligatory Reinsurances.
(11) Losses arising directly or indirectly out of war, invasion, acts of foreign enemy, hostilities (whether war be declared or not), civil war, rebellion, revolution, insurrection, military or usurped power or confiscation or nationalisation or requisition or destruction of or damage to property by or under the order of any government or public or local authority.
(12) Loss or destruction of or damage to any property whatsoever or any loss or expense whatsoever resulting or arising therefrom or any consequential loss, or any legal liability of whatsoever nature, directly or indirectly caused by or arising from ionising radiations or contamination by radioactivity from any nuclear fuel or from any nuclear waste from the combustion of nuclear fuel.

Third Party:—

(1) Inland, coastal and ocean-going Marine risks.
(2) Airlines, aircraft and the operation of airports, including refuelling, control-tower liability and construction or repair work within the airport perimeter.
(3) Railways other than private sidings, tramways and cable cars.
(4) Gas or Electricity undertakings.
(5) Manufacture, storing, filling, breaking down or transport of:
 (a) Fireworks, ammunition, fuses, cartridges, powder, nitroglycerine or any explosive
 (b) Gases and/or Air under pressure in containers.
 (It is understood and agreed however that the storage and transport of any of the substances above mentioned which is merely incidental to the operation and/or trade of the insured is not excluded from this Agreement).
(6) Quarrying with the use of explosives.
(7) Underground mining.
(8) Construction and maintenance of Dams and Coffer dams.
(9) Construction, operation of maintenance of tunnels, bridges and subaqueous work, unless incidental to operations not otherwise excluded.
(10) Prospecting, extraction and/or refining of liquid or gaseous fuels.
(11) Shipbuilding, shiprepair, shipbreaking, port authorities and risks connected with docks and wharves.
(12) Amusement parks, stadiums and stands.
(13) Professional indemnities.

(14) Products liability, Products Guarantee and/or Products Recall.
(15) Third Party liability in respect of motor vehicles other than those used on the insured's own premises or the site of a contract covered under a General Third Party policy.
(16) Employers Liability and liability under any Workmen's Compensation ordinance.
(17) Excess of loss Insurances and/or Reinsurances.
(18) Obligatory reinsurances.
(19) Losses arising directly or indirectly out of war, invasion, acts of foreign enemy, hostilities (whether war be declared or not), civil war, rebellion, revolution, insurrection, military or usurped power or confiscation or nationalisation or requisition or destruction of or damage to property by or under the order of any government or public or local authority.
(20) Loss or destruction of or damage to any property whatsoever or any loss or expense whatsoever resulting or arising therefrom or any consequential loss, or any legal liability of whatsoever nature, directly or indirectly caused by or arising from ionising radiations or contamination by radioactivity from any nuclear fuel or from any nuclear waste from the combustion of nuclear fuel.

Although the above lists are intended purely for the purposes of illustration and certain of these exclusions would not normally appear in an excess of loss treaty, it will be seen that the drafting of an appropriate list of exclusions involves much care and attention in order to achieve a homogeneous portfolio in which the risks being reinsured are clearly identified. The exclusion list in a treaty forms an essential part of the definition of the business covered thereunder, particularly in view of the modern practice of issuing broad forms of policy wording whereby any risk or peril not specifically excluded would by inference be covered by the terms of the insurance—and, by extension, by the reinsurance treaty. This consideration becomes particularly important where third party business is reinsured or any possiblity arises of an exposure to United States jursidiction. The various exclusions found in excess of loss treaties may be grouped into the following categories:—

1. Totally excluded risks

There are certain types of risk which can not be reinsured at all because of considerations of public policy or the existence of market agreement or the absolute catastrophic nature of the risk. A prime example is the invariable exclusion of War risks. Prior to the Second World War this was not a standard exclusion either in direct insurance policies or in reinsurances. The growth in military technology during the 1930s led to what is known as the London Waterborne Agreement of 1937, whereby insurers agreed to insure certain risks of war under policies of marine insurance but not to insure or reinsure war risks on land. Since that time, major disturbances have led to the extension of the exclusion to civil war and the arbitrary exercise of power by authorities (whether ruling under law or by the force of arms). A further example is reflected in the exclusion of Nuclear Risks. Originally this started off as a simple exclusion of business written by Nuclear Pools because at that time all such risks were of a major nature and written by pools of insurers. Since then however the increased nuclear presence in economic and social life has led to the need to draft an increasingly complex exclusion. The most recent form of wording in use in the London market is the "Nuclear Energy Risks Exclusion Clause 1984". The most recent forms of exclusions relating to War and to Nuclear Energy risks are contained in the specimen treaty wordings appearing in the Appendix.

In this context the exclusion of what are known as "Target" risks represents somewhat of an indefinable area. These are not risks which are totally excludable because of the kind of considerations of public policy, etc. Rather this is the kind or risk where, at the time of placing, the sum insured is so great that many insurers need to be involved, often in many parts of the world, in order to secure the capacity necessary to insure the whole of the risk. As each of these insurers needs to effect reinsurance, it is possible that a reinsurer could experience an accumulation of risk as each of these insurers cedes part thereof to the same reinsurer. These "Target" risks are generally listed in the appropriate exclusion, and, naturally, the list changes as, due to new technology and erosion of values, new target risks appear and risks previously so designated become merely large risks of their kind.

2. Where an additional premium would be chargeable

A general scrutiny of exclusions of this type shows that they relate in the main to classes of risk in which the catastrophe hazard especially predominates, and where the chance of a heavy claim falling upon the excess cover is consequently above the normal. It is for this reason that such risks are excluded from the normal treaty. This does not mean that in no case can they be included, for since they must be insured, reinsurance facilities need to be provided. Those reinsureds which write these risks can quite readily get them included in their excess of loss treaties. It is all a matter of premium rating, for many of them would carry a much higher reinsurance rate than that applicable to a less hazardous account. Those reinsureds which do not write such risks can, if they agree to their being excluded, obtain more favourable terms for their treaties than would otherwise be possible. Reinsurers, if they are to agree to the deleting of the exclusions, prefer to do so in favour of reinsureds which write these risks on a fairly wide scale, for such companies will have an extensive experience of the business and will write enough of it to give a fair average. It should be noted however that reinsurers will often agree to cover, without penalty, risks coming within this category if such risks are merely incidential to the main risk being reinsured.

3. Specific to the reinsured

The excluded risks in this category would be similar to those outlined in 2 above. However, such hazardous risks are much more dangerous to an excess of loss treaty if the reinsured does not ordinarily accept them, but writes one or two to oblige particular connections. In such event the possible additional premium which could be charged would not be commensurate with the imbalance caused by the increased exposure. Such risks should be excluded from the treaty and reinsured facultatively.

4. Which are insurable under other classes

It would not normally be expected that losses arising on insurances such as Employers' Liability or Public Liability would be covered under a motor excess of loss treaty. Nor would Public Liability insurances be expected to cover motor third party losses. In this context, however, the wording of this type of exclusion needs to cope with the overlap which can occur between different types of insurance policy lest, by mutual exclusion, the reinsured is not covered by any treaty. Thus, for example, building contractors do use motor vehicles on-site as items of plant and equipment and need to insure the third party risk, so that the exclusion relating to Motor business in a Public Liability treaty has to be adapted to apply solely to the road risk.

A word may be said as to the exclusion of insurances and reinsurances accepted on an excess of loss basis. The treaty normally applies to the whole of the business accepted by the reinsured whether written direct or accepted by reinsurance, though the lists reproduced above each contain a further exclusion of "Obligatory reinsurances", i.e. treaties. The reasons for this latter exclusion arise primarily from the considerations outlined in paragraphs Nos. 2 and 3 above, but the current reaction against retrocession business is also a factor. Where inwards reinsurances, whether facultative or treaty, are allowed to be covered, such reinsurance acceptances must be on a sharing basis carrying a share of the original premium. The treaty premium is fixed at a percentage which can only be related to original premiums. But reinsurances on an excess of loss basis are themselves rated at a percentage of some original premium and the treaty rate would not be adequate if based on that percentage. An example will make this clear. Suppose the treaty be placed for the excess of £10,000 at a rate of 5% on original premium and suppose further that the reinsured accepts a risk of the excess of £5,000 at 10%. If that risk were reinsurable under the treaty at a rate of 5% that would mean a rate of 5% of 10%, i.e. one-half per cent. on the original premium, whereas the treaty would have to bear any loss in excess of £5,000 plus £10,000, i.e. £15,000. But if an excess of £10,000 be worth 5% (for example) it cannot justly be said that an excess of £15,000 is worth as little as one-half per cent. The same reasoning applies where the original insured, in return for a substantial reduction in his premium, agrees to bear a heavy excess under his policy, as often occurs in third party business.

Nevertheless, without abating any part of the principle involved, it must be said that the practice of the business needs to be sufficiently flexible to meet modern needs. The point mainly arises under retrocession treaties, and then only when these refer to a whole range of business of a mixed nature, some sharing treaties and some excess of loss. If these were retroceded separately, then each would be dealt with on its merits in accordance with the foregoing rules. But where it is desired to take out an excess cover over the whole range, then obviously one rate of reinsurance premium must be devised. This is calculated by taking a view of the whole business—its past claims experience; the proportion of the business which is already on an excess of loss basis and whether this proportion is stationary or rapidly increasing; the underwriting reputation of the reinsured in regard to this class of treaty and so on. The resulting retrocession rate must to a large extent be empirical and the factors which govern subject to constant change.

A special word must also be said in regard to the normal exclusion of Products Liability for this is a branch of insurance which has come much into demand in recent years and for which reinsurance facilities have been provided. This is usually done by adding a clause called an Aggregate Liability Extension Clause. In view of the way in which claims arise under a products liability policy, there is often difficulty in deciding what amount of loss is due to any one event, and the practice has developed of ignoring this factor altogether and providing a certain aggregate liability up to which the policy will pay in the aggregate during the year. This would then apply to the sale of the product in question irrespective of who the claim came from, thus avoiding any question of having to decide the exact cause of the relevant claims. To make the excess of loss reinsurance effective, the clause is worded in somewhat the following terms:—

> "Notwithstanding that this Agreement is effected on an any one event or occurrence basis it is agreed that where any policy or policies of insurance in respect of the same original insured provides for a limit of indemnity during this period of such insurance on an aggregate loss basis this Agreement shall indemnify the Company up to the amount of the ultimate net loss provided herein in excess of the Company's retention by aggregating all claims arising during the annual period of such policy of insurance. Further it is agreed that notwithstanding that this Agreement is effected on a losses occuring basis such aggregate losses shall be allocated to this Agreement if the commencement date thereof (or a subsequent anniversary date) occurred during an annual period hereof. For the purposes of computation of such losses each such commencement date or subsequent anniversary date as may be applicable shall be related to the relevant annual period of this Agreement."

This addition would merit some extra premium. No general schedule of rates can be given for this is a matter for negotiation depending on the facts in each case.

Where, as is usual, this aggregate liability cover is an extension of an ordinary excess cover based on one event, the reinsured is normally allowed the option to extract any individual loss or losses which are identifiable under an aggregate liability, as being due to one event or occurence, and occurring during the same year of insurance. The losses thus extracted would be then accumulated with any other loss due to the same event, but not under aggregate covers, so as to enable the eventual loss due to that event being attributed to the main contract. In that case it would not of course fall on the aggregate liability extension.

An appropriate paragraph is added to the Aggregate Liability Extension Clause where this provision is required.

Before taking leave of the discussion on the business covered, whether such be described by positive definition or by exclusion, it is necessary to make reference to a further clause which has begun to find its way into the wording of excess of loss treaties in recent years. At the time the treaty is negotiated, the reinsured and the reinsurer should have a clear idea of the original business being covered, both as to the types of risks being insured and the normal limits per risk accepted. A material change in the underwriting policy of the reinsured after the inception date of the treaty could substantially increase the exposure of the reinsurer. The following "Change of

Underwriting Policy" Clause is being found in an increasing number of treaties:—

> "The Company undertakes not to introduce without the prior approval of the Reinsurer any change in its established acceptance and underwriting policy which is potentially capable of materially increasing or extending the liability or exposure of the Reinsurer hereunder."

Because the practice in proportional reinsurances of the reinsurer "following the fortunes" of the reinsured this type of clause would not be found therein. However, the modern practice whereby the reinsurer receives few details, if any, of changes in underwriting policy between the time of negotiation of the contract and the time of renewal negotiations could mean that even for the proportional reinsurer the cost of changing fortunes could be considerable.

Article No. 3 is referred to as the net retained lines clause. Its purpose is to give effect to the intention of the parties that the treaty shall apply only to that portion of any insurance or reinsurance which the reinsured retains net for its own account. So, in computing the amount of any loss in excess of which the treaty is to apply it will be necessary first to deduct any share of the risk in question which may have already been reinsured.

Although the form of treaty under discussion is normally used as the principal method of reinsuring the class of business to which it applies, that does not prevent the reinsured, in the exercise of its underwriting judgment, from reinsuring a proportionate part of any particular risk or risks. Some risks may be of such a nature that the reinsured does not wish to hold at its own risk the whole of the underlying retention, and it may accordingly desire to give away a share of that risk. Or it is possible that some kind of sharing arrangement, either by surplus or quota share, may be made over the whole range of the business. There is nothing in this which is contrary to the spirit of the excess of loss cover, but it must be made clear that cover is to operate only in respect of that portion of the business retained by the reinsured.

To this rule, however, there are exceptions, and it is not uncommon when the reinsured has reinsured, say, a quota share of its business, for it to take out an excess of loss treaty to operate over the whole of the gross business, and so to limit the loss not only of the reinsured, but also of its quota share reinsurers. This is known as "reinsuring for common account". The treaty is made with the original reinsured only, but is declared to be for the common account of that company and its quota share reinsurers. In that event the reinsurance premium is calculated on the original gross premiums and the appropriate share is charged by the reinsured to each of the quota share reinsurers. The excess loss is then computed on the original gross loss, so that the underlying retention applies as the maximum liability of the reinsured and its quota share reinsurers. In that case the net retained lines clause is not included in the treaty, the reinsurance for common account clause being substituted. However, it should be noted that in equity each quota share reinsurer should be given the opportunity to decide whether or not it wishes to participate in the common account reinsurance.

Whichever system be adopted, a paragraph is added to the clause providing that the reinsurer's liability shall not be increased by reason of the inability of the reinsured to collect from any of its other reinsurers any amount which have become due from them, whether on account of the insolvency of such other reinsurers or otherwise. The reason for this is that if a share of a risk has been reinsured elsewhere, it is to that extent taken out of the range of the excess of loss treaty. It is therefore no concern of the excess of loss reinsurer if for some reason that outside reinsurance fails, and any loss which might thereby fall on the reinsured is not a loss within the meaning of the excess of loss treaty. It would indeed be unreasonable that the reinsurer should suffer through the default of any of the reinsured's other reinsurers, as it could have no knowledge of them nor any control over their financial strength.

It will be seen from the operative clause that the reinsurer assumes liability for the excess of the reinsured's "ultimate net loss", and this term calls for exact definition. This is provided in Article No. 4. The term "ultimate net loss" is defined to mean the sum or sums paid by the reinsured in settlement of all losses arising out of one event, including any litigation or other expenses incurred in connection therewith, but excluding any charge for the services of any salaried employee of the reinsured in connection with the investigation of claims. In this connection it should be noted that, in certain jurisdictions where the legal process can be protracted, interest may be allowed on the amount of the award and such interest would be included in the computation of the loss settlement. From the aggregate cost of such claims, there must be deducted all recoveries, whether by way of salvage or otherwise, and all sums recoverable under other reinsurances which may inure to the benefit of the treaty, irrespective of whether or not such reinsurances are actually recovered. This definition shows clearly the origin of the expression, for the figure upon which the excess is to be based is the total of the ultimate cost of all the claims arising out of one event, but with the deduction of all amounts which go to reduce the reinsured's loss, thus arriving at the ultimate net loss. It should be noted that the

"Ultimate Net Loss Clause" is intended to relate purely to the summation of the amounts which comprise the loss. Whether any amount does or does not form part of the indemnity granted by the treaty is a separate issue and is covered in greater detail in the discussion above on the "Operative Clause" and the explanation below on the "Claims Clause".

This definition is not, however, intended to prevent the reinsured from making any claim on the reinsurer until the ultimate net loss has been ascertained and a clause in this Article so provides. It may often happen that the complete and final settlement of every claim arising from one event will take a very considerable period of time. This is frequently the case in third party liability insurances, for example. If the reinsured has already paid more than its underlying retention, it would not be reasonable that it should be unable to make any claim on its reinsurer merely because some small part of the claim remained to be settled. The reinsurer may therefore be asked for payment of an amount on account without prejudice to the right of the reinsured to claim further sums as and when further claims are settled.

But, similarly, the reinsurer has certain rights, for if, after a claim has been completely settled and the excess amount paid, some recovery is subsequently made the reinsurer is entitled to the benefit thereof, until the amount of the excess paid has been extinguished—if the recovery goes so far. This is, of course, obvious, for if the reinsured were to be permitted to retain recoveries for itself, its ultimate net loss would be reduced below the underlying retention provided in the treaty and would to that extent defeat the purpose of the contract. The right of the reinsurer to be credited with subsequent recoveries is generally expressly provided, but there is undoubtedly an implied obligation on the reinsured to account for such recoveries without any express provision to that effect.

The next clause of the treaty—Article No. 5—deals with the consideration for the contract, i.e., the reinsurance premium. This is a matter of much importance and requires detailed examination. The continuance of the treaty on lines satisfactory to both parties will obviously depend on the manner in which the premium paid for the cover is arrived at, for if it be too high, that throws too heavy a charge on the reinsured's account, while if it be too low, it will eventually cause a loss to the reinsurer. Various methods are in use for the computation of the reinsurance premium, and the commonest of these provides for a fixed percentage of the total net premium income derived by the reinsured from the class of business covered by the treaty. In the case of a motor treaty the net premium income is defined as gross premiums less cancellations, returns, bonuses, and premiums paid for reinsurances which inure to the benefit of the treaty. This last of course would not apply to a treaty for common account. The purpose is to obtain the true net premium income retained by the reinsured for its own account. The whole income derived from the business in question must be included, even though some of the policies might be issued for an indemnity lower than the underlying retention—as happens sometimes in third party business—but premiums on policies in respect of any excluded risks are not to be included. It should be noted that in some cases the definition of net premium allows also for the deduction of agents' commission (this is usual in marine insurance) and for local premium taxes. This problem of premium taxes can cause confusion, particularly where the taxation system extends to reinsurances. Thus there could be one or more premium taxes which would affect the calculation of the reinsured's net retained premium, upon which the reinsurance premium would be calculated. The reinsurance tax would subseqently be deducted from the amount of such reinsurance premium. In fixing the reinsurance rate it is of course essential to know which system is being adopted and to fix the rate accordingly.

The determination of the rate of reinsurance premium to be applied to the treaty is a matter which presents something of a problem and it is not possible to lay down any scale of rates which could be relied upon. The general conditions which govern the matter are liable to change, so that rates which might be considered to be adequate today may become quite wrong tomorrow, and the problem calls for continual consideration. Some general factors may, however, be set out as governing the matter.

In the first place the rate must depend on the level of the underlying retention and the limit of liability of the reinsurer. A treaty under which the reinsurer accepts say £400,000 in excess of £100,000 any one occurrence, is obviously worth a higher rate than one for £400,000 in excess of £200,000. Yet it is difficult to assign any mathematical relationship to these different excesses. It is not possible to say that an excess of £100,000 is worth double the rate of an excess of £200,000, for the element of chance enters too greatly into the matter. It is probable that the chance of a claim exceeding £100,000 is rather more than twice that of it exceeding £200,000, but the uncertainty in this respect illustrates one of the problems of rate-making.

Another factor affecting the rate is the range of the business and whether or not the treaty includes a full list of exclusions. Where a treaty is issued without exclusions, or without some of them, this may be provided for by increasing the rate over the whole business or alternatively a normal rate may be charged on the ordinary business and an increased rate on the hazardous risks. Where this is done the increase may be substantial according to the classes of hazardous risks to be included. For public hire vehicles for example, the rate may be as much as four or five times the normal.

A further factor which may affect the rate of premium is the amount of cover required, i.e, the aggregate top limit of the whole treaty. This is more clearly seen in contracts fixed at high priorities, such as an excess of £1,000,000 for example. Though in this context it may be pointed out that the concept of a "high priority" is a relative term dependent upon the reinsured's portfolio of business. It is also a term relative to time in that a period of inflation will deflate quite high layers of cover, previously intended purely as a catastrophe protection, towards the level of a "working layer". The assessment of the rate will vary according to whether the limit of liability is say £1,000,000 or £5,000,000 or £50,000,000, even though there cannot be so very great a difference in the chance of loss at the higher levels. This also depends upon the reinsurance market available. No reinsurer will put a risk on its books, no matter how remote the exposure, without at least a premium of some significance, and it may cost appreciably more in proportion to arrange reinsurance cover for the larger limit.

On the general question of arriving at a normal reinsurance rate, considerable importance is naturally attached to the past experience of the business. The reinsured will supply its figures over a period of years, so as to show its net annual premium income each year and the number and cost of all claims which have exceeded the amount of the underlying retention. From these figures it is a simple matter to calculate the percentage of the premiums which have been absorbed by the excess claims. This may be regarded as the pure claims cost, which would then have to be loaded by some proportion in order to arrive at the reinsurance rate. However this simple description needs to be very heavily qualified and expanded before it becomes serviceable as a guide to the calculation of premium rates for excess of loss treaties. Thus, for example, the value of the previous loss experience to the rating of the various layers of reinsurance can be extremely variable in that:—

(1) The premium rating for a working excess of loss layer, which is subject to a regular level of loss, tends to be closely related to the past loss experience. For the higher layers or catastrophe excess of loss treaties, the past loss experience may be irregular or even non-existent. Therefore, certain other approaches to rating may need to be used, such as the reinsurer applying a rate based on the average loss experience over a whole portfolio of similar layers (if its account is of such a size as to develop valid information of this nature) or basing the rate upon a mathematical probability model or on its years of

experience and feeling as to the "right" rate or merely charging what the market will bear.

(2) This previous loss experience may be incomplete. This problem arises particularly with classes of business considered as being of a "long-tail" nature, which term is normally applied to those insurances where losses may arise in a particular treaty year but not appear for many years after the expiry date. Thus the loss experience for the current and the previous year, and probably for at least the past four years, would not be complete. It is normally expected that losses of this nature would arise on one or other of the various forms of third party liability insurance, though many classes of business which are reinsured do have a "tail" of varying length. The losses which may have arisen but which may not be apparent for perhaps years to come are usually referred to as IBNR losses—Incurred But Not Reported.

(3) The past loss experience may not be a sure guide to the future. A period of inflation in itself would serve to ensure a higher monetary expenditure on losses in the future—though this may be offset by an equivalent increase in premium income. However other social and economic factors also have an influence.

These considerations will be covered in greater detail in the following pages. Suffice to say, at this stage, that many and various statistical models which have been designed in an attempt to try to develop a valid loss experience from the information on past claims so that the reinsurer can quote premium rates on basis of such experience.

However, before proceeding, we need to consider the nature and function of the loading applied to the pure claims cost, usually referred to as the "burning cost", to obtain the reinsurance premium rate. In this loading no amount would be required for commission, because except in rare instances, excess rates are always quoted net. There is no particular reason why this should be so, nor any principle involved; it is just that the practice has so developed and so continues. However, with the increasing use of intermediaries in the transaction of reinsurance the size of the loading would need to allow for the brokerage which will be deducted from the premium payable to the reinsurer, if the treaty is placed by a reinsurance broker. Some proportion must be allowed for profit, but the loading must go farther than this, because the reinsurer needs to create a fund to protect itself against the possible heavy catastrophe to which it may be liable and this fund must go much beyond any normal calculation for unexpired risks. Where the treaty is for the lower layers of deductible and limit of indemnity, such as the working layers, where the size of the reinsurer's exposure on a single loss is comparatively limited this problem is not so great, though it nonetheless still exists since an untoward and unexpected increase in the frequency of losses in a single year could have the same catastrophic effect. However, an examination of the application of the loading to the higher layers leads us to what is the major problem in the rating of such excess of loss treaties. The nature of these layers is such that the incidence of the claims must be expected to be highly irregular. These are catastrophe covers; they are designed to meet the larger claims and these must occur with less frequency than the smaller claims. And even those which do occur fall into two categories, those which only exceed by a small amount the underlying retention and do not therefore involve the reinsurer in an amount beyond which its incoming premium can stand, and those much less frequent claims which are of a real catastrophic character and may cost the reinsurer many times its premium income for that year. It follows from this, then, in looking at its results under a single treaty of this nature, the reinsurer is likely to find a wide variation year by year. In some years there may be no claims at all, in others very few, and again in others a claim cost of some hundreds per cent. The experience therefore must be looked at as a whole to see if the complete period shows a reasonable surplus. Both parties to the contract need to keep this point in view. If the treaty runs for a few years at a very low claims cost it is not reasonable for the reinsured to require too soon a reduction in rate. On the other hand, if the disastrous year happens to come in the early years of the treaty, the reinsurer cannot immediately claim that the rate is inadequate. This feature is greatly accentuated by the very high priorities, which in modern practice have come increasingly into use. These are super catastrophe covers where the reinsurer's premium may be calculated in small fractions of one per cent. of the limit of liability and the whole of the premium for each year of the contract is no more than a contribution to a catastrophe reserve.

Following this line of argument to its logical conclusion, it is clear that to conduct excess of loss business on a profitable footing, it is necessary for the reinsurer to spread its business as widely as possible, and to accept treaties on as extensive a scale as may be posssible consistent with sound principles of underwriting, so as to ensure a better chance that the bad year under one treaty will synchronise with a good year under another, thereby preserving a more or less even balance over the whole account. The average which is produced from the inclusion of the whole portfolio of business under one treaty, is not in itself sufficient to even out the excess of loss results; thus this requires the assistance of a number of treaties.

In the same way in order to deduce a satisfactory scale of rates applicable to various excess levels, it is, in theory at all events, necessary to take the past experience, as displayed over as large a number of treaties as could possibly be obtained and taken over as long a period of years as might be available. This would seem to give mathematically a claims cost which would be proof against any of the variations which might arise from the methods of different ceding companies and sufficient to allow for good fortune as well as bad due to the incalculable element of chance. In practice, however, it does not work out quite so simply as that. Certain factors arise from time to time in the life of a community which have a seriously deranging effect on this question and throw out of gear any calculations which are based on the experience of past years. Such has been the situation applying to most forms of third party insurance during recent years. Thus in motor insurance, for example, a number of factors—such as the great increase in traffic, the advance in what is called "claims consciousness" on the part of the public, the continuous upward trend in the level of damages awarded, the introduction of new ideas, such as the allowance of interest on Court awards and so on—have combined to bring about a great increase in the number and cost of the larger claims, throwing a consequently enhanced burden on to the excess of loss treaties.

There is a further important factor which operates to increase the difficulty of arriving at an accurate system of rating and this is the inevitable "time lag" which must occur between the happening of a claim and its eventual cost of the treaty (which are referred to as IBNR losses—Incurred But Not Reported). This is clearly shown in the notes to Article No. 7 (see below) dealing with the notification of claims. Sometimes it will take several years to determine what claims will eventually fall upon each year's premiums and this must unavoidably delay the working out of the "burning cost" as it is commonly but not always accurately called. For this reason rates of premiums under excess of loss contracts have a tendency to lag behind the claims experience and only with difficulty to catch up with it. This has been a pronounced feature of the past thirty years or so. It is a feature which is likely to be prominent, as has happened in the most recent past, at a time when keen competition for the business is accompanied by derangements in the social and economic life of the country.

Thus as a consequence of these economic and social factors the excess cost, viewed over a period of years, would usually be greater during the later years of that period than during the earlier years, and this on a business which in volume and quality had undergone no material change during that period.

The delayed effect of IBNR losses, may, however, so disguise this increase in the later years that, superficially, the loss experience for the whole period would show very little change.

Clearly this state of affairs plays havoc with the mathematical estimation of risk already referred to. If a reinsured submits its statistics for the past five years only, a certain claims cost will be disclosed which will certainly be much altered if ten years' experience be given and even more altered on a fifteen years' record. The position thus arises that the longer the experience, the more the claims cost thereby deduced departs from the present-day position, and yet it must be the present likelihood of claim upon which the reinsurer must base its rate. On the other hand changes in the underwriting policy of the reinsured and general economic circumstances make this loss experience of the earlier years unreliable as a guide to the future. This is a very real difficulty in rating excess of loss treaties covering third party business, especially as it has upset many preconceived ideas and has led to many revisions of rates. It might be felt that no regularity can be assigned to these factors since they operate in an irregular manner with some degree of chance and subject to unforeseeable factors. Therefore what seems like sound theory does not always square with actual practice.

Yet the effort needs to be made. The days are long gone where the rating of excess of loss reinsurance was believed to be subject entirely to blind chance. Accumulation of information and the development of statistical tools over the years have enabled a great amount of quantifiable analysis to be made so that the areas of uncertainty, which are not yet amenable to quantification, have been much reduced, though it is doubtful whether they will ever be entirely eliminated. For the time being it is possible to apply only qualitative judgments to these areas of uncertainty, even though these qualitative judgments may be expressed in quantified terms. Modern practice in the calculation of premiums for excess of loss reinsurances, therefore, considers both the loss experience for the portfolio as a whole as well as the past experience of the individual treaty. Thus deviations from the general experience can be identified and taken into consideration when establishing the appropriate premium rate. The procedure followed requires firstly that the relevant claims data is collected and tabulated in a form capable of interpretation. This claims information needs to be capable of presentation in an "as if" form. Thus, for example, the past claims information may have been prepared for layer for £40,000 in excess of £10,000 but if the treaty is now to be placed as a layer for £75,000 in excess of £25,000, this information needs to be re-interpreted in a form "as if" the new layer had been in existence in these past years. The figures then need to be projected to the level of their ultimate full development, i.e. when all losses to that year have been ascertained and settled. Losses relating to the past years also need to be revalued to current monetary values since the insurance is being placed at these values. As previously mentioned the burning cost is then expressed as the percentage which the aggregate cost of all claims which have exceeded the underlying retention bears to the premium income.

A series of examples will illustrate the procedure followed, as well as some of the problems encountered.

Assume that, in connection with the renewal for 1985, the reinsurer is presented with the following details of losses on a treaty covering Employers' and Public Liability business for the layer up to £75,000 in excess of £25,000 each and every event. The figures are for a period of five years and exclude 1984 because no losses have been reported to date. Thus the Loss experience could show the following:—

The ABC Insurance Company Limited
Liability first excess of loss treaty
Layer for £75,000 in excess of £25,000
All figures in sterling as at 5th October 1984

Year	Claims P/D	Claims O/C	Incurred	Reinsured	Loss Ratio
1979	1,396,202	1,395,000	2,791,202	1,119,037	10.15%
1980	883,596	653,000	1,536,596	950,385	7.81%
1981	512,885	1,249,829	1,761,714	959,714	8.27%
1982	1,150,975	1,660,333	2,811,308	970,379	10.04%
1983	539	2,415,500	2,416,039	735,500	7.58%

The average Burning Cost (the ratio of the claims cost to the Layer expressed as a percentage of the reinsured's applicable Premium Income for the year concerned) over the past five years would amount to 8.77%. In the past this figure would have been simply increased by the amount of the loading which had been agreed to produce the reinsurance rate for the following year. Thus, on a basis of a loading of (say) 100/80, the premium rate would amount to 10.95%—say 11%. This premium rate would exceed the reported loss figures for all the years shown and apparently allow the reinsurer a surplus on its underwriting of the treaty.

In this context it must be pointed out that, in modern practice, unless there were overriding reasons for so doing, the deductible would not be set at a level which would generate such a consistently high level of "burning cost" and resultant premium. Setting the deductible at this level would merely result in the reinsured paying for its own losses—plus the amount of the loading. This phenomenon is generally known as "dollar swapping". In the absence of other considerations, therefore, the amount of the deductible should be set at a level which would minimise, if not eliminate, this phenomenon.

Although this approach does have the advantage of excluding the 1984 year, where including the Burning Cost for that year of 0.00% would have reduced the six year average to 7.31% and the premium rate to 9.14% (and thereby guaranteeing a loss to the reinsurer in at least two years), the arithmetic does not identify the essential disparity of the data being compared. Thus, at 5th October 1984, the losses relating to the 1979 treaty year would have reflected the situation as at the end of the 69th month after inception of the treaty, the losses relating to the 1980 treaty year would have reflected the situation as at the end of the 57th month, the 1981 treaty year would have reflected the situation as at the end of the 45th month and so on. Therefore the figures for the later years would not have yet developed fully. On the long-tail classes of business, of which this is an example, even the earlier years may not have developed fully, as may be seen in the above example where 50% of the losses on the 1979 year are still outstanding.

Thus a pattern of development has to be established. This needs to be established initially at the level of each individual loss, as will be seen from the development of five losses on the 1979 year, thus:—

1979 Treaty Year

Loss Reference No.

	EL/579	EL/179	EL/879	EL/379	PL/879
Losses as at the end of 9 months (end of September 1979)					
Paid	0	0	0	0	0
Outstanding	45,000	21,374	0	0	0
Incurred	45,000	21,374	0	0	0
Retained	25,000	21,374	0	0	0
Reinsured	20,000	0	0	0	0
Losses at the end of 21 months (end of September 1980)					
Paid	0	21,374	0	0	0
Outstanding	45,000	0	42,500	0	0
Incurred	45,000	21,374	42,500	0	0
Retained	25,000	21,374	25,000	0	0
Reinsured	20,000	0	17,500	0	0

	EL/579	EL/179	EL/879	EL/379	PL/879
Losses as at the end of 33 months (end of September 1981)					
Paid	63,950	21,374	0	42,056	0
Outstanding	0	0	65,000	0	0
Incurred	63,950	21.374	65,000	42,056	0
Retained	25,000	21,374	25,000	25,000	0
Reinsured	38,950	0	40,000	17,056	0
Losses as at the end of 45 months (end of September 1982)					
Paid	63,950	21,374	50,000	42,056	0
Outstanding	0	0	0	0	65,000
Incurred	63,950	21,374	50,000	42,056	65,000
Retained	25,000	21,374	25,000	25,000	25,000
Reinsured	38,950	0	25,000	17,056	40,000
Losses as at the end of 57 months (end of September 1983)					
Paid	63,950	21,374	50,000	42,056	0
Outstanding	0	0	0	0	65,000
Incurred	63,950	21,374	50,000	42,056	65,000
Retained	25,000	21,374	25,000	25,000	25,000
Reinsured	38,950	0	25,000	17,056	40,000
Losses as at the end of 69 months (end of September 1984)					
Paid	63,950	21,374	50,000	42,056	0
Outstanding	0	0	0	0	65,000
Incurred	63,950	21,374	50,000	42,056	65,000
Retained	25,000	21,374	25,000	25,000	25,000
Reinsured	38,950	0	25,000	17,056	40,000

It will be seen that, in respect of these five losses alone, the liability of the reinsurer has increased from £20,000 at the date of the first reporting (30th September 1979) to £121,006 at the latest date (30th September 1984). By summation of all the individual loss figures, the full loss development pattern for each of the five years under consideration would therefore appear thus:—

The ABC Insurance Company Limited
Development of liability first excess of loss treaty
Layer for £75,000 in excess of £25,000
All figures in sterling as at 5th October 1984

Treaty Year	1979	1980	1981	1982	1983
Losses as at the end of 9 months					
Paid	0	50,584	0	718,340	0
Outstanding	641,374	140,000	100,000	491,660	1,137,500
Incurred	641,374	190,584	100,000	1,210,000	1,137,500

Treaty Year	1979	1980	1981	1982	1983
Losses as at the end of 9 months (*continued*)					
Retained	421,374	100,000	50,000	910,000	775,000
Reinsured	220,000	90,584	50,000	300,000	362,500
Loss Ratio	2.00%	0.74%	0.43%	3.10%	3.74%

Treaty Year	1979	1980	1981	1982	1983
Losses at at the end of 21 months					
Paid	105,748	84,789	0	769,878	539
Outstanding	917,500	569,000	870,000	1,556,660	2,415,500
Incurred	1,023,248	653,789	870,000	2,326,538	2,416,039
Retained	820,374	325,000	400,000	1,335,000	1,680,539
Reinsured	402,874	328,789	470,000	991,538	735,500
Loss Ratio	3.65%	2.70%	4.05%	10.26%	7.58%
Losses as at the end of 33 months					
Paid	559,529	94,789	360,648	1,150,975	
Outstanding	970,260	1,053,000	1,697,556	1,660,333	
Incurred	1,529,789	1,147,789	2,058,214	2,811,308	
Retained	887,638	485,000	827,000	1,840,929	
Reinsured	642,151	662,789	1,231,214	970,379	
Loss Ratio	5.82%	5.45%	10.61%	10.04%	
Losses as at the end of 45 months					
Paid	746,539	445,629	512,885		
Outstanding	1,581,271	982,585	1,248,829		
Incurred	2,327,810	1,428,214	1,761,714		
Retained	1,392,638	585,687	802,000		
Reinsured	935,172	842,527	959,714		
Loss Ratio	8.48%	6.93%	8.27%		
Losses as at the end of 57 months					
Paid	1,133,317	883,596			
Outstanding	1,436,271	653,000			
Incurred	2,569,588	1,536,596			
Retained	1,517,680	586,211			
Reinsured	1,051,908	950,385			
Loss Ratio	9.54%	7.81%			
Losses as at the end of 69 months					
Paid	1,396,202				
Outstanding	1,395,000				
Incurred	2,791,202				
Retained	1,672,165				
Reinsured	1,119,037				
Loss Ratio	10.15%				

The development of the Burning Costs would then be summarised as follows. The method of presentation of the loss experience in this format is usually known as a "triangulaton".

Treaty Year	1979	1980	1981	1982	1983
Loss Ratio					
At 9 months	2.00%	0.74%	0.43%	3.10%	3.74%
At 21 months	3.65%	2.70%	4.05%	10.26%	7.58%
At 33 months	5.82%	5.45%	10.61%	10.04%	
At 45 months	8.48%	6.93%	8.27%		
At 57 months	9.54%	7.81%			
At 69 months	10.15%				

It will be seen that the Burning Cost for each year increases significantly over a period of time. Thus, when each year has developed fully, it would probably be seen that the reinsurance premium rate of 11% contemplated above would have resulted in an underwriting loss to the reinsurer in each of these years (except possibly 1980). Another benefit of the triangulation is that it indicates possible anomalies to the reinsurer. For example, the decrease in the loss experience between the 33rd and the 45th month on the 1981 year could be due merely to the file on a previously advised loss being closed as "no claim".

One of the major reasons for this development stems from the effect of inflation. This factor and the application of the Index Clause were described above. If the loss experience used in this example were to be recalculated on the basis that the treaty had been subject to an Index Clause for each of these five years, the revised trangulation would appear as follows:—

Loss development after application of the index clause

Treaty year	1979	1980	1981	1982	1983
Loss ratio					
At 9 months	2.00%	0.60%	0.39%	3.19%	3.72%
At 21 months	3.09%	2.02%	3.89%	9.80%	7.83%
At 33 months	3.62%	4.04%	10.42%	9.96%	
At 45 months	5.79%	4.88%	8.06%		
At 57 months	7.25%	5.54%			
At 69 months	8.94%				

It will be seen that, even over these limited periods, this adjustment for inflation makes a significant difference. But as the usual form of Index clause provides for increases not only in the level of the deductible in accordance with the rate of inflation but also in the nominal limit of liability of the reinsurer, the benefit to the reinsurer could be much reduced. For example, the occurrence of a number of losses which would normally have "burnt through the layer" and fallen to the reinsurer on the Second layer of the excess of loss treaty, could revert to the reinsurer on the First layer so that a total loss of £75,000, when the Wages Index was at 100, could now become a loss to the reinsurer of £90,000 when, after a few years, the Index at the date of settlement is 120. In this context of the difference between "nominal" and "real" values, it should be noticed that even the values and Burning Costs as revised in the above Table for the effect of inflation cannot be used, as they stand, for the calculation of a reinsurance rate. This is because the losses on the 1979 year are now related back to the monetary value of the coverage existing at the inception of the treaty at the beginning of 1979, the losses on 1980 are related back to the monetary value existing at the beginning of 1980 and so on. To be able to calculate a premium rate for the 1985 year these earlier losses need to be re-expressed in the monetary values existing at or near the beginning of 1985.

The factors governing this loss development, therefore, and the problems of IBNR losses, are not restricted solely to the effect of inflation but are many and various, and the effect of each differs considerably. These factors may be grouped as follows:—

(1) *Specific to the Reinsured* (in which grouping should be included the actions of any reinsurance intermediary operating on behalf of the reinsured). These factors would include communication delays arising from their location, lack of technical expertise, administrative breakdown and sometimes (fortunately rarely) even deliberate act. These are not normally amenable to statistical analysis. Action taken would need to be of a more qualitative nature.

(2) *Specific to the Method of Reinsurance.* The various forms of reinsurance have their own inherent causes for delay. Even quarterly accounts under a surplus treaty require time for staff to prepare, typists to type the copies necessary for the various participating reinsurers and for supervisors to check. At the other extreme losses on LMX business (excess of loss reinsurances and retrocessions of Lloyd's Syndicates and London Market companies) can take years to make an appearance and to resolve.

(3) *Specific to the Class of Insurance.* As a general rule, property insurance losses tend to be reported quicker and also settled faster. There is generally a greater delay with liability business. Among the major reasons therefor may be listed—that it may be some time before anyone becomes aware that a claim could arise (due partly to the effect of the Statutes of Limitation

applicable in various countries), liability has to be established (often through legal process and the Courts) and so has the amount. In this connection it must be noted that this delay factor can vary as between one type of third party liability and another. As a general rule, losses on a motor third party treaty tend to have a shorter "tail" than losses on a treaty covering products liability business. But the delay may also be specific to the class of risk being covered, such as may happen when a third party liability insurance covers an equipment manufacturer. Then, for example, an item of equipment may lie in store or in a wholesaler's warehouse for years before being sold, and through defect, cause injury or damage. This could increase the delay inherent in the chain of liability and recourse back from the retailer, through the wholesaler to the manufacturer. In this regard a change from the method of the direct insurance, say, from issuing policies on a "losses occurring" basis to "claims made" or the inauguration of a regime of strict liability for losses to third parties, could have profound effects upon the length of the "tail".

(4) *Arising from the economic environment.* The major factor arising in respect of this characterisation is that of Inflation, though fluctuations in the rates of exchange between currencies can also have adverse effects upon the reinsurer's ultimate liability. The effects of inflation have been one of the major influences on the reinsurers' writing of excess of loss reinsurances in recent years. However, in this regard, it must be noted that although there is a relationship between court awards for third party bodily injuries and the wage index it is not necessarily a close and direct relationship. Rather it is the judge's perception of inflation which is the relevant factor so that awards may sometimes lag behind the rate of inflation and sometimes be in advane thereof. In addition, there is often a different relationship between the wage index and the direct liability insurance claim and between the wage index and the loss to the reinsurance layer. Thus, although in reinsurance terms the problem tends to be dealt with by means of the operation of the Index Clause, the operation of this Clause may not be exactly co-incident with the actual process of inflation.

(5) *Arising from the social and political environment.* This arbitrary distinction between economics as in (4) above and social life is intended to highlight certain phenomena such as inflation which are generally recognised as being amenable to measurement and certain other effects which may be less so. By way of example one may indicate the social influences acting upon

court awards to be more generous in levels of award, heads of damages, and the interpretation and application of the law relating to liability (though these could all change in a different social environment). Medical care improvements are increasing treatment costs and at the same time keeping alive more seriously injured people. New industrial processes bring with themselves a whole new range of hazards for their operators. The effect of this grouping tends to be described as "super-imposed" inflation and left at that. However no adequate statistical interpretations can be developed unless the separate strands are disentangled.

In the past various attempts were made to resolve the difficulty experienced by many reinsureds in arriving at their loss experience for the reason that in respect of many losses their liability would be indeterminate due to the prevailing tendency towards legal proceedings and therefore, through no fault of their own, the estimates given to the intending reinsurers could be incorrect. Nowadays, however, it is recognised that there would be some degree of loss development in most classes of insurance business. The premium rate quoted for an excess of loss reinsurance treaty would therefore be based not so rigidly upon the losses for the past years as are currently known but rather upon the level of the expected developed losses for these years. An example of such an earlier approach may be seen from the "Special Records" clause which was sometimes included in treaty wordings to minimise the effect on the premium rating if the loss experience provided by the reinsured were found to be inaccurate. A draft of this clause is given as follows:—

"This Agreement is entered into on the understanding that, during the period commencing on the day of 19 and expiring on the day of 19 and after making full allowance for all outstanding claims as at the latter date the total amount of the liability sustained by the Reinsured in excess of £ any one accident in connection with policies which would have been protected by this Agreement had it been in existence is less than £ in all. Should circumstances arise whereby such liability as aforesaid in excess of £ exceeds the sum of £ then the premium payable under this Agreement and any renewal hereof shall be increased proportionately, or by such lesser proportion thereof as may be agreed by the parties hereto."

The effect of this clause is to give the reinsurer the right to amend a rate of premium which the course of events proves to have been founded on false premises. However, nowadays, the clause tends to be used only where the claims data originally supplied is patently deficient for some reason or another.

The reinsurance premium calculated on this basis is normally expressed as a rate per cent. of the original premium written by the reinsured during the period of the treaty and retained for its own account. Reference has been made in greater detail elsewhere to the variations which can be encountered in the definition of the premium income of the reinsured. As an alternative to this fixed rate per cent method of calculating the reinsurance premium, there are various methods of premium rating which seek to relate the level of premium more directly to the actual loss experience of the treaty period itself rather than to the developed experience of prior years. These methods form part of the "burning cost" or "automatic" scale of rating. This consists in basing the rate on the actual percentage which the excess claims occurring during the period of the treaty bears to the reinsured's written premium for the period and adding an agreed loading to provide the necessary margin for fund and profit. This loading is computed by multiplying the claims cost by an agreed factor varying between 100/60 to 100/85 according to the circumstances of the case. Perhaps the factor most commonly used stands about midway at 100/70. Under this method the rate is adjusted each year until all losses applying to the treaty period have been ascertained and liquidated. Since the claims cost depends so greatly on the cost of settling outstanding claims and since an accurate estimate of these is not easy to make, it is usual to delay the initial calculation of the claims cost and the resultant reinsurance premium until at least the twenty-fourth month after the commencement of the treaty period. This means that the reinsurance rate for any given year cannot even be initially determined until the close of that year, i.e., the year following the treaty period. This being so, an estimated reinsurance premium is agreed and paid at inception of the treaty period by way of a "deposit premium" and which is adjusted as may be necessary when the required rate has been ascertained. Although the reinsurance rate varies with the claims cost, there must always be a minimum rate and a maximum rate, agreed between the parties. If there were no minimum then if there were no excess claims—as could be possible—the reinsurance rate would disappear, while if there were no maximum, the reinsured would not in effect be reinsured at all since it would have to pay—by an adjustment of the rate—for all its losses.

This method of premium rating is open to various degrees of criticism. Thus, if the loss experience of the reinsured remains below the maximum rate applicable then the company is not only still paying for its own losses but also paying an additional loading. Furthermore, other than the limitation imposed by the level of the maximum rate, there is, for the reinsured, very little minimisation of the untoward fluctuations in loss experience which might occur as between one year and another. Attempts have been made in the past to stabilise these possible fluctuations by calculation of the reinsurance premium rate on the basis of a three-year or four-year or five-year average. The methods of operation varied from rating the treaty on the average loss experience of the current period plus the previous two, three or four years, as the case may be, to building up to the three-year or four-year or five-year average. In this latter variation the premium rating for the initial treaty period was calculated on the loss experience of that year only, the premium rating for the second year of the treaty was calculated on the average loss experience of that year plus the previous year and so on. This system of rating is rather complicated and involves a lot of adjustment, but it does overcome the difficulty of rating due to violent fluctuations in experience. It can, however, only act fairly between the parties and fulfill its function if the contract is continued for a reasonable period of time.

A further attempt to achieve a measure of stabilisation and to simplify the burning cost method of premium calculation consisted in basing the rate on the actual percentage of the excess claims during the three years *immediately preceding* the commencement of the treaty and adding an agreed loading to provide the necessary margin for fund and profit. Under this method the rate was adjusted each year, according to the claims cost of the three years preceding. It was also usual to delay the working of the claims cost for any given three-year period until the close of the following year when it was expected that outstanding claims would be settled or could at least be estimated with reasonable accuracy. Until the reinsurance rate for the given year was finally determined the premium was paid at the previous year's rate and adjusted as may have been necessary when the required rate had been ascertained. In the first year of the treaty an agreed rate was paid. As with other forms of treaty rated on a burning cost basis a minimum rate and a maximum rate was always agreed between the parties. This variation was intended to reduce the administrative burden of continual recalculation of premium rates, but its distinguishing characteristic whereby no cognisance was taken of the actual loss experience of the current treaty year, other than in the premium calculation for a treaty covering some future year, quickly led to this form falling into disuetude. Furthermore, the modern volatility in treaty reinsurance programmes, both in regard to changes in reinsurer and to alterations in deductible and limits destroyed the continuity which was a precondition for the successful operation for all these variations on the burning cost form of premium rating.

These points illustrate a serious difficulty in operating the adjustment of premiums assessed on a burning cost basis. This necessitates each year's claims record being kept distinct, and the eventual claims cost cannot be worked out accurately until all outstanding claims occurring during that year have been settled. This may, and nearly always does, take many years, during which the parties must wait for the final adjustment. This is both laborious and time wasting, especially as the reinsurers on the contract will have changed considerably in the meantime. The point is sometimes met by taking a time limit—generally 5 or 10 years—at the end of which time the remaining outstanding claims will be assessed by agreement between the parties and the final rate for that year computed accordingly. But in this connection it is for each party to decide whether the potential added burden which might result from such a commutation would justify the reduction in administrative costs.

It would be of interest to mention a further method of rating originally adopted for the catastrophe excess covers of many Lloyd's Underwriters and called the "fixed premium" system. This method of premium calculation is also known as a "premium in full".

Under this method the reinsurance premium is calculated in similar manner to that previously described, with the essential difference that such premium is expressed as a fixed amount and not as a rate percentage of the premium income, and therefore it follows that with this method there will be no calculation or adjustment required at the expiry of the contract.

In this context it should be noted that Lloyd's Underwriters are subject to a triennial system of accounts, i.e., their accounts are kept on a three-year basis, and if the reinsurance premium is a rate percentage of the original premium income the annual adjustment could not take place until the completion of the account year in question, i.e., a period of two years after the expiry of the account year. This would be cumbersome, and the "fixed premium" method is adopted to avoid that difficulty.

It should be noted, however, that this system can only be used satisfactorily in respect of annual excess contracts for the reason that the "fixed" reinsurance premium does not, as in the case of a contract subject to a rate percentage of the premium income, make any allowance for subsequent alterations in the gross premium income of the reinsured, which could give a corresponding alteration in the liability under the contract.

For some types of general catastrophe covers or high layer excess of loss treaties, where the underlying retention has been built up to a very high level, the fixed rate of premium may be computed on the amount of the indemnity (a "rate on line") and bear no relation whatever to the original premium income. Such covers are always yearly contracts, the terms to be reconsidered each year in the light of the existing circumstances.

The accounts to be rendered under the treaty are provided for in Article No. 6. The procedure is comparatively simple and this is one of the advantages of this type of reinsurance, because its simplicity effects a considerable saving in administrative cost. No bordereaux or other particulars of risks ceded are required, since no individual risks are given off. The treaty applies to the whole business and to give bordereaux for the whole of the class of business covered would be inconvenient to the reinsured and of no practical value to the reinsurer. An exception might be made where the excess cover applies only to a specified section of a business, such as Third Party fire risks for example, where it may be agreed that the reinsured shall submit monthly bordereaux of the risks ceded. This, however, is not the usual procedure and a clause in this Article relieves the reinsured of the necessity of advising any risks.

The Article lays down the manner in which the reinsurance premium is to be paid. As a general rule the accounts under an excess of loss treaty provide only for the payment of premium and differ in that respect from accounts under a surplus treaty, which include all transactions relating to a quarter. Under an excess of loss treaty, all losses are treated as cash losses, payable on demand and not in account; there is no commission, as rates are always net; and it is seldom that such treaties contain a premium reserve deposit provision.

Profit commission is not usually payable under excess of loss contracts, and in view of the general irregularity of possible results it should not be payable, unless those results are averaged over a very long period. It would be easy for the loss in one year to wipe out the profits of the ten preceding years and it would be inequitable if those profits had been reduced by profit commission and the reinsurer were left to recoup its heavy loss from the profits of future years. Nevertheless this rule tends to be relaxed during periods of competition and profit commission is sometimes agreed to.

This development leads sometimes to awkward results. In computing the profit of any year an estimate for outstanding claims must be made. But in view of the "long tail" which some classes of business incur, these estimates may prove to be totally inadequate so that a year which seems to show a profit eventually produces a heavy loss. It would then turn out that the profit commission ought not to have been demanded. This would not matter so much under a continuous treaty, where the position would right itself by provisions in subsequent years, but difficulties arise from the fact that frequent alterations are experienced in the identity of reinsurers, so that over a period of years, any revisions of outstanding losses from back years may well work out to the advantage of the wrong reinsurer. To meet this situation provision may be made to compute profit commission separately for each year of account so as to ascertain in due course the exact results of each year when all outstanding claims have been settled. This may be a protracted business, but in equity there seems no way of avoiding it. In order to reduce the work involved it is sometimes provided that the first computation of profit commission shall not be made until two or three years after the close of the year of account, thus increasing the likelihood that all claims belonging to that year will have been notified and most of them settled. This will not obviate, however, subsequent adjustments having to be made to those few claims that are not settled, and no doubt a weakness in this approach—equitable though it be—is its cumbersome and costly operation.

There is some variation in the methods in use for the payment of premiums. That most usually provided in past years is the quarterly system, under which a statement of all premiums on insurances falling within the scope of the treaty is to be rendered by the reinsured within three months (or other agreed period) after the close of each quarter, i.e., the period of three months usually ending 31st March, 30th June, 30th September and 31st December in each year. This statement includes premiums on all policies issued or renewed during the quarter, and the reinsurance rate is calculated on the total amount of such premiums. This statement also shows the amount due to the reinsurer for the quarter, and that amount is payable within a fixed period—say 15 days after confirmation. Under this system it will be seen that no premium is paid in advance, at the inception of the treaty, but each quarter is finally disposed of by its relative account.

Under another method, which is nowadays the more commonly in use, a premium is payable in advance, based upon an estimate of the anticipated premium to the treaty, and at the end of each year, within a period of three of four months after the close of the year, a statement of the actual premium income of the reinsured for the treaty year is rendered and any adjustment that may be necessary is made in the reinsurance premium. If this deposit premium were to be established in conjunction with a burning cost form of rating then the annual adjustments would need to be continued until all losses to that treaty period have been identified and liquidated. The premium payable in advance may be for the whole year and paid at the commencement of the treaty or it may be paid in four equal quarterly instalments, one at the beginning of each quarter. In regard to the annual adjustment it may be noted that excess of loss contracts are quite frequently effected at a minimum premium, so that no adjustment will be made if, when the actual premium has been ascertained, the minimum premium has not been reached. Although less common than the minimum reinsurance premium stipulation, the reinsurer may sometimes require an undertaking to be given as to the maximum original premium income to be written by the reinsured during the treaty period. This is not normally due to the reinsurer being averse to an increased reinsurance premium which could result from the application of the fixed rate per cent. to such an increased original premium income. However, an excessive increase, beyond the premium income originally estimated by the reinsured during the negotiations prior to inception of the treaty, could imply that the increase had arisen from an extension into insuring other types of risk or a lowering of the underwriting standard, and which could lead to an increase in the reinsurer's exposure beyond that which had been originally contemplated.

Such warranties as to the maximum original premium to be written should be distinguished from what is now the more common form of premium warranty, i.e. that relating to payment of reinsurance premiums. Although all types of treaty, proportional and non-proportional, have traditionally provided for accounts to be submitted and premiums to be paid within well defined time limits, these limits have often been breached in recent years. Thus, there is an increasing tendency on the part of the reinsurers to require a warranty as to the date of payment of reinsurance premiums. Such warranty would normally provide for premiums to be paid at, or within a fixed period after, specified dates. Dependent upon the wording of the warranty, breach of the warranty renders the treaty cancellable from the date of the breach or, even, voidable from inception. Although it may be somewhat difficult to apply such a warranty to the submission of accounts under a surplus treaty or to the premium adjustment under an excess of loss treaty, where the amount due to the reinsurer is unknown until advised by the reinsured, the payment of initial deposit premiums under excess of loss treaties is highly susceptible to this approach. In this context it must be noted that the intention of the warranty is that the premium shall be received by the reinsurer at the date or within the period stipulated. Thus, for example, if the reinsured had paid the premium to its reinsurance broker within the warranty period but the broker failed to transfer the premium to the reinsurer this would constitute a breach of the warranty.

In the case of a treaty including foreign business the premiums of the reinsured upon which the reinsurance rate is to be based will be derived to some extent from foreign currencies, and provision may be made for the conversion of these into sterling so as to arrive at necessary total in the home currency. This is a matter for agreement between the parties, but as a rule currency premiums are converted at the rates of exchange used by the reinsured in its own books. If the currency is not actually converted into sterling the rate may be agreed at the prevailing rate on the last day of the quarter to which the account refers, or it may be taken at the average of the rates current during the quarter, or otherwise as agreed. The intention is that the reinsurer shall, as possible, take its share in the actual premium coming to the benefit of the reinsured in its accounts. It is desirable, however, that whatever method is to be adopted should be clearly understood.

Article No. 7 of the treaty sets out the procedure to be followed in the event of losses; and certain special provisions have to be made as being particularly applicable to the excess of loss method of reinsurance. As the treaty applies only to losses which will, when the ultimate net loss is ascertained, exceed a certain figure, it will include only a small proportion of the losses which will arise under the class of business in question. The reinsured will not always know, when a claim first occurs, whether nor not the loss will reach a figure bringing it under the treaty. This is especially so in regard to third party claims, where the eventual cost is often very uncertain. An apparently trivial accident may on occasion result in a heavy claim for damages, whilst it may happen that a really serious accident may in the eventual settlement cost very little to one side or the other. Yet it would not be reasonable for the reinsurer to be left in complete ignorance of a claim for which it might be liable, until such a time as the liability was fully ascertained. The reinsurer is entitled to know its expected liabilities, if only approximately, so that it may see how its business is running and also because it may in turn have to notify its own reinsurers. A reinsurer often gives off a share of its liability by means of retrocession. To meet this point it is stipulated that the reinsured shall advise the reinsurer as soon as reasonably practicable of any accident or occurrence which may reasonably be considered as likely to give rise to a claim under the treaty, i.e. to exceed the amount of the underlying retention. This provision must of course be interpreted with a certain amount of latitude and it will not be construed to the prejudice of the reinsured if a claim which eventually exceeds the retention was not notified at the time it occurred. So long as the reinsured exercises a reasonable judgment in the matter it will not be expected to possess the gift of prophecy. However, as has been pointed out above, the effect of inflation is such that over a period of time it can increase the value of even comparatively modest losses to a level which might exceed the deductible. Thus, many reinsurers have adopted a form of Loss Advice clause which requires the reinsured to give immediate advice of all losses where the estimated amount exceed a sum lower than the deductible. This sum is generally fixed at a level of some 60% to 75% of the deductible. Thus, if a treaty covered losses in excess of £25,000 any one event, the Claims Advice clause may require immediate advice of any accident or event where the estimate of the potential loss exceeds £15,000.

The Loss Advice obligation may be further extended. There are certain types of bodily injury where the nature of the injury is such that a severe potential claim could arise to both the reinsured and the reinsurer, no matter how small the original loss estimate may be. Reinsurers prefer to be advised of these so that progress can be monitored. Article No. 7 of the specimen wording appearing in the Appendix contains a list of the kinds of potential loss which are of interest to the reinsurer.

At one time it was usual under excess of loss treaties for the reinsured to reserve to itself the right to conduct the settlement of all claims, whether such settlements were made under strict policy conditions or otherwise, though it was also generally provided that the reinsured would conduct the settlement of claims as conscientiously as if it were liable for the whole amount. However, on occasion, the reinsurer tended to feel that the reinsured's interest in minimising the loss diminished once the amount of such loss had exceeded the deductible. Thus there is nowadays a greater tendency to insist upon cooperation between the parties in the conduct of losses which might involve the treaty. In addition, the absolute right to make loss settlements outside of the strict policy conditions has become more circumscribed in that the reinsurer is, nowadays, prepared to accept under the treaty only those "ex gratia" payments made with its consent. Clearly this does not prevent the reinsured from making "ex gratia" payments to its insureds, but it is felt to be only equitable that if the reinsurer is to bear such a loss under the treaty then its consent should be obtained.

In regard to this matter of loss settlements being made which are not in accord with strict policy conditions, some remarks are necessary on the problem of what are commonly known as ECO (Extra Contractual Obligation) losses. This problem arose some years ago, primarily in the United States of America, from the practice of certain Courts making exemplary awards in addition to the claim for bodily injury, etc. made by the plaintiff. These "punitive damages" awards were made because of some real or apparent dereliction of duty on the part of the insurer arising from frivolous defence, tardiness in settlement or otherwise. Because of the form of Claims Clause in use at the time there was considerable confusion as to whether or not such damages could be included in the amount of a loss under the treaty. It is clear, however, that the contract of reinsurance is purely one of indemnity so that unless otherwise agreed the reinsurer is liable only for losses made under the strict terms of the insurance policy covered by such reinsurance. Therefore, if Extra Contractual Obligation losses were to be covered under the treaty a suitable clause would need to be included in the contract wording.

So far as claims which are capable of settlement are concerned, the matter is a simple one where the reinsurer with every confidence entrusts its interests to the hands of the reinsured and the reinsured consults with the reinsurer on the difficult or complicated losses. But when, as sometimes happens in all classes of business and not infrequently in third party business, it becomes necessary or desirable to contest a claim by litigation, the position can become more complicated since there are differing ways in which the claim can be dealt with.

It will be remembered that the definition of ultimate net loss given in Article No. 4 included any litigation expenses incurred in connection with a claim, and this fact gives rise to certain considerations of an important character. If a claim is contested in the Courts, it would be quite easy for the costs thereby incurred to mount up to a very substantial sum, possibly even larger than the amount of the damages involved. It is therefore possible for the reinsured, if unlucky in its suit, to double the cost of settling claim for the sole reason that it contested the claim rather than settled it by agreement. This may often have the effect of bringing the reinsurer in for a share of a claim which it would otherwise have escaped, and the question arises how, if at all, the reinsurer can protect its interests. In this matter there are various methods of procedure. That which is contained in the specimen form of the treaty given in this book may be taken as representing the more modern usage and is based upon the reinsured undertaking to cooperate with the reinsurer in the conduct and settlement of *all* losses, whether litigated or not. But there are also other approaches designed to give complete protection to the reinsured while safeguarding the reinsurer as far as reasonably possible.

Under the first method all litigation expenses go to the ultimate net loss, whether they be incurred by the reinsured on behalf of its insured or whether they be awarded against the company on behalf of a successful claimant. But since the reinsurer must have a vital interest in the matter, it is given a right to be consulted in the matter before litigation is undertaken, and its consent obtained thereto, though that consent must not be unreasonably withhheld. The wording of this part of the article—commonly known as the "costs clause"—may be quoted here to show the practice:—

> "The Company shall not without the consent of the Reinsurer contest a claim which may reasonably be considered likely to give rise to a claim under this Agreement, but such consent shall not be withheld unreasonably and shall not be withheld if, having regard to the generally accepted practice in connection with claim settlements and to any special circumstances in respect of the claim in question, it would be reasonable for the Reinsurer or the Company (if liable for the whole amount of the claim without reinsurance) to contest the claim."

The effect of this is to give the reinsurer a voice in the matter without depriving the reinsured of its reasonable discretion, which may be an important consideration where a claim arises in a foreign country and where the question of contesting must depend upon local conditions known only to the reinsured's representative in that country. With this clause the reinsured can never pay less than its underlying retention (if the total claim plus litigation costs exceeds that figure), but on the other hand can never pay more, thereby ensuring that the purpose of the treaty shall be given effect to.

The second method proceeds on a different assumption. In the first place it provides specifically that the term ultimate net loss shall exclude all costs incurred in litigation. The Costs Clause then runs as follows:—

> "In the event of a loss arising to which the Reinsurer may be liable to contribute, no legal costs shall be incurred on its behalf without its consent first being obtained, and if the Reinsurer so consents it shall contribute to the said costs in the proportion that the said loss as finally settled bears to the total sum payable by way of damages. If, however, a settlement of the loss be practicable before taking the case into Court, whether by compromise or otherwise, for a sum not exceeding £   (i.e., the amount of the underlying retention) no legal costs shall be payable by the Reinsurer.
>
> No settlement of a loss by agreement shall be effected by the Company for a sum in excess of   (the underlying retention) without the consent of the Reinsurer."

It will be seen that this version of the clause is more favourable to the reinsurer. Litigation costs are to be dealt with as something apart from the damages, costs of repairs or other items making up the claim. No such costs may be incurred on behalf of the reinsurer without its consent, which means the reinsurer will not be liable for its share of any such costs if they are so incurred. No provision is made giving the reinsured a right to incur costs on the reinsurer's behalf if consent is unreasonably withheld. Of course, no prudent reinsurer would in fact withhold its consent without reason, though it might be otherwise if the reinsurer were in liquidation and the consent had to be given by the liquidator. As and when consent has been given, the reinsurer will be liable for its share of the cost, but only for its share. The costs are not added to the claim, so as to make up one total from which the reinsured's retention may be deducted. The costs are to be shared between the parties to the treaty in the proportions of their respective liabilities in the claim which was the subject of the litigation. An example will show how this is worked. Suppose the treaty is for an excess of £20,000 and a claim is contested in the Courts under which the reinsured is found liable to pay £30,000 as damages and costs come to £6,000. The damages are then payable as to £20,000 by the reinsured and £10,000 by the reinsurer, i.e., two-thirds and one-third respectively. The costs are then allocated in the same proportions so that the reinsured pays £4,000 and the reinsurer £2,000. The effect is that of the total cost of the claim of £36,000, the reinsured pays £24,000 and the reinsurer £12,000, so that with this Costs Clause the reinsured is not able to limit its loss under one occurrence in all circumstances to the amount of its underlying retention.

This method of dividing the costs applies whether damages are actually awarded in the action or whether, after proceedings have been commenced, the case is settled out of Court. But a further paragraph provides that if the loss could be settled for a sum not more than the underlying retention, the reinsurer is to escape costs altogether, the idea being that if the reinsured does not choose to settle a claim at its underlying retention or less, it must be considered as serving its own interests only, in an endeavour to obtain a more favourable verdict, and in that case it is but fair that it should bear the costs itself, whatever may be the result of continuing the action. It should be noted that this restrictive provision applies to nothing but the costs, and the reinsurer would be liable for its share of any damages that might be awarded, whether or not the case could have been settled out of Court.

A further paragraph provides that no claim shall be settled by the reinsured, by agreement with its insured, for a sum exceeding the underlying retention without the reinsurer's consent. This may be regarded as not unreasonable since, before an agreed settlement is made, the reinsurer may be reasonably ask for an opportunity to consider whether or not the claim should be resisted.

This more stringent form of costs clause was at one time almost always included in excess of loss treaties, but it is fair to say that modern practice tends more and more away from it.

Article No. 7, besides laying down the methods of dealing with claims, also provides for the payment of the proportion falling to the charge of the reinsurer. Generally all losses under an excess of loss cover are treated as cash losses and are payable by the reinsurer within an agreed period—say 15 days—after demand by the reinsured, such demand being accompanied by the loss papers in support thereof. This practice developed from a time when losses under such treaties were comparatively few in number and often for substantial amounts, so that the cash loss system was the more suitable.

The Article concludes with a provision for the reinsured to supply the reinsurer with a statement of the individual outstanding losses as at the 31st December of each year or such other date as may be agreed. This statement is required for a number of purposes, among which may be mentioned the reinsurer's need to keep its own retrocessionaires up to date and the need for an up to date listing of unsettled losses in which it might be involved for its own underwriting accounts.

Article No. 8 defines the period for which the treaty is to run and the exact manner in which it is to apply. Since the treaty applies to the whole of the business of a given class, and the premium thereon is based on the annual premiums derived by the reinsured from that business, there are obvious advantages in making the period of the treaty coincide with the reinsured's business year. Thus the treaty will commence in the ordinary way on the 1st January and will continue yearly thereafter, for an indefinite period, subject to cancellation by either party by a fixed period of notice—three months or six months—to expire on the 31st December in any year. There is, of course, no necessary uniformity in this practice, as excess treaties may run for any period, or may be renewed every year, or may be terminable on short notice or otherwise as may be agreed. But the method outlined above is the more usual, since contracts of this nature are intended to be reasonably permanent.

It is likely that many treaties would include in this article a war clause providing for automatic cancellation in the same form as under a surplus treaty. In its early days this class of business was placed to a great extent in its country of origin and no war clause was required. The position has changed completely today and the practice of excess of loss reinsurance is just as world-wide as any other, its nature being such that the wider the geographical spread, the safer the whole portfolio becomes. Treaties placed in this way would of course contain a war cancellation clause.

In the method of application of the treaty to the business to which it refers, there are two distinct systems in vogue, each having its advantages in certain directions. It is not possible to say that either system is the more correct, since both are in use and either may be used according to the view held by the reinsured as to the form of its requirements.

Under one of these two systems the treaty may be constructed on what is called a "losses incurred" basis. The underlying idea of this is to segregate the affairs of each year as it were and to make the treaty apply to all losses occurring within that year, irrespective of any question of unexpired liability or whether the policy under which the loss occurred was issued in a previous year. The merit of this system is its simplicity. Each treaty year is self-contained. There is no portfolio to be taken over at the beginning of the year, nor to be surrendered on cancellation of the treaty at the end of a year. In effect the unexpired liability coming over from previous years is attached to the year of account and goes on in that way from year to year, so that at the end of a year there is no unexpired liability to fall on to an outgoing reinsurer; it automatically goes over to the new reinsurer. No question of portfolio premiums arises as it is an integral part of the arrangement that the reinsurance premiums of the year shall apply as consideration for the obligation to pay the claims of that year, so that no premium is paid to the reinsurer for the unexpired liability which it must take over, but at the end of its term it escapes any obligation to return any unearned premiums, since its liability terminates. The wording of the clause makes this position clear.

> "This Agreement shall take effect from the First day of January 19   and shall continue in force for an indefinite period unless otherwise agreed. Either party may, however, terminate this Agreement by giving three months notice in writing to expire on the Thirty First day of December of any year. The Reinsurer shall remain liable for all losses occurring up to and including the date of termination. Thereafter the liability of the Reinsurer shall cease outright other than so far as outstanding claims are concerned."

Thus all claims arising during the year, no matter when they are eventually settled or when the relevant policy was issued, fall on that year's reinsurer, but no other claims whatsoever, hence the expression "losses occurring".

The method by which the year's premium covers the year's losses is not entirely accurate, for those losses do not strictly relate to the year's written premium. The losses arising in any year relate to the original premiums written during the year, plus the unearned premiums from the previous year less the unearned portion of the written premiums of the year. On a stable income this adjustment would make no material difference, as the earned premium would correspond approxmately to the written. But if the income was fluctuating this would not be so. Suppose the premium income in a given year amounted to £10,000,000 and this has risen from £5,000,000 in the preceding year. Then the earned premium, assuming the usual 40% for unexpired liability, would work out as follows:—

Written premiums	£10,000,000
Add earned premiums from previous year, being 40% of £5,000,000	£2,000,000
	£12,000,000
Deduct unearned premiums of current year, being 40% of £10,000,000	£4,000,000
Earned premiums	£ 8,000,000

But under the "losses occurring" system, the reinsurer would receive a rate of premium based on £10,000,000 though running the risk of claims based on a premium exposure of £8,000,000 only. If however the premium income were falling, the written premiums would be less than the earned, and the reinsurer would suffer accordingly. In the long run and provided the reinsurer remains on the treaty for a period of years, the arrangement compensates itself and the reinsurance premium will fairly represent the extent of the risk. This is another reason why it is desirable that treaties of this nature should be of a reasonably permanent nature and not subject to too frequent changes in the reinsurers. There is, of course, nothing to prevent the reinsured and its reinsurer agreeing that the reinsurance premium under the excess of loss treaty shall be calculated at a rate per cent. of the "earned" premium during the period rather than the "written" premium. After all, in these days of electronic data processing, calculating the true earned premium can be no more complicated than calculating the written premium.

Apart from its simplicity the "losses occurring" system possesses a certain advantage in enabling the reinsured to cut off the reinsurer's liability short at the end of the year, for then no complications can arise as between an old and a new reinsurer.

If the outgoing reinsurer were required to run off all unexpired risks at the end of its treaty, then in regard to claims under policies issued in the preceding year the old reinsurer would be responsible until each policy expired or fell due for renewal. A new reinsurer would then come on risk for claims under all policies issued or renewed during the new year. The position might then arise under a motor treaty, for example, in which two cars were involved in one claim, both insured with the same reinsured, one under a policy running off from the previous year and one under a policy issued during the new year. Although the aggregate liability would fall on the one reinsured, it would be necessary to allocate this as between the two policies, so as to determine the respective liabilities of the two reinsurers. This would be difficult enough, but, what would be worse, the reinsured would be obliged to deduct the amount of its underlying retention from each reinsurer's liability so that it might find itself saddled with a double retention on the one claim. It may be admitted that the risk is not a very heavy one since it depends on a combination of circumstances not likely to occur very often. But there is a risk, and this is entirely avoided under the losses occurring method.

Yet that method may have one definite disadvantage to the reinsured arising out of the fact that the reinsurer by terminating a treaty escapes all further liability after the expiry of the notice to cancel. If the business happens to be running badly—and this would be the most frequent reason for a reinsurer to cancel—the reinsured may find itself in the position of having to run off the unexpired portion of the business either without any reinsurance cover or with a cover at a very high rate. Even if a new reinsurer could be obtained, it would probably stipulate that all previous business should be excluded. In practice this is perhaps not a very serious matter, since it would not happen very often. In any event if the business was running so badly that the treaty could not be put right by an adjustment in the reinsurance rate this would point to something radically wrong with the reinsured's methods, which it could hardly expect to continue to the prejudice of a reinsurer, but which it would have to put right at its own expense. Nevertheless, the fear of being left without reinsurance, at the caprice of the reinsurer, does sometimes deter a reinsured from adopting the "losses occurring" system.

From what has been said it will be clear that the second system of applying an excess of loss treaty is related to the portfolio or earned premium basis, in which respect it follows the practice of the surplus treaty. Under this system the reinsurer may or may not take over a portfolio on coming on to a treaty. If it does it will be responsible for claims arising in respect of the running off of the previous year's business; if not it will be responsible only for policies issued or renewed during the year of the treaty. But in either case—and this is the important difference—the reinsurer will be responsible at the end of the year in respect of all policies issued or renewed during the year until their expiry, unless arrangements are made for the withdrawal of the portfolio with an appropriate return of premium by the reinsurer. Under this system the clause would be worded somewhat as follows:—

> "This Agreement takes effect in respect of all policies issued or renewed on or after the 1st day of January 19 . On the termination of this Agreement the obligations of the Reinsurer hereunder shall remain in full force until the expiry of the then current insurances and the settlement of all liabilities arising hereunder."

Provision may then be made for the withdrawal of the portfolio, either by mutual agreement or at the option of the reinsured, but not as a rule against the consent of the reinsured. The method of computing the amount of the portfolio under an excess of loss treaty requires a little consideration. It would, of course, be possible to compute this pro rata, but as the treaty applies to the whole of a business this would generally be quite impracticable, and a fixed percentage is usually agreed. In arriving at this, however, it has to be remembered that the customary 40% as the value of a portfolio is arrived at under a surplus treaty by an approximation of the gross unexpired premium at something about 50% and then deducting the reinsurance commission. But since excess rates are almost always on a net basis this method will not apply, and the rate would have to be based on the gross return without deduction of commission. To base a net rate on a net return premium would be in effect to deduct the commission twice and so unduly reduce the portfolio value. The portfolio premium is, therefore, usually calculated at 50% of the premiums ceded under the treaty during the previous year and though this is not necessarily exact, it is probably not far out. The rate will then be credited to a reinsurer who takes over a portfolio or debited if the portfolio is withdrawn.

The portfolio system has the advantage of assuring the reinsured of its reinsurance cover until the normal expiry of its policies but is not so simple as the first method. It complicates the accountancy to some extent by requiring claims records to be kept in separate series, while there is also the possibility of a duplicated retention already referred to. It will be obvious that such differences as exist between the two systems only come into play when there is a change in the reinsurer. As long as a treaty remains in force there is no great practical difference.

Nevertheless it is fair to say that the excess treaty on a "losses occurring" basis, tends more and more in modern practice to supplant any other form because on balance it has so many advantages.

In recent years, however, a further development has taken place in that some excess of loss treaties have been issued on what is known as a "claims made" basis. This type of excess of loss treaty follows the increasing practice for various types of liability risk to be insured on a "claims made" or "losses discovered" basis. Under these contracts the date of loss is the date of the first report of a loss to the insured or the insurance company, and such loss is covered only if the report were made during the period of the policy of insurance. The "claims made" form of excess of loss treaty operates on the date of the first report of a loss being made by the reinsured to the reinsurer. Such contracts have been developed in an attempt to shorten the "long-tail" which arises for insurers (and reinsurers) on certain types of liability risk. Obviously, over an extended period of time the coverage under such a "claims made" treaty would be little different to that provided by a treaty on a "losses occurring" basis. However, where a change in reinsurance arrangements takes place some provision may need to be made for the effect of the transition. Thus, a reinsurer accepting a new share of a "claims made" treaty incepting at say the 1st January 1987, would not wish to be exposed to losses which may have occurred many years ago but which might be reported for the first time during 1987. Thus the treaty may contain some form of "prior acts" limitation to the effect that coverage would apply only to claims made during 1987 under policies of insurance issued on or after a specified date (or in respect of losses occurring on or a specified date) or as may be negotiated. In the same way some form of "sunset" clause may be required for losses which may be reported after termination of the treaty, such as the reinsurer agreeing subject to receipt of an additional premium to cover losses which occurred during 1987 and which are reported during the ensuing twelve months. Apart from this method of establishing the date of the loss event so covered by the reinsurance, all the other terms of the excess of loss treaty would be similar to those discussed above. It should be noted that an excess of loss treaty can be issued on a "claims made" basis to indemnify the reinsured in respect of losses arising on policies of insurance which it issued on a "losses occurring" basis. In such event, however, the reinsured would need to pay particular attention to the possible "run-off" problems which might arise in respect of losses which do occur during the period of the reinsurance but which are only reported long after the treaty has terminated.

The foregoing survey completes the description of the special features of the excess of loss treaty as applied to the reinsurance of liability risks. In addition the contract wording contains certain Articles dealing with such matters as errors and omissions, the reinsurer's right to inspect books, the parties' right to give immediate cancellation, provisions for alterations and notices, confidentiality, communications and an arbitration agreement. These Articles will be found in the specimen form given in the Appendix. They follow in all respects the corresponding Articles contained in a surplus treaty and do not, therefore, call for further comment here.

Chapter 8
Reinsurance by Treaty
III—Property Excess of Loss

Perhaps one of the outstanding features of the development of the reinsurance business in recent years has been the way in which the excess of loss method of reinsurance has been adapted beyond its original scope. This makes for greater flexibility in method, and plays its part in fulfilling the needs of the reinsured. Naturally in such extended use, the parties have to feel their way as it were, to experiment with premium ratings, and to make such special provisions as the circumstances may require. Thus we find the excess of loss treaty is used with increasingly frequency in fire, personal accident, hail and marine business. The previous chapter concentrated on the protection of the liability classes of insurance by excess of loss treaty reinsurance since this was originally the commonest form of excess of loss. In such earlier times the excess of loss form was, with few exceptions, the major method of reinsuring liability risks while the surplus treaty was the major method of effecting property reinsurance. In this context the term "property reinsurance" can encompass a wide range of classes of insurance covering objects which can be lost, damaged or destroyed. In this Chapter, however, we shall also be considering certain forms of benefit or pecuniary loss insurance, such as Personal Accident, where the reinsurance practice is more similar to that applying to property rather than to liability risks. In the abovementioned earlier times excess of loss reinsurance of property risks was used purely as a form of catastrophe protection, in the sense of limiting an untoward accumulation of retained losses. The application of excess of loss reinsurance to the various forms of property insurance has however increased greatly in recent years. This has very largely been brought about by the emergence of what is termed the "risk excess" of loss reinsurance. The practice of catastrophe reinsurance has not altered significantly other than in the size of the exposures being covered.

A "risk excess" may be placed facultatively or as a treaty. In this Chapter we shall concentrate on its operation as a treaty reinsurance.

The "risk excess" of loss treaty may be considered as being of the nature of the "working" excess referred to Chapter 7 above, in that a reinsurer would anticipate that a number of losses would arise thereon in each year. Risk excess of loss reinsurance protects individual risks and is therefore used as an alternative to surplus reinsurance. This development of risk excess reinsurances arises from the same impetus which gave rise to excess of loss treaties, i.e. the administrative ease and comparative cheapness of the cover. In addition modern practice tends toward the establishing of retentions on an Estimated Maximum Loss (EML) or Probable Maximum Loss (PML) basis rather than on the Sum Insured. Although this practice may provide the reinsured with an added capacity under its surplus treaty, the accuracy of the EML assessment could give cause for anxiety so that a single risk protection would be necessary to limit the effect of possible errors. Such a cover may also be used to protect the surplus treaty by limiting the exposure on a major single risk ceded thereto.

Although the risk excess of loss cover can be used as described above to operate behind the surplus treaties to correct an EML assessment or otherwise, the system tends to apply nowadays as the main method of reinsurance and not merely as an addition to the surplus treaties. Such types of risk excess treaty are sometimes called "underwriting" covers to distinguish them from pure catastrophe covers. In such case the underlying retention must be fixed at a lower figure to correspond with what the reinsured can afford to run in respect of a fire or other peril causing loss to an individual risk. The cover does not operate to limit the cost of a catastrophe but is a method of limiting the cost of one fire at one risk.

The underlying retention will not be fixed at an invariable figure as is done with a catastrophe cover, for that would be to impose on the reinsured the same liability for loss in respect of every risk which it accepts irrespective of the class of risk or the hazard involved. This would not be in accordance with sound underwriting principles. The method is to fix differing retentions for various classes of risk and this is most conveniently done by classifying the whole of the fire business according to, say, premium rating. The underlying retention is then fixed on a sliding scale with the highest figure for risks in say class (1) reduced by successive stages for the higher rated classes. The exact divisions of the business and the retention to be applicable to each are, of course, entirely matters for arrangement between the parties and will depend to some extent on the nature of the portfolio. It is to be understood that this is a pure excess cover, so that the reinsured will be responsible for the whole of every loss up to the amount of the underlying retention applicable to each class and the reinsurer will be liable for the whole of the excess amount of any loss up to its limit.

This limit is not a fixed amount as in a catastrophe cover but varies according to the class of risk just as does the underlying retention. This is done by making the reinsurer liable up to, say, 5 or 6 or 10 times the underlying retention so that, as this latter reduces, so the maximum reinsurance limit reduces. This has the effect of giving the reinsured a fixed amount of cover for each of the various classes of risk, while reducing the burden falling on the reinsurer in respect of the more hazardous classes.

Where such a "risk" excess of loss treaty is issued, the wording of the Ultimate Net Loss Clause appearing in the contract would need to be amended to refer to "any one claim any one risk" rather than to "claims or series of claims arising out of any one event" and the wording of the Operative Clause would need to be amended to include the following:—

> "The Company shall be the sole judge as to what constitutes one risk, it being understood and agreed that one risk shall mean all property or interest at one location and designated by the Company in its records as subject to one risk retention.
>
> It is warranted that the Company undertakes not to retain on one risk an amount greater than (list the various retentions)."

Under the "any one event" or "occurrence" form of excess of loss reinsurances described in Chapter 7 above there is normally no limit to the number of occurrences covered during the period of the treaty. The payment of the full limit would not therefore exhaust the cover in the same way that a total loss does under a direct insurance policy. Thus there is an individual, not an aggregate, limit to the reinsurer's liability. However, excess of loss treaties of the risk excess type provide for a limit for any one loss occurrence and a separate (and sometimes larger) aggregate limit for any one year. This approach also applies in catastrophe excess of loss reinsurances covering business such as fire and marine which provide for a single limit for any one occurrence and for any one year, but allow for reinstatement of the cover upon payment of an additional premium. Such catastrophe covers are explained in greater detail in the following pages. However, such limitations are beginning to be found even on excess of loss treaties where, traditionally, the coverage provides what are in effect "unlimited free reinstatements".

This annual aggregate limitation to reduce the effect of an untoward accumulation emphasises one of the major differences between the surplus form of treaty and the risk excess. Under a surplus treaty the reinsurer is liable for a share of a theoretically unlimited number of losses. But for that liability it receives a proportionate share of all the applicable premiums of the ceding company. Under the risk excess the premium to the reinsurer generally represents a comparatively minor rate per cent. of the reinsured's premium income. Such premium paid to the reinsurer contains little, if any, element for a catastrophe exposure.

The risk excess cover for fire business has been adopted for many of the larger insurance companies, which by reason of their high accumulated funds feel able to retain a much higher limit than was customary under the surplus treaty. Thus, an excess cover might be arranged for a priority of say £250,000, £500,000 or even more, so that the reinsured would retain at its own risk all claims below the priority. The incidence of the more hazardous or very large risks may then be dealt with by facultative reinsurance, or by taking out a treaty to operate not before but after the excess cover is filled.

It is sometimes necessary to make specific exclusion in respect of certain classes of insurance transacted in various territories. A good example of this found in modern times is earthquake insurance in New Zealand which is subject to collaboration with the New Zealand government. A clause may be inserted in the treaty specifically excluding liability in respect of this business.

> "This Agreement does not extend to cover any liability attaching to the New Zealand Government or to the Earthquake and War Damage Commission of New Zealand in respect of insurance under the Earthquake and War Damage Act, 1944 or regulations made thereunder or under any subsequent act, regulation, order or amendment covering earthquake damage."

As with all other forms of excess of loss reinsurance, the rating of risk excess of loss treaties is a complex matter and no schedule of premium rating can be given for treaties of this kind, since each has to to be dealt with on its merits. The discussion of premium rating in Chapter 7 above explained some of the various methods used in the calculation of premium rates under excess of loss treaties, including the approaches based upon past loss experience. There are significant differences in treatment in risk excesses covering such as property business, however, because of the more minor effect of inflation and because there tends to be a lesser delay in the advice of losses under most classes of insurance other than liability (i.e. these classes of business have a shorter "tail").

Rather than calculating the premium rate on the prior years' loss experience, the reinsurer may base this premium rate upon its risk exposure under the treaty. This "exposure rating" may also be used as a check on the premium rating obtained by the "burning cost" method. The first stage in this approach requires the construction of a "Risk Profile" of the portfolio of business being insured. This Risk

Profile consists of a table classifying the insured risks according a range of sums insured. The ranges may also be based upon EML estimations but this may give rise to a degree of uncertainty as to the measures of the exposure. The following is intended to be a simple representation of such a Risk Profile:—

Range of sums insured	Ave. value at risk	Number of risks	Agg. value at risk	Aggregate premium
£0–25,000	£18,000	3,000	£54m	£360,000
£25–50,000	£38,000	5,500	£209m	£1,100,000
£50–100,000	£75,000	1,000	£75m	£300,000
£100–200,000	£150,000	300	£45m	£120,000
£200–500,000	£350,000	200	£70m	£120,000
TOTAL	100%	10,000		£2,000,000

On the assumption that the reinsured is seeking, say, an excess of loss treaty to pay losses up to £450,000 each and every risk in excess of £50,000, the next stage would be to estimate the degree to which the coverage under the treaty would be exposed to these various ranges of Sum Insured. Obviously, at this level of coverage no account would need to be taken of the premiums relating to the two ranges of risk with Sums Insured less than £50,000 since no claim arising on any risk represented by such an insurance policy could expose the treaty to loss. If all the losses arising under the policies represented by the other ranges of Sum Insured were to be total losses, then the premium due to the reinsurer would be directly related to the exposure. Thus, in the range of policies with Sum Insured exceeding £200,000 up to £500,000 the average Sum Insured at risk is £350,000. On the basis of a deductible of £50,000 the reinsured would be entitled to retain a premium equal to one-seventh of the written premium for the range, and the premium rate to the reinsurer would need to generate a reinsurance premium equivalent to six-sevenths of that original premium. However, partial losses also do arise which reduce the total exposure of the reinsurer and, accordingly, the strict mathematical allocation of premium. The percentage allocations of premium which are used are often negotiated between the contracting parties. Thereupon the following schedule would be constructed to calculate the total of the reinsurance premium expected by the reinsurer. The percentages used in this allocation are intended for the purposes of illustration only.

Range of sums insured	Ave. value at risk	Aggregate premium	Reinsurance percentage	Reinsurance premium
£50–100,000	£75,000	£300,000	25%	£75,000
£100–200,000	£150,000	£120,000	50%	£60,000
£200–500,000	£350,000	£120,000	75%	£90,000
TOTAL	100%			£225,000

On a gross written premium income of the order of that used in the example the reinsurer would therefore expect to be paid a reinsurance premium of some £225,000. In the usual manner of attempting to preserve a relationship of reinsurance premium to exposure, as represented by the premium written by the reinsured, the reinsurance premium rate would be expressed as 11.25% of such written premium. In practice, it is more correct to construct these tables on the basis of the applicable "risk premium", i.e, the gross premium less acquisition costs and premiums paid away for priority reinsurances if any, rather than the gross written premium. In such event the reinsurer would need to increase this "risk" reinsurance premium by an adequate expense, profit and contingency loading.

It normally happens that a cover of this nature, though adjustable in accordance with the original premium income, provides for a payment by the reinsured of an initial and minimum premium at the inception and subsequent renewal dates of the cover. The wording of the relevant Premium Clause closely follows that described in Chapter No. 7 above and contained in the specimen excess of loss treaty wording appearing in the Appendix. In this context, however, it will often be found that the term Gross Net Premium Income of the Company is used as the basis for calculation of the reinsurance premium. The term "Gross Net Premium Income" is no different to the term "annual premium income" as used in the specimen Premium Clause in that it is intended to mean the gross premiums less only cancellations, returns, bonuses and premiums on reinsurances which inure to the benefit of the Agreement. This rather curious expression denotes that no agents' commission has been deducted from the premiums, thus distinguishing it from the term "net premium" used in marine insurance.

Under a Liability Excess treaty which deals with indemnities there is no exhaustion of the sum insured; the indemnity is payable as often as claims may occur throughout the year. This practice applies likewise to excess of loss treaties covering a number of other forms of a third party liability. However it should be noted that the practice in the fire and other departments provides for the sum insured to be automatically reduced upon the payment of a claim and catastrophe covers covering these risks tend to be drafted to conform with this principle. Thus a clause may be inserted into the treaty which provides for the reinstatement of the sum insured upon the payment of a loss subject to a provision that the total claims paid by the reinsurer must not exceed more than twice the total sum insured or as may otherwise be agreed between the parties.

To give effect to these provisions a clause may be inserted in the treaty as follows:—

> "In the event of loss or losses occurring under this Agreement it is hereby mutually agreed to reinstate this Agreement to its full amount of not more than £1,000,000 (one million pounds) from the time of occurrence of such loss or losses until expiry of the Agreement and that an additional premium calculated at pro rata premium for the period from the date of such loss or losses to expiry of this Agreement shall be paid by the Company upon the amount of such loss or losses and that this additional premium shall be paid by the Company when any loss or losses arising hereunder are settled, but nevertheless the Reinsurer shall never be liable for more than £1,000,000 (one million pounds) in respect of any one fire, conflagration or disaster or series of fires, conflagrations or disasters arising out of one event or occurrence or £2,000,000 (two million pounds) in respect of all losses occurring during the currency of this Agreement."

It will be noted that the additional "reinstatement" premium referred to above would be calculated by applying the reinsurance premium or premium rate to the amount of the loss and charging to the Company a pro rata portion thereof for the unexpired period from the time of occurrence of such loss or losses until expiry of the Agreement. Such a method of calculating reinstatement premiums are known as being "pro rata" both as time and to amount. However it may be negotiated that the reinstatement premium would be pro rata as to amount alone. In such event the amount of the reinstatement premium would be proportional to the size of the loss but would be paid for the full annual period rather than merely the unexpired part thereof. Further variations may be negotiated. Thus, the first reinstatement may be "free", in the sense that no additional premium would be chargeable, a second reinstatement may be chargeable at 50% and a third at 75%. These latter represent percentages of the original reinsurance rating which are to be used in calculating the reinstatement premium. In the Clause quoted above the reinstatement premium calculation would have represented a 100% Additional Premium provision. It is, sometimes, possible for the reinsured to purchase an insurance against its liability for reinstatement premiums.

The premium for this insurance enables the reinsured to quantify exactly the total cost of its reinsurance programme at the commencement of a year, rather than be exposed to the uncertainty whether additional premiums might become due at some future date when a loss occurs and the reinstatement premium provisions become operative.

In fire business the excess of loss treaty is used extensively as a conflagration cover and some reference has already been made to this. However the application of excess of loss reinsurance to such a use is not confined to fire business. "Catastrophe" excess of loss cover will be found to be purchased in all classes of insurance business where it is necessary for the reinsured to purchase protection against a major loss arising either by way of the great size of a single claim or by an untoward accumulation of retained losses. In its essentials catastrophe excess of loss reinsurance differs very little from the form already described. It covers the excess of a certain fixed amount, at a premium which is a percentage of the total premium of the business to which it relates. But the purpose of the cover is quite different. In fire business it operates behind the surplus or risk excess treaties and is fixed, therefore, to commence at a reasonably substantial figure. It does not stand in the first line of the reinsured's reinsurance defences for that would be to set up a retention which was the same for every class of risk irrespective of hazard. Its purpose is to give protection against the unavoidable risk of accumulation in one fire—unavoidable even after every precaution has been taken to maintain reasonable limits. It is usual for such covers to be placed over the whole fire account, or at least over the whole of a section such as home or foreign, though preferably over both. United States business is, however, always dealt with separately as in the surplus method and for the same reasons.

Nevertheless a reinsured may sometimes need to make a substantial provision for catastrophe and means have been devised to secure this. This is done by constructing excess of loss covers in layers one above the other so that in total a large indemnity is secured. For example, a cover might be placed for, say, £250,000 in excess of £250,000 thereby providing cover up to £500,000. The second layer might be for £500,000 in excess of the first £500,000 thus providing for a catastrophe costing up to £1,000,000. Then there might follow a further layer of, say, £1,000,000 in excess of £1,000,000 and so on up to the amount required. This enables the reinsurance to be spread amongst a large number of reinsurers without imposing too heavy a burden on any one. It also provides reinsurers with an opportunity to choose the level at which they wish to become involved. Thus certain reinsurers may wish to participate in the lower layers where premium levels are higher, although there is of course the concomitant higher incidence of losses under the treaty. Other reinsurers prefer to participate in the higher layers where, although there may be a lower volume of premium, the risk of a claim arising on the reinsurance is also, hopefully, very much lower.

The modern accumulation of risks together with the depreciation in the value of money have led to the limits being very considerably increased. Contracts which relate to a mixed account may run up to several millions of pounds, and a top layer may well be constructed to cover, say, £50,000,000 in excess of £100,000,000. These are matters for negotiation and the availability of reinsurance capacity. The principle remains the same no matter how large the amount of the cover, but the practice shows how the reinsurance market responds to the demands upon it.

The establishing of a suitable premium rating for a layer of catastrophe excess loss reinsurance requires a considerable degree of underwriting experience and technical knowledge. Obviously, by its very nature there would be little, if any, prior year's loss experience upon which a rate for such a treaty could be based. Very often the level of premium will be based upon what the market will bear. However, as a general rule the level of deductible and the limit of the reinsurer's liability will be of considerable importance. Thus, it would be expected that a premium rate would be lower for an excess of loss treaty where the deductible represented an accumulation of three retentions of the reinsured as against a coverage where the reinsurer became liable for a loss in excess of a level of two such retentions. Where it is possible to calculate an exposure rating, as has been described above, this method will be used. But often the necessary information may not be available. The reinsurer will then, of necessity, need to rely upon an assessment of the probability of a loss arising which would involve the treaty. Probabilities would need to be calculated as to the frequency of loss and the probable total of the claim should such a loss arise. In recent years much technical data has been obtained on climatic and geological conditions throughout the world in order to estimate, for insurance purposes, the probabilities of earthquakes, hurricanes and the like. Where such data is insufficient or inappropriate the reinsurer will resort to a "payback" approach to premium rating. After making an assessment of the likely maximum loss exposure over the whole portfolio of business of that nature, the reinsurer would make a subjective assessment of how often a loss will arise. A level of premium would then be charged which would be adequate to fund the level of expected losses over the number of years included in the assessment. The premium quoted for each treaty within that portfolio would represent that treaty's contribution to the fund plus a margin for the reinsurer's profit, expenses and contingencies. Where it is intended that the indemnity under the treaty shall be reinstated to its full limit after a loss has accurred, reinstatement premiums may become payable in the same way as described above.

Some observations on the exact meaning of the expression "any one event" have been made on a previous page in connection with the excess of loss reinsurance of liability risks. It will be obvious from what has been said that some provision must likewise be made to determine the definition of a loss arising on a catastrophe excess of loss treaty from a disturbance of nature such as tornado, cyclone, hurricane, windstorm and the like. It is not often possible to say what damage is due to one and the same event so that it is quite frequent for these points to be left to be considered in each individual case. However, such an approach can lead to dispute at the time of a loss. An example of the difficulties which may arise may be illustrated by a claim which involved two marine casualties. The LASH carrier Munchen was lost with all hands at about 11.00 a.m. on the 13th December 1978 and no trace was found, other than some debris north of the Azores. The floating dock SIMA 109 sank off the French coast near Brest, some 1,300 miles away at about 17.35 p.m. on the same day. In a dispute between the Hannover Reinsurance company and its retrocessionaires the Court of Arbitration found that the losses were due to the same "storm" as they took place on the opposite sides of the same severe atmospheric depression and that the storm was a single event. Obviously where it is possible to identify a single proximate cause for a loss then no dispute would arise. But where a number of separate such causes can be identified then the amount of the loss would need to be allocated among the separate loss occurrences arising from such proximate causes. In order to minimise these uncertainties the practice has developed whereby the position is dealt with in advance, so far as it is possible so to do, by stipulating a series of agreed definitions of a "loss occurrence" for perils of this type. Clauses dealing with this point are usually known as "Hours Clauses" because of the method of delimiting such disasters or catastrophes by defined periods of time. Many variations have been produced over the years. However, the clause drafted by the Reinsurance Offices Association is now generally used throughout the London market. The ROA Clause operates on the basis that the Insuring Clause in the treaty wording expresses the coverage under the catastrophe excess of loss treaty as indemnifying the reinsured for that part of its ultimate net loss which exceeds the designated retention on account of each and every loss occurrence. The term "loss occurrence" is then defined along the following lines:—

"For the purposes of this Agreement the words 'loss occurrence' shall mean all individual losses occurring during any one loss period arising out of and directly occasioned by a single catastrophe (which is understood to mean a sudden physical disaster) and the words 'loss period' shall mean:—

72 consecutive hours as regards Windstorms, Tornados, Tempests, Cyclones, Hurricanes, Typhoons, Rainstorms and/or Hailstorms arising out of or caused by the same atmospheric disturbance.

72 consecutive hours as regards Earthquakes or Seaquakes having the same epicentre, Tidal Waves and/or Volcanic Eruptions.

72 consecutive hours and within the limits of one City, Town or Village as regards Riots, Civil Commotions and Malicious Damage.

72 consecutive hours as regards Bush Fires in Australia originating in or spreading through trees and/or grasslands.

72 consecutive hours as regards Flood arising in a territory forming one and the same river basin (river basin being defined as the catchment area of a river including all its tributaries).

168 consecutive hours as regards any other catastrophe of whatsoever nature provided that if an individual loss or losses caused by one of the perils mentioned above are included among the claims made by the Company against the Reinsurer in respect of such a catastrophe then the loss period applicable thereto shall be 72 consecutive hours.

and no individual loss which occurs outside such period or areas shall be included in the claims made by the Company against the Reinsurer in respect of any such period.

The Company may choose the date and time when any loss period commences and if any catastrophe is of a greater duration than the appropriate loss period, the Company may divide that catastrophe into two or more loss periods provided that no two loss periods overlap and provided no loss period commences earlier than the date and time of the happening of the first recorded individual loss to the Company in respect of that particular catastrophe."

With regard to the periods quoted in the above clause it should be noted that these are given purely by way of example, since the parties involved will fix such periods as they think best for their own purposes.

This definition of a "loss occurrence" is capable of further development. In recent years the severe winter conditions which have arisen in various Northern European countries have been a major source of losses under property insurances. The damage caused has arisen not so much from the initial onset of the snow and ice but from the results of the thawing process when the weather became warmer. It is the contention of the reinsurers that the basic intention of the catastrophe treaty is to provide a protection against sudden, violent and external happenings. Thus the catastrophe treaty should not, ordinarily, cover loss caused by, e.g., water damage which is the result of a gradual process, i.e. the thawing of ice and snow. This problem is therefore resolved by the inclusion of an Optional Aggregate Clause within the terms of the treaty should such coverage be required. The wording of this Clause would be as follows:—

> "This Agreement is extended to include individual losses from collapse caused by weight of snow, and water damage from burst pipes and melting snow, as follows. The Company shall have the option to deem the aggregate of all such individual losses which occur during 168 consecutive hours within one continent as having occurred during a loss period arising out of a single catastrophe. No such loss period may commence earlier than the date and time of the occurrence of the first recorded individual loss to the Company in such a catastrophe and two or more such loss periods (in the same continent) may not overlap. (It is understood and agreed, however, that if the Company exercises the option set out in this paragraph then the amount in excess of which this Agreement attaches shall be increased for the catastrophe or catastrophes involved by the greater of £ or % of the Company's premium income for the period from .)"

A further problem related to the types of peril discussed above arises from this extended period of the loss occurrence. Thus, for example, the treaty may terminate while the catastrophe is in progress. In order to clarify the normal practice that the whole of the loss occurrence is covered by the treaty, the following Extended Expiration Clause may be included in the contract wording:—

> "If this Agreement should expire or be terminated while a loss occurrence covered hereunder is in progress it is understood and agreed that subject to the other conditions of this Agreement the Reinsurer is liable as if the entire loss or damage had occurred prior to the termination of this Agreement provided that no part of that loss occurrence is claimed against any renewal of this Agreement or replacement hereof."

In workmen's compensation insurance, reinsurance was, formerly, not required to the same extent as in other classes of insurance. In Great Britain, as in many other countries, workmen's compensation is covered by the State and no reinsurance is therefore required. The business is now confined to the common law liability of an employer towards his workpeople. However, as a matter of historical interest, and also as applying to overseas business, some observations are submitted on workmen's compensation reinsurance. To a considerable degree, each individual workman consititutes a separate risk and, as the cost of each such claim is regulated by statute, it is in the usual way well within the compass of the direct writing company. Occasionally a hazardous type of risk may be reinsured but this is not often necessary and surplus treaties are not in common use. There is, however, a certain "catastrophe" risk attaching to the business, when the trade is such that a considerable number of workmen may be killed or injured as a result of a single accident and this is just the type of claim to which an excess of loss cover is suitable. The same applies to those common law claims which are sometimes made against an employer and in which damages may be awarded for a large amount since, here, there are no statutory restrictions. These aspects of the business have been somewhat prominent of late owing to a number of substantial claims at common law. Such losses have encompassed not only large awards to a single person, but also the accumulation of awards to groups of workpeople suffering industrial diseases such as may arise from the inhalation of dust, etc.

In arranging an excess of loss treaty for employer's liability or workmen's compensation business, two methods are in use.

(1) To cover the excess of a certain fixed amount or
(2) To cover the excess of a certain number of fatal accidents.

Where the excess of a fixed sum is covered, the treaty follows the usual terms as has been described in greater detail in Chapter 7 above. The cost of one claim will be made up from one accident or series of accidents due to the same cause and will include the cost of any fatal claim and any non-fatal claim, whether for permanent or temporary disablement. Some delay may arise in arriving at the ultimate net loss, owing to the possible difficulty of settling non-fatal claims and it is sometimes provided that a permanent disablement claim shall be assessed on an annuity value basis, with a right of recovery by the reinsurer if a more favourable settlement is eventually made. This is a matter for mutual arrangement, but the intention of the treaty is that the reinsured shall pay its agreed ultimate net loss, but not more. Under many workmen's compensation treaties, no limit is fixed to the reinsurer's liability, the idea being that the statutory limits to the amount of compensation are sufficient to safeguard the reinsurer's position. The growth of common law claims, however, led to the imposition of a limit in most cases so far as that section of the business was concerned so that this became more generally the practice.

Under the second method the excess of loss cover may refer to the cost of fatal accidents only. The reinsured may agree to hear the cost of one or two fatal accidents arising out of the same cause, the reinsurer to be responsible for the remainder. Such a cover may be applied only to certain classes of risk, unlike the excess of a fixed sum which generally applies to the whole business. Certain trades, such as collieries or sea risks or explosives factories, are particularly susceptible to fatal accidents and for these such an excess cover is well adapted to the requirements of the reinsured. Such a treaty must contain a provision as to the computation of the reinsured's liability, in view of the fact that the cost of fatal accidents varies according to the circumstances and the statutory provisions relating thereto. Although the reinsured bears its own risk, say, the first accident, this is not meant to be the first which actually happened in point of time by reason of the accident. The cost of all the fatal accidents must be added together as soon as all the settlements have been made and an average struck. The reinsured then pays its one (or more) fatal claim at the average cost and the reinsurer pays the remainder.

In regard to workmen's compensation excess treaties generally, the contract will contain a certain number of excluded risks, as is customary in treaties of this type, which the reinsurer is not willing to carry at the normal rate of premium. A typical list of such exclusions would be, collieries, firework manufacturers, explosives manufacturers, sea risks, quarries, well sinkers, demolition risks, and work on towers, steeples or chimney shafts. Some of these exclusions would not be possible in an excess of fatal cover, for the reason that they are the very risks in which that cover is most required. The reinsurance rate has then to be computed so as to allow for these risks.

These remarks so far as this country is concerned are largely matters of historical record, for since the passing of the Industrial Injuries Act in 1948, the purely workmen's compensation hazard has been taken over by the State, leaving to the employer only his Common Law Liability which would fall under a General Third Party cover. However, in many countries overseas, Workmen's Compensation Legislation still remains in force.

Returning to the application of excess of loss reinsurance to special classes of reinsurance, the next to be considered is personal accident business. Here again the reinsurance is intended to be a catastrophe cover to protect the rensured against the chance of more than one of its insureds being concerned in the same accident, or to limit the cost of a claim to the original sum insured. Certain factors in the character of the business come into play here. Such a cover will apply mainly to the capital sums only, for weekly benefits, being limited to a certain period, only come into the aggregate cost of a claim if they accumulate with a death or permanent disablement claim. Now it is clear that as a personal accident insurance is a benefit policy, there can be no question of the cost of a capital sum claim. If the insured is killed the sum payable is £10,000 (or whatever is the sum insured) and nothing else. It would not be possible, therefore, for the rensured to reinsure, say, an excess of loss of £5,000 at a small percentage of the premium, since in effect the reinsurer would be liable for half the cost of the claim.

When, therefore, the underlying retention under such a treaty has been fixed, the reinsured is required to warrant that it will not hold at its own risk more than an agreed amount payable as a capital sum in respect of any one person. Thus for an excess of £10,000 it may be warranted that not more than £10,000 will be retained on one person, and if a larger policy is issued the surplus will be separately reinsured. A recent feature in personal accident reinsurance is the issue of large policies to cover, for example, the incidence of death duties imposing a heavy liability on an individual life. These could not be thrown wholly on to the excess cover and the reinsured's liability must be reduced to an agreed limit by means of a surplus arrangement. The excess cover then operates in its true sense as a catastrophc cover and protects the reinsured in two ways. First it will limit the loss if more than one insured is killed or injured in the same accident and secondly it will keep the loss down to £10,000 if the original sum insured has been increased by the action of the double benefits clause or by cumulative bonus. The operation of these clauses is to some extent a matter of chance which may properly be dealt with by means of an excess cover.

Excess of loss treaties of this nature always contain a limit to the reinsurer's liability which is fixed at a reasonably moderate figure, say, £50,000, though this will depend on circumstances. This limit is usually sufficient for the reinsured's requirements, since the contingencies which give rise to a claim do not lead to such large claims as is possible in other classes of business, in view of the limited amount at risk on any one life. In special circumstances, however, a limit may have to be enlarged, as when a number of persons are insured for a special trip by aircraft or boat or train, causing an extended possibility of catastrophe. Such cases are generally dealt with specially at higher rates of premium. The development of aviation has added greatly to the catastrophe hazard in personal accident insurance and reinsurers have had to allow for it. Modern developments in travel have had to be met in this type of reinsurance. By aircraft or by ship, or coach or train, the tendency is all in the direction of the accumulation of hazard. All normal personal accident insurance policies now include the risk of air travel as a fare paying passenger on regular airlines or chartered flights. Obviously excess protection must be provided. Sometimes the arrangement is for the excess of one life, and reinsurers will fix a limit on known liability any one aircraft, ship or coach. This is to give the reinsurer a basis for fixing its rate, but the cover would of course have to include any unknown liability up to the limit provided in the treaty and this would have to be taken care of also in the rating. All top limits in the cover are much greater than they used to be in order to provide the degree of protection which modern conditions demand.

In regard to aviation risks it should be noted that the Aviation market now takes a considerable volume of personal accident flying risks, and to the extent that it does so those risks would be excluded from the excess of loss treaty issued in the personal accident department.

This Chapter has concentrated on the considerations determining the deductible, the indemnity and the premium under risk and catastrophe excess of loss reinsurances. As with surplus treaties and excess of loss for liability risks, the contract wording would need to contain various Articles covering such necessary matters as errors and omissions, the rensurer's right to inspect books, inception and termination of the treaty including the parties' right to give immediate cancellation, provisions for alterations and notices, confidentiality, communications and an arbitration agreement. These Articles follow in all respects the corresponding Articles discussed in greater detail in Chapers 6 and 7 above.

Chapter 9
Reinsurance by Treaty
IV—Special Forms of Excess of Loss

As mentioned in the previous chapters, the commonest types of excess loss reinsurance treaty are those which provide reinsurance cover for losses in excess of a fixed amount any one event or any one risk. The excess of loss form of reinsurance lends itself to adaptation in many ways, and over the years many reinsurance coverages have been developed out of the excess of loss principle. Most of these variations tend to have very brief careers and are soon totally forgotten. By way of example the following types of treaty have, at one time or another, had a certain following:—

(1) The Ecomor Treaty. This was an excess of loss reinsurance paying the balance of each and every loss above a retention. This retention varied. Briefly the reinsured established the retention at the level of a particular claim, say its twentieth largest claim in the year. The reinsurer then paid the balance of each loss above this retention with the limit of liability for any loss being a multiple of so many times the retention. The reinsurance premium was also related to the amount of the retention and the number of the claim represented thereby.

(2) The Loss Ratio Stabilisation Treaty. Under this form of coverage the reinsurer undertook to pay an amount representing the difference between the loss ratio of the year reinsured and the average loss ratio of that year plus the previous four years. Similarly the reinsurer was paid any amount by which such loss ratio was less than the average loss ratio of that year and the previous four years. The intention was that over an extended period of time the receipts and payments would balance. The reinsurer was remunerated by way of a fee for its provision of such an equalisation service.

(3) The Lutfall (Nationale) Treaty. This form of coverage was intended as a substitute for a surplus treaty with the intention of reducing the costs of administration. In effect it operated as an

> unlimited stop loss treaty in excess of an agreed underlying loss ratio. The premium calculation included a loading to enable the reinsured to take credit for ceding commission. Another feature of the premium was a maximum limitation on the amount paid by the reinsured in any year, with the balance being deferred for payment in a following year. In the interim, interest was paid on the outstanding amount.

The prime objective in the designing of these forms of contract was the attempt to secure a measure of equalisation in the underwriting results of the reinsured by minimising fluctuations in the loss experience between one year and another. However few of these appear to have been properly thought out either as to the consequences for each of the contracting parties, the reinsured and the reinsurer, or as to performing a proper statistical analysis of the possible operation of the cover.

The form of excess of loss treaty which differs materially from the common form, and which has survived, is that known as a "stop loss" cover, as it is most commonly called, though the terms "aggregate excess of loss" and "excess of loss ratio" are also used. Under this form of treaty the reinsurer is not responsible for the excess of the amount by which any individual claim exceeds a fixed amount. Its liability does not rise in that way at all. Such a treaty operates in respect of the annual loss ratio incurred on a particular branch of insurance business. The reinsurer will not be liable for any losses until the loss ratio for the year reaches an agreed percentage of the premiums. Thereafter the reinsurer is responsible for all losses, great or small, until its limit of liability is reached. The limit is also expressed in the form of a loss ratio. For example the treaty may cover the amount up to 120% in excess of 80% loss ratio so that as soon as the losses exceed 80% the reinsurer pays all further losses until the total amount paid by the reinsured and reinsurer together reaches 200%. Thereafter the liability would revert to the reinsured. It is not uncommon for the reinsured's retention and the reinsurer's liablity also to be fixed in amount. These amounts would be fixed in accordance with the size of the business and would usually be computed at approximately the relevant percentage of the business as it existed at the time the treaty began. The purpose is to prevent a substantial expansion of the portfolio which might be against the reinsurer's interests.

The loss ratio upon which the excess cover depends is computed on the annual results of the business. It is computed by relating the claims incurred to the earned premiums. At the end of each business year the claims paid during the year are increased by the estimate for claims still outstanding and decreased by the reserve for outstanding claims brought forward from the previous year. This gives the amount of the net claims incurred. The earned premiums are computed in the same way by adding to the written premiums the reserve for unearned premiums brought forward from the previous year and deducting the reserve for unearned premiums at the end of the year. In this country this could be done on the usual 40% basis, but it may be agreed otherwise if the circumstances in which the business is written so require. The percentage of claims to premiums thus disclosed shows the amount for which the reinsurer is responsible and payment would be due accordingly. Thus, if payment is called for under the treaty, it is usually made once a year after the accounts are ascertained. It does not follow, however, that the reinsured must necessarily wait till its annual accounts are published before it can make any claim under its excess cover. The clause found in the ordinary excess of loss cover to the effect that "nothing in this clause shall be construed as meaning that losses are not recoverable until the ultimate net loss has been ascertained" applies with equal force in this form of cover. Therefore, if it be found during the course of the year that the claims paid have exceeded the agreed loss ratio, even after due allowance for the loss reserve brought forward from the previous year, the reinsurer may be called upon to make a payment on account. This is subject, however, to the proviso that when the actual claims ratio is ascertained at the end of the year, the reinsurer would be entitled to the benefit of any improvement that might have resulted from the remainder of the year's working by a refund if necessary of the whole or part of what it had paid. The intentions of the treaty must be carried out so that the reinsured bears at its own risk the agreed loss ratio.

It is obvious that a material fact in a treaty of this kind is to know how the outstanding claims reserve is constructed since this is the one fact that is uncertain. This illustrates once again the importance of the principle of utmost good faith in reinsurance transactions.

A special provision is usually found in treaties of this kind by which the reinsurer accepts responsibility for only 90% (or some such proportion) of the aggregate liability arising under the treaty, the reinsured being required to warrant that it retains the remaining 10% at its own risk. This provision is sometimes found in other forms of conflagration or catastrophe cover, but is invariable in the excess of loss ratio cover. The reason for it is clear. It will be noted that the excess loss ratio is fixed at a high figure because the treaty is meant only to give protection in a bad year. At such a time it will generally be obvious to the reinsured some time before the end of the year that the agreed loss ratio will be exceeded. Thereafter, all losses would fall wholly on the reinsurer and each for its full amount. It is, however a well-established reinsurance principle that it is not wise, except in very special circumstances, to accept liability for the whole of a claim or series of claims, the settlement of which is left entirely in the hands of the reinsured. Such a condition of affairs, without any reflection whatever on the honesty of the reinsured, is likely to lead to some relaxation in the methods of claim settlements to the prejudice of the reinsurer. To avoid this it is stipulated that the reinsured shall retain, say, 10% of the excess cover, so that it shall have at least that interest in every claim which has to be dealt with. This is the more important in that there may be quite a large number of such claims of many different kinds. In a fire catastrophe cover the same point arises, though perhaps in rather less degree, since the various claims concerned must all arise out of the one catastrophe and the retention of a share by the reinsured is not always insisted upon.

The rate of premium for such a cover is computed at a net percentage of the premium income in the same way as is usual for other classes of cover. No general scale of rates can be given, for these depend upon many different factors, the character of the business, the previous experience, the limits of cover and so on, so that each proposal must be rated on its merits. However, it will often be found that in setting the rate of reinsurance premium, the reinsurer will seek to establish a particular level of reinsurance premium to limit of indemnity, i.e. a target "rate on line". The system of rating according to the claims cost over a three-year period, with a loading for contingencies and profit, as already described in Chapter 7, may be used in this class of treaty. For the purposes of this form of reinsurance it often happens that that system is particularly convenient to produce an equitable rating.

The description of the cover outlined above represents merely one of the forms in which stop loss reinsurance may be transacted, although the underlying princple of limiting the effect of an aggregation of losses remains unaltered. Thus, for example, the retention of the reinsured and the limit of liability of the reinsurer may be expressed in terms of both loss ratios and fixed monetary amounts, thus:—

> "The Reinsurer shall pay 90% of all losses in the aggregate applicable to the 1985 Year of Account in excess of 150% of the Company's retained premium income or £750,000 whichever be the greater up to a further 100% of such premium income or £500,000 whichever be the less."

Such a formulation will tend to be used where this form of cover is being sought for a new or untried class of business or insurance company, such as a captive insurance company. If the actual premium income for the period is considerably less than the estimated premium then the reinsurer's exposure could be considerably increased. Thus, in the above example, the reinsurance could have been placed on the assumption that the reinsured's underwriting acceptance (or retention) would be limited to, say, £50,000 any one risk. On the figures as presented the reinsurer would become liable only after 15 total losses had been exceeded (150% multiplied by £500,000 and divided by £50,000). However, if the reinsured's premium income amounted only to £300,000 then the priority of 150% thereof, i.e. £450,000, would represent only 9 total losses.

Where the reinsurance is structured purely on the basis of fixed monetary amounts it will tend to be termed as an "aggregate excess of loss" reinsurance rather than "stop loss".

The definition of the period to which the reinsurance relates is worthy of some closer consideration. The period of the reinsurance as described above is based upon the reinsured's accounting period. In such a formulation the basis for calculation of the priority and the reinsurer's liability is based upon the relation which the premium written (as adjusted by changes in the unearned premium provision) bears to the claims paid figure (as adjusted by movements in the estimates for outstanding losses). The reinsurance premium rate would also be based upon this earned premium income. Such an approach does not find favour nowadays, primarily because of the reinsurer's exposure to fluctuations in the outstanding loss figures especially where these represent losses which may have occurred in years well prior to the period of the reinsurance. It will be more commonly be found that a stop loss treaty is placed on a "losses occurring" basis. In this format the liability of the reinsurer will be calculated solely upon losses which arise during the period of reinsurance with no adjustment for losses which arise in any other period. If necessary, claims under the treaty may need to be recalculated until all losses arising in the period have been finally liquidated. The reinsurance premium is usually calculated as a percentage of the "earned premium", i.e. the premium written by the reinsured (net of any priority reinsurances which inure for the benefit of the stop loss coverage) adjusted by changes in the unearned premium provision.

Another possible approach is to structure the stop loss reinsurance on an "issued or renewed' or "underwriting year" basis so that the reinsurer is liable for the aggregation of losses arising on all policies issued or renewed in the year of account. As many of these policies would in the normal course of business expire in the year subsequent to the period of the reinsurance, the reinsurer could find himself on risk for more than twelve months. As with all reinsurances constructed on a "issued or renewed" basis, the administration of the treaty would be increased by the need to relate each individual loss to the relevant policy year in order to ascertain whether such loss forms part of the aggregation or not. The position would also be complicated by alterations in priority reinsurances as between one year and another, so that the retention on a loss occurring in 1985 on a 1985 policy might be quite different to the amount forming part of the aggregation if a loss on such policy were to occur in 1986. Nevertheless, a stop loss reinsurance constructed in this basis can, on occasion, fulfill a valuable function. Thus, for example, a reinsured entering a new or untried class of business could prefer such a cover to be placed on an "issued or renewed" basis in order to secure some continuity—at least until the first renewal date of the insurances. A treaty placed on a "losses occurring" basis and not renewed would leave the reinsured without reinsurance protection for the remaining period of the unexpired risks.

The excess of loss ratio/stop loss/aggregate excess of loss treaty can be applied to any class of insurance. Its original use, however, arose most frequently in hail insurance. Both quota share and surplus treaties may be applied to hail business, but when an excess of loss is desired, then it is usually the excess of loss ratio. It is easy to see why this should be so. An excess of a fixed amount must apply to the cost of one occurrence, but when a serious loss occurs though hailstorm it is extremely difficult to say exactly what is one occurrence, where the one storm begins and ends. Attempts have been made to define one storm either by the time factor, as by including therein all damage caused in a given area within twenty-four or forty-eight or seventy-two hours or whatever, or by limiting the areas in which a storm shall be regarded as one occurrence to a definite width and length of territory. These are not, however, very satisfactory and are liable to lead to dissension between the parties. The excess of loss ratio avoids any trouble in this respect and enables the reinsured to regulate the results of the year's business as a whole, not perhaps to avoid any loss on the year, but to keep it within reasonable bounds. The same considerations apply to any type of weather insurance, to which full reference has been made on a previous page in regard to the definition of any event. Another type of cover is products liability, which has become of increasing importance in modern times, and under which the possibility of a widely spreading loss is always present. The stop loss cover is very suitable for this also.

This is perhaps an essential feature of this type of treaty, for it is not meant to give the reinsured a guaranteed profit. This would not indeed be possible, for if the excess of loss ratio were fixed at too low a figure so as to allow an apparent margin after charging expenses, the insurance rate would have to be increased considerably, thereby reducing the margin available to the reinsured. In this, as in all forms of reinsurance, the gross account must provide a reasonable chance to profit for both reinsured and reinsurer, which must of necessity involve a possibility of loss from time to time equally to both parties and cannot guarantee a profit to either of them.

Chapter 10
Reinsurance by Treaty
V—Miscellaneous

Although the surplus treaty and the various types of excess of loss treaty to a great extent cover the ground of treaty reinsurance, there are nevertheless other forms of treaty which will bear description.

Reference may first be made to the quota share treaty. As its name implies this is a form of treaty under which the ceding company is bound to cede and the reinsurer to accept a fixed share of every risk which the ceding company may insure in an agreed section of its business. The operative clause of such a treaty would run on somewhat the following terms:—

> "The Company binds itself to cede and the Reinsurer binds itself to accept a fixed share of   per cent of each and every insurance undertaken by the Company against the risk of fire in any part of the world, provided that the Company shall retain for its own account not less than   per cent of every such insurance."

This is given as a specimen only, and it would be drafted according to the exact class of business to be covered and the area from which it was derived. The quota share treaty is clearly a form of reinsurance which is favourable to the reinsurer. It provides for a cession of a share of every risk, great or small, good or bad. There can be no sort of selection against the reinsurer, for it shares in the business on exactly the same footing as the original company. Very frequently a limit is imposed on the amount to be allotted to the reinsurer, so that, for example, the ceding company might cede 5% of every insurance, but not exceeding £5,000 on any one risk. In that case the operative clause would contain a provision to that effect. The limit acts as a safeguard to the reinsurer in preventing cessions of very large amounts on any one risk. There is, however, a natural safeguard in this matter due to the fact that the proportion of each risk which the ceding company undertakes to keep for itself is usually much larger than the proportion allotted to any one reinsurer, so that if a substantial amount were ceded to the reinsurer the ceding company would be obliged to keep a much larger amount. When a quota share treaty is used in fire business it would be quite common for the ceding company to retain, say, 50% or 40% of the business and to allot the remainder of the quota among, say, ten reinsurers, giving them 5% or 6% each, or in varying proportions, as the case may be. The proportions to be retained and ceded may be varied as thought necessary, just as is done in arranging a surplus treaty. But there is this distinction in the quota share treaty that these proportions are fixed by the contract and thereafter apply to the whole of every policy issued. There is no discretion allowed to the ceding company in fixing its retentions.

Owing to the more favourable spread of business, quota share treaties will tend to command the most favourable terms of commission. They may be arranged so that the reinsurer pays its due share of the original acquisition cost with a small overriding commission to the ceding company, but the more usual practice in fire or accident business is to allow a fixed rate of commission. This is perhaps more satisfactory to the reinsurer as enabling it to judge the situation of its treaty more accurately. There is not, however, the same objection to an overriding commission when the ceding company retains a substantial part of the business as there is when the quota share reinsurance is large and the retention small. There are many reasons why the stipulated retention of the ceding company is a material fact in the negotiations leading up to the formation of the contract, and this is one of the most important as past experience has shown.

A form of quota share treaty sometimes used is called an "original cost" treaty. This means that the quota share reinsurer pays its proportionate share of the cost of acquiring the original business including commission and expenses. This form of treaty is often used by a ceding company to deal with its own retained lines in addition to the use of surplus treaties. The quota share reinsurer stands in with the ceding company and shares the retained business on identical terms, but care must be taken to ensure that the expenses relating to the buisness are fully defined, so that the reinsurer bears only what may be properly charged. This is a matter for arrangement when the contract is being negotiated. Such a treaty is not common and is used only to meet special circumstances.

The use of the quota share treaty in fire or accident business is comparatively restricted. It would never be used by a large or powerful ceding company since it involves giving away a great deal of business which can quite safely be retained. It may have to be adopted sometimes by a new company which, having no past results to show, may be able to obtain reinsurance facilities on its contract only on terms most favourable to reinsurers. Even this, however, is nowadays truer in theory than in practice. Again, if a company has experienced a run of very bad results which seem to be due to errors of judgment in its reinsuring methods, it may have to offer a quota share to retain its reinsurance connections. Sometimes, too, this form of treaty is used for special kinds of reinsurance which are passing through a difficult phase so that the ceding company itself desires to keep its commitments on a modest footing. This has happened for example in regard to motor and third party business in some countries, though it is a condition of things which usually does not last long and passes away very quicly when the business begins to improve. An important use of the quota share form of reinsurance, however, arises from its function within the overall financial management of the ceding company. This function is generally termed "surplus relief". Thus, in certain markets the domestic insurance industry may be under-capitalised in relation to the premium volume available. Or an insurance company may wish to increase premium rates after a period of competition which considerably reduced its net assets. In such instance the imbalance of total premium income to the capitalisation available could infringe solvency requirements and could not be reduced by any other method of reinsurance. Finally, the quota share treaty is used very largely for retrocession as will appear on a later page.

Some remarks may here be offered as to a former application of the quota share treaty in relation to marine reinsurance. As mentioned in Chaper 6 the subject of marine reinsurance is dealt with in detail in "Marine Reinsurance" by Messrs Robert H. Brown and Peter B. Reed, published by Witherby & Co. Ltd in 1981.

The use of the quota share treaty developed in marine business during the years immediately after the First World War under conditions which gave rise to certain difficulties. The system developed so as to provide a very large volume of reinsurance cover. The ceding company's retention might be fixed at a very low percentage, say 5%, giving reinsurance facilities for 95% of every risk and thereby enabling the ceding company to write for gross account a volume of business very large in relation to its net account. The quota would be placed, as is usual in marine business, at original net rates, i.e., policy premiums less commission and brokerage, subject to a reinsurance commission calculated on the net rates at rates which varied between 2.5% and 7.5% or occasionally even more. Treaties so placed came to be known as "profit" treaties, because of the profit which the ceding company derived from the reinsurance commission. The system produced an effect which in the circumstances was inevitable. On a 5% retention and a 95% quota share reinsurance, the ceding company collected reinsurance commission on nineteen times the volume of net premium appearing in its accounts. Putting the rate of reinsurance commission at 5%, this means that the recovery on this account would amount to a sum equal to 95% of the net premiums, and, since all commission and brokerage had been deducted from the cessions, this sum would be pure profit subject only to a charge for expenses of management, which would not be likely to exceed 20% of the net premiums. This profit obviously put the ceding company in a highly advantageous position, for a claims cost well in excess of 100%, would still leave a handsome profit to the ceding company while burdening the reinsurers with heavy losses. Yet a claim ratio exceeding 100% indicates that the original rates of premium are inadequate, but unless both ceding company and reinsurer share equally in the burden thereby created, there is likely to be some delay in the revision of rates, especially if the business is being keenly competed for. This is in fact what happened, with results disastrous to reinsurers. The position became so acute that the system of profit treaties had to be largely discontinued for want of reinsurance facilities. This did not entail the disappearance of the quota share treaty, but it was reconstructed on an "original cost" basis. The overriding commission disappeared and the reinsurer paid its appropriate share of the whole acquisition cost, including commission, brokerage and management expenses, thereby doing away with any undue source of profit to the ceding company and setting up that community of interests between the parties which is the basis of sound reinsurance. In addition the reinsurer would pay a profit commission, out of which the ceding company would derive the benefit to which it would be entitled for skilful underwriting. The effect of this alteration very greatly improved the reinsurance results, as was to be expected, though it would not of course abolish loss on the business if the original rates proved to be inadequate; it merely secured a more equitable distribution of the loss as between ceding company and reinsurer. A specimen form of marine quota share treaty is given in the Appendix.

Another form of treaty which is occasionally met with is what is called a mixed quota and surplus treaty. This is sometimes found on the Continent of Europe, but must be very rare in this country. It gives, as it were, more scope to the ceding company to deal with its reinsurances, by giving the right to cede both a quota and surplus on the same risk. Mixed treaties are constructed in different ways. The ceding company may, for example, allot a quota share of every risk up to a maximum agreed figure on one risk to a quota share treaty, retaining, say, 20% for itself and giving the balance amongst, say, five quota reinsurers. The remainder of any risk which might exceed the agreed figure is then reinsured as a surplus, a share being allotted to each of the quota share reinsurers on a surplus basis up to an agreed proportion of the ceding company' s line. The arrangement is rather a complicated one and may best be made clear by an example. The quota may be limited to, say, £50,000 in all on any one risk. Every insurance which does not exceed that figure will then fall entirely into the quota in the agreed proportions, leaving nothing for the surplus. So on a risk of £50,000 the ceding company will retain 20% for itself, or £10,000, while the balance of £40,000 divided amongst, say, five reinsurers will give them £8,000 each. Now if the surplus has been constructed to give each of the reinsurers one line, then each will, if the risk exceeds £50,000, receive one-fifth of the surplus up to £10,000, the amount of the ceding company's retention. Therefore a further £50,000 could be placed under the surplus, giving each reinsurer £18,000 on the risk. If, however, the risk were to be insured for £60,000, then the surplus is only £10,000 and the reinsurers receive £2,000 each or a total cession of £10,000 on the risk. This shows the difference from the pure quota share treaty, since the reinsurer's proportion is not always the same.

The mixed treaty may also be constructed, as it were, the other way round. The ceding company may set up first, say, a ten-line surplus treaty, but with this proviso, that, instead of reserving an absolute discretion in the amount of its retention, it will agree to a scale of fixed amounts of rentention on various classes of risk. It will then reserve the right to cede a part of its retention by way of quota share without prejudice to its surplus treaty arrangments. The retention out of which the quota is given is sometimes called the "priority", a name which denotes that this part of the business stands in front of the surplus and may be dealt with at the discretion of the ceding company. Another term often used is "gross retention". In that case a share of the priority may go with a share of the surplus, or it may possibly be given to a favoured reinsurer who does not take a share of the surplus. As has already been mentioned, this expression "the priority" is also now in common use in excess of loss treaties. Its meaning is always to denote something which comes in front of something else.

There is nothing fixed in the form of these mixed treaties, for they may be adapted in any way suitable to the ceding company's requirements and on such terms as the quality of the business may command, though the quota share will always obtain better commission rates than the surplus. The mixed treaty is used only when the special circumstances of the ceding company require it, and its use is probably decreasing in volume.

A further development which arises out of a desire to combine both an increased retention with a saving in administrative cost is a combination of a quota share and excess of loss contract. Under this method the cèding company will fix its priority at a figure considerably larger than it intends for its own account, reinsuring the balance by means of quota share treaty. The increased net retention, which will be a fixed proportion of all gross acceptances, is then protected by an excess of loss cover, the underlying priority of which is the amount which the ceding company wishes to retain absolutely net for its own account.

There are two main advantages in changing to this type of mixed treaty reinsurance:—

(1) The administrative costs are reduced to a minimum. Since it is not necessary to consider reinsurance on every policy individually, the administration becomes basically a simplified accounting operation.
(2) The quota share treaty may be used as an instrument for reciprocity so that the ceding company is able to retain intact its relations with its former reinsurers.

Nevertheless although the basic treaties are orthodox quota share and excess of loss treaties, it is necessary to build certain safeguards into the quota share treaty because if this were the sole form of protection, the retention of the ceding company for its proportion of the gross acceptance might well be excessive on the larger type of industrial risk and the corresponding cost of excess of loss protection would in consequence be prohibitive. It is therefore necessary in practice to apply a limit to the gross acceptances, all policies over a certain figure being reinsured by means of a form of surplus treaty or a facultative open cover based on the number of the ceding company's retentions.

This pattern of reinsurance is particularly attractive to the company with several agencies in any one particular country, since it obviates the necessity to make frequent amendments to the reinsurance cover on any one policy following alterations to the original insurance, and since the effect of a deterioration in the business will be more readily reflected in the ceding company's net retention it is therefore of some advantage to the reinsurers. The ceding company will of course have to give away much business it might formerly have kept, but against this it gets protection against all smaller losses which come a little below its former net retention and which may aggregate to a quite considerable sum during any one year, as for example an unprecedented number of claims due to adverse climatic conditions.

Here it may be convenient to refer to a special method of reinsurance, viz.—the pool method, which is particularly well adapted to cover extra hazardous risks. A pool is the name given to any arrangement whereby a certain number of insurers agree to contribute a defined business to a common central association between themselves and to divide such business among them in certain agreed proportions. Such a contribution may be made in the form of the whole of a business, or of a surplus over and above a fixed retention, or of an agreed excess of loss. As a method of sharing risks by way of reinsurance, a pool is the most flexible and adaptable arrangement, lending itself to many different variations, provided a sufficient number of members are available. In effect each member of the pool cedes its risks to the pool and receives back a share of its cessions and also of the cession made by all the other members, so that a complete system of reciprocity is inherent in it. It is a very good way of dealing with extra hazardous business, because each member is liable for only a small share of a wide spread of business, thereby conveniently applied to such risks as workmen's compensation in collieries, aviation risks, credit risks, and the like, and is especially valuable when the business is new and untried. Pools have existed for the sharing of motor risks on an excess of loss basis but this method of reinsurance in that class of business is not now in common use.

A point of nomenclature may be noted here. Many offices accepting reinsurance treaties on a wide scale desire to retrocede some portion thereof, usually by quota share. It is a common practice to aggregate all treaties coming from a given area, or having some other feature in common, into a pool, as it is then called, and out of this "pool" retrocessions are then made of a percentage over the whole group. This is not a true pool because only one company—the reinsured—puts business in, so that the reciprocal element of a true pool is lacking. However, the intention is clear enough, and what is provided by such a type of pool is well enough understood in modern practice.

The greater spread of business which is derived from a pool makes it possible to deduce a reasonable reinsurance rate for excess of loss, even though a pool is subject to those modern factors which affect this particular hazard. Of course a pool does need to make a profit, and though it is desirable that it should balance its acccounts and in the long run produce results which are of the same pattern throughout its whole membership. A pool could not succeed if one member's business gave continual bad results even though the pool as a whole might balance, for that would mean that the good business of the remaining members was being used to support the bad business in question. But of course a long view must be taken since the purpose of the pool is to protect the members against annual variations in the experience. It is of the essence of a successful pool that it should be composed of companies of the same kind and conducting their business on similar lines, and of course, at similar rates of premium.

Subject to this proviso the pool is an extremely convenient method of reinsurance and capable of application to many different purposes, both on surplus and excess of loss lines.

Some explanation may now be given of what are called retrocessions and the manner in which they are effected. A retrocession is a reinsurance of a reinsurance. The term arises from the assumption that every reinsurance is made by means of a cession by the original company to the reinsurer, and if the reinsurer in its turn wishes to give off a share of the cession which has been ceded to it, it is said to retrocede, i.e., to cede again, and the transaction is a retrocession. The expression is not quite exact, since the prefix "retro" means "back" but a retrocession is not the giving back of a reinsurance to the reinsured from which it came but the passing on of the reinsurance, or a part thereof, to some other reinsurer. It is also not exact with regard to retrocessions of loss reinsurance since, in excess of loss reinsurance, there is no original cession as such. The reinsurer so accepting a retrocession is called a retrocessionaire, this being a term imported from the French for which there is no English equivalent.

Retrocessions play an important part in the business of reinsurance, especially as carried on by professional reinsurers. These derive the whole of their business from reinsurance, and if they are to carry on their affairs on a widespread scale, they are bound to accept many treaties from the same country. This must inevitably lead to a certain accumulation of risk and the aggregation of a large volume of liabilities. They must accordingly safeguard their position by retroceding some part of their acceptances, and the accounts of reinsurance companies show in some caes that a substantial proportion of their gross business is disposed of in this way.

Retrocessions may be made by any one of the methods used in reinsurance. Thus it is possible to retrocede facultatively by giving off each risk individually or it may be done by treaty. Retrocession treaties may be quota share or surplus or excess of loss, as the case may be, and these treaties possess the same characteristics in retrocession as in reinsurance. There is, in fact, no difference in principle between reinsurance and retrocession, though some variation is found in methods to allow for differing circumstances.

The surplus retrocession treaty is not in such common use as the surplus reinsurance treaty, and is perhaps decreasing in importance as time goes on. Such a system of retrocession involves the original reinsurer in the task of indexing or otherwise recording all the risks it has accepted by way of reinsurance, fixing its retentions on each, and retroceding its surpluses as required. This is a very difficult and costly matter, further complicated by a constant succession of alterations in cession, with consequent alterations in the retrocession. The great deal of detail work involved in the matter makes it very difficult to attain complete accuracy in the working out of gross commitments and the allocation of surpluses. It is one of the drawbacks of the surplus retrocession treaty that it does not always achieve the object it sets out to attain because of the lack of reliable information. This, under modern practice, makes the surplus retrocession treaty almost of historical interest only, for the issue of complete bordereaux, in sufficient detail to permit of the proper working of a surplus retrocession treaty, has been generally discontinued, and the required information is not therefore available.

In addition, when business is retroceded on a surplus basis, it follows that the original reinsurer will have gone through its risks, will have selected those which it desires to keep, and will have retroceded those which are too large or too hazardous to be fully retained. But the reinsurance business out of which such reinsurer makes its retrocession has already been selected once by the reinsureds, so that a surplus retrocession treaty is subject, as it were, to a double selection which must necessarily be of an adverse nature for the retrocessionaire. This is naturally reflected in an increasing claims ratio and this in turn adversely affects the rate of commission which such treaties can command. In effect the original reinsurer must either be prepared to submit to a loss on commission in respect of the business retroceded on a surplus basis, or to run the risk that those treaties will prove unremunerative and result in a difficulty in finding adequate retrocession facilities. There is indeed a considerable dislike towards surplus retrocession treaties amongst retrocessionaires generally, making it more and more difficult to find a satisfactory market for such business.

For the reasons stated the quota share treaty is much more common in retrocessions. It should be understood that this differs from the quota share reinsurance treaty in that it does not comprise a share of every risk written by an original insurer. A quota share retrocession treaty is a means of giving off a proportionate share of a treaty which the reinsurer has accepted and of which it does not desire to retain the whole. Thus the nature of the quota share retrocession treaty will depend upon the kind of reinsurance treaty to which it relates, and it may be a quota share of a quota share, or of a surplus, or indeed of an excess of loss, as the case may be. Most quota share treaties provide for the retrocession of a fixed part of a surplus treaty, since this is generally the commonest form of business in the reinsurer's portfolio. The purpose of such retrocession might be to reduce the reinsurer's liability in respect of a given treaty, where the original reinsured's lines are known to be heavy and to impose a greater single liability on the reinsurer than it cares to retain. Or it may be used to reduce the reinsurer's aggregate liability in a given area which may have mounted up because a large number of treaties have been accepted. This is often done by constructing a pool into which the reinsurer puts all its treaties in a given class of business derived from reinsureds in a certain area. It may then retain varying shares of each treaty and the remainder falls into the pool. The whole pool will then be allotted amongst a number of retrocessionaires in such shares as may be agreed. This a pure quota share arrangement and not a surplus, for each retrocessionaire receives a clean quota of each treaty concerned in the pool and is interested in its due proportion of every risk which is ceded to the original reinsurer. This is a convenient way of limiting the liability in any particular territory and retrocession arrangements of this kind are carried out in greater variety. This type of pool must be distinguished from the true pool already explained on a previous page, whereby a group of reinsureds arrange between themselves for the reinsurance of certain classes of business.

Under such a retrocession treaty the retrocessionaire receives its proportionate share of the original reinsurance premium and pays the same share of claims and commission, with generally a small overriding commission to the original reinsuer varying between 1% and 2.5%, according to circumstances. This is not always charged however, for reinsurers in modern practice have found the quota share retrocession treaty a convenient means of meeting demands made upon them for reciprocity and in that case it is a frequent thing to dispense with an overriding commission, since the consideration for the bargain is found in the reciprocity. A quota share retrocession treaty when placed on original terms is equal in value to the reinsurance treaty from which it is derived, and as such it can be used as reciprocity either for other treaties of the same nature or for direct reinsurance treaties. A great deal of business has been exchanged on these terms in recent years.

Where the original reinsurer has accepted a number of contracts on an aggregate loss basis, the clause in the retrocession contract will provide that any losses occurring under more than one of such contracts, shall be deemed to be part of one aggregate loss, provided all such losses arose from one and the same cause.

A specimen form of retrocession treaty providing for the giving off of a quota share of a specific treaty is given in the Appendix.

Certain clauses of this treaty wording call for mention.

Article No. 1 provides for the retrocession by reference to the specified treaty or treaties which are to be retroceded. No details of the actual retrocession appear in this Article but particulars are included in the treaty schedule which is incorporated and deemed to form part of the Agreement. It is perhaps becoming more common, where a part of a single treaty is being retroceded, for a copy of the full contract wording to be attached to the retrocession agreement.

By Article No. 2 the retrocessionaire is given the right to inspect the original treaty and documents relating to the transactions thereunder. This follows the usual practice as found in reinsurance treaties.

Article No. 3 absolves the original reinsurer from providing any bordereaux or loss advice lists since it would be impossible to incur the labour and expense which the supply of bordereaux would involve, even if indeed the information were available from which to compile such bordereaux.

Article No. 4 is the accounting article and it will be seen that accounts follow, as indeed they must, the accounts under the original treaty or treaties.

Article No. 5 provides for a premium reserve deposit, the details of which would appear in the schedule.

Article No. 6 is the clause providing for the method of cancellation. The important point about this is that the retrocession agreement will automatically expire if the original treaty is cancelled but that it may also be cancelled by notice between the parties. In that event the retrocessionaire giving notice is required to make that period of notice four months instead of three so as to give the original reinsurer the opportunity to replace the retrocession, if it so desired. This provision is not, however, invariable.

By Article No. 7 the original reinsurer reserves the right to withdraw a portfolio and this is an option which must always be so reserved because the reinsurer must be free to deal with this matter according to the way in which it may itself be dealt with in the event of the determination of the original treaty.

The remaining Articles of the treaty follow the usual form.

As has already been mentioned retrocessions may also be effected on an excess of loss basis and this may be applied to any kind of reinsurance business as circumstances may require. This method of retrocession is, however, applied in a specialised form to reinsurance accepted on an excess of loss basis and consists in building as it were an excess upon an excess. Suppose for example that a reinsurer has undertaken a reinsurance contract covering £200,000 in excess of £50,000 any one occurrence at, say, 5% of the original premiums. Its total liability may then reach up to £200,000 and even though a total loss is unlikely it will nevertheless desire to limit its liability by retrocession. This problem is approached by the reinsurer in much the same way as by the original reinsured. It may not wish to give away a quota share, as this would mean giving away a proportion of the premium while the reinsurer might feel able to retain any loss which did not exceed a reasonable figure. It therefore retrocedes an excess of loss on its own liablity and will retain for example all losses which do not cost it more than £50,000. This would mean that the retrocessionaires would accept £150,000 in excess of £50,000 in respect of the reinsurer's ultimate net loss. Such an excess of loss cover has certain peculiarities. There are two underying retentions to be taken into account, that of the original reinsured and that of the reinsurer. In the example given the retrocessionaire would not be interested in an original claim until it exceeded £100,000, £50,000 being paid by the reinsured and £50,000 by the reinsurer. Then again the premium computation calls for special consideration. The reinsurer will require to pay a percentage of its premium for its retrocession but this cannot be worked out in the same way as for the original excess of loss cover, because it is to be based on a premium which is itself only a small percentage of the original premium. Thus, although an original excess of loss contract for an excess of £50,000 might be placed at, say, 5% on the original premium, such a rate would obviously be inadequate when applied to a retrocession contract for then it would be based—in the example quoted—on only 5% of the original premium and would be equivalent to only one-quarter of one per cent. on the original business.

It is true the retrocession contract applies to losses only when they exceed £100,000 from the ground, but even so, a premium rate constructed in such a way would be quite inaccurate.

What is done is to arrive at a reasonable rate on the original business, having regard to the fact that there are two underlying retentions and then to relate that rate to the rate payable under the original excess of loss contract. Thus it might be calculated that if this original excess of £50,000 is worth 5% of the original premium then an excess of £100,000, i.e, £50,000 over £50,000, is worth say 1.5% of the same original premium. This would be equivalent to 30% of the premium paid under the original excess of loss cover and that accordingly would be the rate to be paid for the excess of loss retrocession. These are of course hypothetical figures but they serve to show how the excess of loss retrocession is arranged.

Chapter 11
Reinsurance Intermediaries

At the time the earlier editions of this book were published, reinsurance intermediaries played a very small role in the functioning of the business of reinsurance. True, there were a number of well-respected and, in some cases, long-established firms of reinsurance brokers operating in various parts of the world. But the amount of reinsurance business which passed through their offices was but a small proportion of the whole. At that time the normal form of the reinsurance transaction was by way of direct relationship between reinsured and reinsurer. Nowadays this has greatly altered, with a large part of the reinsurance business of the world being transacted through the use of intermediaries.

Reinsurance intermediaries may be classified into two broad groups, thus:—

(1) The agents of the reinsured, in the form of reinsurance brokers who place reinsurances, both facultatively and by treaty, on their behalf. Directive 77/92 of the European Economic Community includes their activities in the following description, "professional activities of persons who, acting with complete freedom as to their choice of undertaking, bring together, with a view to the insurance or reinsurance of risks, persons seeking insurance or reinsurance and insurance or reinsurance undertakings, carry out work preparatory to the conclusion of contracts of insurance or reinsurance and, where appropriate, assist in the administration and performance of such contracts, in particular in the event of a claim,"

(2) The agents of the reinsurer, in the form of underwriting agencies who accept business on behalf of the reinsurer. These agencies may accept business on behalf of a number of reinsurers. In certain markets extensive use may be made of underwriting agencies, and their strengths and weaknesses should be clearly understood.

There are a number of occasions where the two functions may merge, such as where a reinsurance broker has a binding authority from a reinsurer to commit that reinsurer to automatic reinsurance of a specific class of risk or business. Obviously, in certain situations, a conflict of interest could arise.

As the business of reinsurance grows and develops, a greater degree of importance attaches to the work performed by the reinsurance broker. He is, of course, a pure intermediary whose chief function is to bring together the two parties to the reinsurance contract. That is however to state the case in the baldest possible way, for the duties which fall to a broker in reinsurance business go much further than that and require for their proper exercise a high degree of professional skill.

Reinsurance broking is a business of a nature quite distinct from the business carried on by brokers in direct insurance. It requires a different outlook and imports a distinctive technique, only to be fully acquired by long experience in handling this particular type of business. The point is recognised by the fact that reinsurance broking is carried on as a separate business. There have for many years been in existence firms which specialise in the placing of reinsurance business and whose activities do not extend to direct business. At one time practically the whole of the reinsurance business handled by brokers was dealt with through such specialised firms and logically this would seem to be the most satisfactory way of dealing with the business. Modern practice has, however, tended towards some broadening of this original concept, for nowadays very many insurance brokers have added to their activities by including a reinsurance department (or setting up a subsidiary or purchasing a previously independent reinsurance broking company to function as such a subsidiary), a course which has largely been promoted as an indirect effect of the spread of the purchase of reinsurance. The separate nature of the business has been fully recognised, however, for insurance brokers do not as a rule deal with reinsurance as an integral part of their main business but conduct it through a separate department or through a subsidiary concern under the control of men qualified in reinsurance business. This is the only wise course to pursue if the business is to be carried on satisfactorily.

An outline of the duties which fall to be carried out by the reinsurance broker may serve to illustrate the nature of its work. There is no doubt that its usefulness has been greatly increased by the growth of the treaty, which has so largely accentuated the international aspect of reinsurance. When risks were largely reinsured on facultative lines, that was mostly done between offices in the same city, who not only had no need of the services of a broker to bring them together, but would have found its intervention a positive inconvenience to the conduct of their business. In earlier days brokers certainly played a part in facultative reinsurance, because they might represent foreign companies who desired to accept facultative risks in this country. No doubt a large business was done in this way, and this still continues though decreasing in importance. But in that connection the broker was more than a mere intermediary, for within the scope of its authority, it acted as agent or manager for the reinsurer.

It was with the development of the treaty that the broker's services became of real significance, because treaties are not widely shared between offices in the same city, but are distributed on an international basis throughout the world. For this purpose some machinery for bringing into contact parties domiciled in different parts of the world is an obvious necessity, and it is in this way that the reinsurance broker plays its most important part. It will be clear that the first and most vital need of the reinsurance broker is to have a thorough knowledge of insurance markets in different countries. This implies a number of things connected with the business. It requires an acquaintance with the leading companies in each country, their standing and reputation, their managements, their methods of doing business and their financial stability. It requires also a knowledge of the general experience of different classes of insurance business in various countries, with some idea of premium ratings, claims experience and acquisition costs. It has to be remembered that all these factors are variable in character and what is true today may be quite otherwise tomorrow. This indeed has been only too obvious during the unsettled conditions of the past twenty years. It is not, therefore, sufficient for the broker to fortify itself with a thorough knowledge of its markets at any given time; it must keep itself up-to-date with all the alterations and developments which may occur. To do this the broker ought to travel frequently and to be acquainted with at least some of the principal languages in which the business is transacted and the language of the country which travellers visit. It must acquire some knowledge of the laws of different countries affecting the transaction of insurance and reinsurance business. This has been a prominent point in recent years, when so much new legislation has been passed laying down regulations for carrying on business in various foreign countries, with rules as to deposits, taxation, government returns and so on. This is apart from the special laws such as those providing for compulsory third party insurance or strict third party liabilities or setting up a State reinsurance company which whilst not necessarily regulating the actual conduct of reinsurance business, has a very important bearing on it.

The work of keeping abreast of the prevailing conditions in the international insurance field is clearly no light matter and calls for intensified study of a specialised nature. A reinsured which desired merely to place a line of its treaty abroad might well look upon such an undertaking as too burdensome to be worthwhile. But it is in this way that the broker can render real and effective service, for this knowledge is part of its everyday business; it does not have to make enquiries specially for each treaty, it is available for all its connections as and when required, and serves the same purpose for them all. In this connection the broker requires its knowledge and experience for a two-fold purpose, because it can act for either party to the transaction. It must know its markets from the two distinct points of view of the reinsured and reinsurer respectively. At one moment it might be required to find a good sound reinsurer, and at the next moment it must be prepared to advise a reinsurer on the merits of a particular treaty. This particular aspect of the broker's work has been affected to some extent by the system of reciprocity which exists in reinsurance business, for the plain issue of finding a suitable reinsurer to supply the needs of a reinsured has been obscured by the further necessity of contriving that each of the proposed parties shall be able to contribute an acceptable exchange of treaties. It is often said that reciprocity must be an advantage to the broker in that it gives it two treaties instead of one. In actual practice, however it does not often give that advantage. For one thing it greatly complicates the broker's work and adds to its cost, and for another thing it is extremely doubtful whether a broker adds materially to the aggregate number of treaties it handles, merely on the score of reciprocity.

It is not, of course, to be supposed that the broker's work is completed when it has brought together the parties to a reinsurance transaction. From one point of view that is only the beginning, for the services of the broker will be required as long as the treaty relationship continues. In the first place the contract must be completed by both parties after the form of wording has been agreed. As the practice grows of placing shares of treaty contracts with a larger number of reinsurers it is becoming more common for the broker to be required actually to draft the wording, especially in regard to new kinds of treaties. In addition it will have to be ready to explain and reconcile any differences that may arise in regard to the wording, and in particular to make comprehensible the customs and usages of different nations in regard to these matters. Subsequently it will act as intermediary for the transmission of accounts, collection of balances due, settlement of cash losses and other matters of detail which arise in the working of the treaty. Where, as often happens, a broker deals with several lines of a treaty, placing them with a number of different reinsurers, it assists the reinsured to a material extent by acting as its agent for the whole of its interest. Thus settlements due to reinsurers are made in one sum and divided by the broker among the interests concerned. Similarly cash losses and other payments can be collected from the various reinsurers and remitted as a whole to the reinsured. In effect the work of that part of the treaty is centred in the broker, with a resultant saving in the detail work and cost of operating the contract.

In summary therefore, there are, from the perspective of the reinsured, six principal reasons for using the services of a reinsurance broker, thus:—

(1) Consultancy—To advise the management of the reinsured on the design, formation and maintenance of a sound reinsurance programme; to furnish the reinsured with a continuous reference of market changes, new forms of reinsurance coverage available and possible ways to improve existing facilities.
(2) Market Selection—To locate sound reinsurers best suited for a long term relationship with the reinsured consistent with the need to obtain the best terms for the client. Although, nowadays, seldom achieved, continuity should, nevertheless, always be an aim.
(3) Negotiating—To arrange the necessary reinsurance capacity at terms equitable to both parties.
(4) Contract Supervision—To prepare reinsurance contract wordings clearly expressing the intentions of the parties. Where wordings are prepared by the reinsurer, these need to be examined and analysed on behalf of the reinsured.
(5) Administration—To oversee all transactions, handle collection of balances and obtain prompt reimbursement of losses due to the reinsured; to provide a practical outline of the accounting and statistical procedures to be followed; to maintain records and statistics adequate for renewal negotiations.
(6) Independence—A major part of the justification in not dealing directly as between reinsured and reinsurer is the legal presumption that the reinsurance transaction is between professionals. But the reinsured, although a professional in its own field, may not be an expert in reinsurance. Thus, using a broker, not only supplies a further, expert, opinion, but the impartiality of such advice is guaranteed by the fact that it is not one of the parties to the reinsurance contract.

Reinsurance brokers, like their colleagues in the direct insurance business, tend to be members of professional and trade associations such as the British Insurance Brokers Association and the Lloyd's Insurance Brokers Association. However the Insurance Brokers (Registration) Act 1977 set up an Insurance Brokers Registration Council and provided for all insurance (including reinsurance) brokers to be registered. The IRBC was also required to draw up a Code of Conduct and to ensure that registered insurance brokers held professional indemnity insurance policies. The terms of the Code of Conduct are as follows:—

(a) Insurance Brokers shall at all times conduct their business with utmost good faith and integrity.
(b) Insurance brokers shall do everything possible to satisfy the insurance requirements of their clients and shall place the interests of those clients before all other considerations. Subject to these requirements of interest insurance brokers shall have proper regard for others.
(c) Statements made by or on behalf of insurance brokers when advertising shall not be misleading or extravagant.

These are internal rules by which the insurance broker must conduct its business and are additional to its common law obligations in contract and in tort.

In addition to the locally incorporated companies and the authorised branches and subsidiaries of international reinsurers, there are various other forms of organisation which can be adopted in order to give effect to a participation in the reinsurance business of a local market. These forms are generally included under the term "underwriting agency". An underwriting agency is a person or organisation which undertakes to perform one or more of the following functions on behalf of insurers or reinsurers:—

(1) To underwrite contracts of insurance or reinsurance on behalf of the participants.
(2) To reinsure such contracts in full or in part.
(3) To collect premiums, invest funds, maintain reserves, handle and settle claims.

There are a number of reasons for a reinsurer wishing to participate in an underwriting agency. Thus, for example, the company may wish to develop an understanding of a particular geographical area or a particular form of business, such as reinsurance, or even a particular way of doing business, e.g. the London market system. It may also be felt to be important for the reinsurer to have a presence in a certain market and a good working knowledge of the operations therein. Furthermore companies domiciled elsewhere who rely upon submissions from (say) the United Kingdom to be sent to them by mail or telex may feel that they are shown business which is surplus to the available market in London and therefore either of an inferior quality or of the nature of target risks. Setting up a fully fledged operation on its own can not only be very expensive, but could also imply a full commitment which had not originally been intended.

There are a number of ways in which a reinsurer may participate in an underwriting agency system, thus:—

(1) The reinsurer may participate in a share of broker's binder whereby it delegates authority to accept reinsurances of a certain class up to agreed limits. However problems could arise not only from conflicts of interest of the broker being the agent of both the reinsured and the reinsurer for the same transaction, but also since the reinsurer will tend to see the major part of the business from that broker, which may lack a spread of risk. In addition, the requirements of the Insurance Companies Act, 1982 may cause problems for a reinsurer not authorised to transact business in this country.

(2) The reinsurer may set up a contact or representative office whereby all acceptances are "subject to approval" elsewhere, so that the underwriting is seen to be completed outside the United Kingdom, and all documents likewise have to be signed outside the U.K. The contract of insurance will then not be subject to U.K. law and the company will not be considered as transacting business in the U.K. This system is open to abuse—and indeed has been so abused—so that a company registered on a Caribbean island, administered from Amsterdam and writing U.K. risks can be considered as not transacting business in any of these places. It is a system which is no longer looked upon with approval and should not be a serious consideration for a respectable company.

(3) Two or more substantial companies may come together to benefit from the economies of size. The joint financial resources permits the agent to write substantial lines with first class security and backing but with the administration costs shared by all the subscribers. Each company operating an underwriting organisation on its own could have the full administrative cost on an income which may be no more than the proportion of its participation in the agency. The income could be even lower as the individual lines may not be as attractive to the broker market as the combined line of all the subscribing companies in the agency.

Thus the structure of an underwriting agency should always be examined very carefully, since the agency is only as good as its construction and management. If properly constructed it will not rely too heavily upon retrocession for capacity and in consequence will offer the aggregate capital and assets of its member companies as security against the written line. Where an underwriting agency makes a practice of ceding away the major part of the premiums written by way of retrocession then it offers only its, often unknown, reinsurance sources as security. A properly constructed agency is merely following the successful formula adopted by Lloyd's with the difference that, instead of the financial strengths of individuals being used to carry risks written, an underwriting agency outside Lloyd's has one or more corporate bodies, already engaged in insurance business, to supply the capital. If the subscribing companies to an agency also own the agency, or at least are substantial shareholders therein, then in the event of the shareholders closing down the agency the question of administration and liability for the "run-off" is no different to a company deciding not to write any kind or a class of reinsurance.

In this connection it may be worth devoting a few words to the subject of "fronting". The term is used where an insurer or reinsurer is unable, for various reasons, to stand in a direct relationship with a client. The policy or guarantee or treaty is therefore issued to such client by an insurer (or reinsurer as the case may be) who has the necessary capability. The coverage is then 100% reinsured to the original company. The "fronting" insurer is remunerated by way of fee or overrider for the use of the facility. There are many perfectly legitimate reasons for such an approach. However, in certain underwriting agencies the quality of the security offered by some of the participants may not be so attractive to clients and to brokers. Therefore the underwriting agent may attempt to use the name of one or two of the more substantial participants to "front" for one or more of the others. In circumstances such as these, it must be remembered as a basic fact of insurance law that the contracts as between insured and insurer and between insurer and reinsurer are entirely separate. Thus, if the reinsurer fails to respond the insurer would still be liable under the terms of its policy. Therefore the company which provides the fronting facility may find that it is committed for 100 per cent. of the liability. The circumstances of the original acceptance will probably be unknown to the fronting insurer and it will need to institute an investigation to collect information and documents to assess the position and the prospects for a successful defence against the claims being made against it. Furthermore, the participants for whom it fronted may be located in various jurisdictions throughout the world and probably worth little, even if they can be engaged in litigation.

Although the term "intermediary" is used extensively in the reinsurance business, the law in general recognises no such thing as a pure intermediary. A person or corporate body acts as an agent either of the one side or of the other. Therefore the law insists that the broker should represent the insured or the reinsured and that principal only in relation to any particular insurance or reinsurance fulfilling the instructions given with due skill and ability. Similarly with the underwriting agent, its duty is to further its principal's business with reasonable skill and judgment within the scope and terms of the authority it is given. The simple legal role of each is often more obscure in market practice. This may be illustrated by consideration of the legal responsibility of the insurance broker for the premium. Under Section 53 of the Marine Insurance Act 1906 the broker is itself liable to the underwriters for the premium and has a lien on the policy in respect of it. In addition, by a special custom of Lloyd's the broker is also liable to the underwriters for the premium and has a lien on the policy in respect of it. It may in such cases be regarded as an agent of the insurers for the purpose only of receiving the premium. This custom is confined to Lloyd's brokers and a broker who was not a Lloyd's broker, and paid on the insured's behalf, was held unable to recover the premium from the insured (Wilson v Avec Audio-Visual Ltd, 1974). On other occasions, also, the reinsurance broker may have ostensible authority as agent of the reinsurer when holding the reinsured covered and issuing cover notes. Thus each situation needs to be judged upon the specific circumstances relating thereto, but always within the basic legal principle stated in Fullwood v Hurley, 1928, that "no agent who has accepted an employment from one principal can in law accept an engagement inconsistent with his duty to the first principal unless he makes the fullest disclosure to each principal of his interest, and obtains the consent of each principal to the double employment ". This judgment was more recently followed in Anglo-African Merchants Ltd v Bagley, 1969, where Lloyd's brokers refused to show to the insured files which they had made available to the underwriter. It was held that this was quite unjustified.

Although the following explanation of the scope and limits of the authority of an intermediary is based largely on the activities of an underwriting agency, much of the law is equally applicable to the operations of reinsurance brokers. Normally the authority of a reinsurance broker to act on behalf of its principal, the reinsured, is of a more informal nature and is inferred more from the conduct of the parties. There is, however, an increasing tendency for formal Letters of Authority to be prepared.

Although underwriting agencies have recently been under something of a cloud because of various abuses and lack of professional expertise which have occurred, the occupation of underwriting agent is well established. Many brokers, insurance and reinsurance companies and specialist individuals, inside and outside Lloyd's, have acted under binding authorities or agency agreements over many years with skill, honesty and integrity. The extent of the authority always depends on the terms of the binder or agency agreement. An underwriting agent's duties under an agency agreement may extend not merely to accepting reinsurances, but also to the collection of premiums and the investment of funds held, the establishment of premium and loss reserves, the settlement of claims and the placing of facultative and/or treaty retrocessions to protect the account. In all of these functions it is the agent's duty to comply with the terms of its authority, i.e., with regard to the classes of business, types, locations and sizes of the risks which it may accept, the premium rates it may charge and the terms of credit it may allow, the types of reinsurance it may effect and the size and type of loss which it may settle. It will also be its duty to exercise its authority with due skill, care and attention. The degree of skill will be determined, in the last instance, by a Court of Law or arbitration determining any dispute on the basis of the evidence as to the standards generally applied or expected in the market.

Unless authorised by its principal the agent may not delegate its authority to others. The general principle by which an agent in all things must be guided is that it is there to promote its principal's, not its own, interests. The business belongs not to it but to its principals. This was clearly expressed in Poland v Julian Praet, 1961. The defendant Praet had represented various foreign underwriters in Belgium for over 40 years and had developed a substantial volume of motor insurance business. In 1937, though the brokers, H. G. Poland, he arranged a binding authority with the Poland Syndicate at Lloyd's. The binding authority was subject to 60 days notice of cancellation at any time. On the Syndicate's behalf, he issued cover under the binder to individual motorists, collected premiums and paid losses. During 1959 Mr Praet met other Lloyd's representatives and decided to change syndicates. He gave notice to H. G. Poland on the binder and sent a notice to each policy holder cancelling the insurance at next renewal date and informing them that they would be insured at the same terms under a new policy to be placed with JP Motor Policies. In the subsequent court action it was held that he had no authority to cancel the insurances and Pearson J held that "In my view the Praet Company committed a breach of contract by the action which they took on the 30th September 1959. That was a breach of Clause 12 of the agreement and of the implied general obligation of the agent to act in good faith towards its principal and not misuse its ostensible authority for the purpose of gaining an advantage for himself at the expense of the principal." This judgment was upheld on appeal with Dankwerts LJ adding that "The policies were the property of the underwriter and however valuable the connection may have been Mr Praet was simply an agent."

In accepting the risk the agent acts for the reinsurer. For better or for worse the reinsurer must accept its judgment. Thus the agent's knowledge will generally be imputed to its principal, and it would not benefit the principal afterwards to query or indicate how material some facts would have been to an underwriter. Thus the careless agent who binds its principal may equally disentitle the principal from recovering under the retrocessions which had been aranged.

The scope of authority depends upon the terms of the agency agreement making it therefore a matter of contractual construction. A company's capacity to contract may be restricted by its constitution e.g. to certain classes of insurance or reinsurance only. Therefore, however hard it, or any agent on its behalf, may try, it cannot validly be bound outside its capacity. Third parties may therefore be well advised to investigate the capacity of any company, foreign or domestic, purporting to carry on insurance or reinsurance. What is also relevant is the capacity of the company as construed within the law applying at the place of authorisation.

One of the commoner areas of dispute in this area of operation arises from a contention by a company that someone purporting to act as its agent acted, in fact, in excess of or without any actual authority in a matter within the company's capacity. A third party seeking to hold the company liable can do so by establishing either actual authority or, in default, apparent or ostensible authority. An agent's actual authority includes (in the absence of express limitation) authority to do whatever is necessary or incidental to the ordinary conduct of the relevant business or transaction in or for which it is employed as well as authority to act according to the usages and customs of the insurance market. If unbeknown to third parties some limitation is placed on its actual authority in this respect then third parties may nonetheless rely upon the apparent or ostensible authority with which it acts. The principal's liability to the third party in such a case is based upon "holding out" or the doctrine of estoppel—the principal has put or allowed the agent to stand in such a position where it appears to third parties to have the usual authority of an agent. Even if it is not possible to identify any relevant usual authority, apparent or actual authority can arise if the principal can be shown to have held out or represented the agent as having authority wide enough to embrace the relevant act or contract. It should be noted that in each case it is the principal, by putting the agent into a position carrying the authority or by any other more specific representation, who must responsible for the holding out. The agent cannot increase its authority merely by holding itself out or getting another party equally lacking in authority so to do. Furthermore, if it actually relied upon the holding out, the third party can seek redress from the principal. If it knew of the actual limits of authority then it would be bound by such limits. In the case of Baines v Ewing, 1866, the defendant authorised an insurance broker to underwrite policies of marine reinsurance in its name and on its behalf, the risk not to exceed £100 by any one vessel. The broker acting in excess of its authority underwrote in the defendant's name a policy in favour of the plaintiff for £150. The plaintiff assured claimed that the broker had such an authority, but it was held that the defendant was not bound since it was well known in the market that in such cases some monetary limit was nearly always put upon the broker's authority. It is doubtful whether nowadays Baines v Ewing is a case which any principal can rely upon if its agent has exceeded its underwriting limits. Ceding companies and the reinsurance brokers seeking to place their reinsurances would certainly be surprised to learn that, when approaching underwriting agents, they were bound to know the limits of the agents' authority. However, in this instance it is worth noting that some underwriting agencies do make efforts to explain the terms and limits of their underwriting authority to reinsurance brokers and potential ceding companies.

Where an agent does act outside or without any authority, whether actual or ostensible, the principal for whom it purported to act can disown any responsibility. Alternatively the principal can ratify the act—provided the act was of a kind within its powers to perform. Where there is neither authority nor ratification the innocent third party is left to seek redress from the agent. The remedy to be sought would be based upon breach of the warranty of authority which every agent is treated in law as giving.

Although the role of the reinsurance intermediary is becoming increasingly important, the relationship of reinsured and reinsurer remains crucial. When the earlier editions of this book were published that relationship was characterised by stability, familiarity and mutual respect. The social and economic changes of the past forty years have introduced a volatility to relationships which has seriously eroded these characteristics. The consequences for the proper practice of Reinsurance are not yet generally apparent.

APPENDICES

NOTES TO THE APPENDICES:—

A. The Specimen Treaty Wordings contained herein are intended purely for guidance. They do not pretend to be complete or usable as they stand for all contracts. For example, the Surplus Treaty wording contains provisions for the submission of bordereaux and the retention of reserve deposits. Their inclusion would be a matter for negotiation. On the other hand, the Excess of Loss Treaty wording omits the Index and Currency Fluctuation Clauses. These should be included as appropriate. Texts for these latter appear in Chapter 7.

B. Over the past twenty years it has been an increasing practice in the London Market to prepare Treaty Wordings on what is termed a "Scheduled" form, whereby the wording consists of a collection of standard clauses plus a Schedule containing the information specific to the treaty such as the name of the reinsured, the business covered, the exclusions, the ceding commission allowed, the provisions for profit commission, the periodicity of the accounts, the provisions for termination, etc., etc. The desire to reduce the administration costs involved in typing and retyping largely unchanging clauses led to this practice. It has also led to inflexibility, cumbersome documents and much cross-referring when reading the contract wording. With the increasing use of the word processors and the ability to produce, at the touch of a key or two, wordings individually tailored to the requirements of each contract, it seems more appropriate to revert to the system of including the variable information in the body of the wording. On this basis it would also be appropriate to include a "Table of Contents" as an indication of the Articles included in the wording.

C. The use of the term "Company" to represent the reinsured party is also deserving of comment. The use of the terms "reinsured" and "reinsurer" has beome increasingly common, since the term "ceding company" is not appropriate for excess of loss treaties where there is no cession of a risk as such. However the use of these terms "reinsured" and "reinsurer" in the same document gives many opportunities for mis-reading or mis-typing. The prime objective being that of clarity, the term "Company" is used herein. Any suitable terms may be used.

FACULTATIVE REINSURANCE

(Chapter 5)

REQUEST NOTE

To the Insurance Company Limited
Reference No. day of 19

The Insurance Company Limited requests guarantee from the day of 19 to the day of 19 for £ a uniform rateable share being the whole (or part) of a policy (or proposal) in the name of for the period from the day of 19 to the day of 19 on and retains £ on the identical property on which this guarantee is requested.

This guarantee is subject to the rules adopted by the Fire Offices' Committee for the regulation of guarantee transactions in home fire insurance business.

TAKE NOTE

Reference No. day of 19

The Insurance Company Limited guarantees the Insurance Company Limited for £ from the day of 19 to the day of 19 being part of its insurance of £ on property insured in the name of situate as per its Request Note No.

This guarantee is subject to the rules adopted by the Fire Offices' Committee for the regulation of guarantee transactions in home fire insurance business.

GUARANTEE POLICY

The Insurance Company Limited

....

Guarantee No.

The Insurance Company Limited hereby guarantees the Insurance Company Limited, subject to the rules adopted by the Fire Offices' Committee for the regulation of guarantee transactions in home fire insurance business to the extent of £ in part of its risk upon property insured under its Policy No. for £ issued to as per copy of policy or the written portion thereof lodged with the said Insurance Company Limited.

The said guarantee is for the period from the day of 19 to the day of 19

Present Consideration

Future Consideration

For the Insurance Company Limited.

SURPLUS TREATY REFERENCE NO.

COMPANY:
OF

REINSURER:
OF

TABLE OF CONTENTS

SURPLUS REINSURANCE AGREEMENT NO.
made between ....
(hereinafter referred to as the "Company") of the one part and
(hereinafter referred to as the "Reinsurer") of the other part.

IN CONSIDERATION OF the payment of the premium as hereinafter provided it is agreed:-

ARTICLE NUMBER 1: The Business Covered

1.1. The Company agrees to cede and the Reinsurer agrees to accept by way of reinsurance a fixed share of % (per cent.) of all surpluses over and above the amount retained by the Company for its own account on all insurances, whether accepted direct or by way of reinsurance, against the risk of Fire or against any other peril which may be insured through the Fire Department of the Company on risks situated in any part of the world excluding the United States of America, provided that the share so ceded shall not exceed % (per cent.) of the amount retained by the Company for its own account.

1.2. This Agreement excludes:—
Loss or liability occasioned by or happening through or in consequence directly or indirectly of war, invasion, acts of foreign enemies, hostilities (whether war be declared or not), civil war, rebellion, revolution, insurrection, military or usurped power or confiscation or nationalisation or requisition or destruction of or damage to property by or under the order of any government or public or local authority.

Nevertheless this exclusion shall not apply to business permitted under the terms of the War and Civil War Exclusion Agreement 1937, and any amendments thereto.

1.3. This Agreement excludes:—
Nuclear Energy Risks, whether such risks are written directly and/or by way of reinsurance and/or via Pools and/or Associations.

For all purposes of this Agreement, Nuclear Energy Risks shall be defined as all first party and/or third party insurances (other than Workers' Compensation and/or Employer's Liability) in respect of:

1.3.1. Nuclear reactors and nuclear power stations or plant,
1.3.2. Any other premises or facilities whatsoever related to or concerned with:—
1.3.2.1 The production of nuclear energy, or
1.3.2.2 The production or storage or handling of nuclear fuel or nuclear waste.

1.3.3. Any other premises or facilities eligible for insurance by any local Nuclear Pool and/or Association but only to the extent of the requirements of the local Pool and/or Association, it being the intention always that the Reinsurer shall follow the fortunes of the Company provided that the Company complies with the requirements of any such local Pool and/or Association.

1.3.4. However this Exclusion shall not apply:—

1.3.4.1. To any insurance or reinsurance in respect of the construction, erection or installation of buildings, plant and other property (including contractor's plant and equipment used in connection therewith):

(a) for the storage of nuclear fuel—prior to the commencement of storage,

(b) as regards reactor installations—prior to the commencement of loading of nuclear fuel into the reactor, or prior to the initial criticality, depending on the commencement of the insurance or reinsurance of the relevant local Nuclear Pool and/or Association,

1.3.4.2. To any machinery breakdown or other engineering insurance or reinsurance not coming within the scope of 1.3.4.1. above, nor affording coverage in the "high radioactivity" zone.

1.4. The Reinsurer shall not be liable for claims arising in respect of the following:—

1.4.1. Industrial All Risks Insurances.

1.4.2. Growing or Standing Crops.

1.4.3. Hail.

1.4.4. Contractors and/or Engineering All Risks.

1.4.5. Boiler and/or Machinery Breakdown.

1.4.6. Credit, Contingency or Contract Guarantee

1.4.7. Obligatory Reinsurances.

ARTICLE NUMBER 2: The Retention

2.1. The liability of the Reinsurer shall commence from the date on which the liability of the Company upon any one risk exceeds its retention as shown in its Tables of Limits, cessions to Reinsurance Agreements in priority to this Agreement, and legal reinsurances, if any.

2.2. The Company, in all cases, shall be the sole judge of what constitutes one risk or hazard and the retention appropriate thereto. The Reinsurer shall accept all alterations, modifications, of cancellations of contracts ceded hereunder, and the consequent adjustment of premium. Subject to the limitations hereunder, the Company shall be at liberty at any time to cancel or alter in any manner it may consider desirable any cession hereunder and to adjust the premium resulting therefrom.

2.3. The maximum retentions of the Company are specified as follows:-

No alteration shall be made to this Schedule of maximum retentions without the prior approval of the Reinsurer.

2.4. The Company shall be at liberty to effect reinsurances elsewhere on any risk normally within the scope of this Agreement provided such reinsurance is in the interest of the Reinsurer. The Company may effect excess of loss reinsurance in respect of its net retention on business ceded under this Agreement.

2.5. It is understood that whenever the Company is compelled by law or Decree to give a priority cession to any Insurance or Reinsurance Institution, state controlled or otherwise then cessions to the Reinsurer shall be made after requirements for such priority cessions have been fulfilled.

2.6. Cessions made hereunder shall not exceed a period of twelve months plus any odd time, which shall in any case be less than a further twelve months.

2.7. In the event of the Company receiving advice of the occurrence of a loss before cession to this Agreement has been determined, the Reinsurer will be liable for its share of such loss based on the usual underwriting policy of the Company relating to this type of risk. If the Company has ceded to the Reinsurer a larger amount on a risk than provided in this Agreement then in the event of a loss the liability of the Reinsurer shall be calculated after the Company has corrected the amount ceded hereunder in accordance with all the provisions of this Agreement.

2.8. In respect of risks or contracts written in currencies other than the currency used in expressing the limits as specified in to this Agreement, the retention of the Company and cessions made to this Agreement are fixed at the date of acceptance of each risk or contract based on the rate of exchange prevailing at that time. The Reinsurer agrees to accept its proportionate share of the liability for risks or contracts ceded in this manner regardless of subsequent fluctuations in rates of exchange. The Company undertakes to correct any anomalies thereby created at renewal of each risk or contract.

ARTICLE NUMBER 3: Bonded Warehouse, etc.

3.1. In the case of policies covering the contents of Bonded Stores, Elevators, Public Warehouses, General Storage Warehouses and Timber and Lumber Yards, and similar risks. It shall not be obligatory for the Company to cede a proportionate amount of each policy to the Reinsurer and the retention of the Company shall not be held to apply to the identical property on which an amount has been ceded to the Reinsurer. In the event of loss however, all cessions on the risk affected though made under specified policy or policies shall, provided that name limits are not thereby exceeded, be deemed to cover proportionately all policies in force on such risk.

ARTICLE NUMBER 4: Self-Insurance

4.1. An insurance effected by the Company wherein the company is named as the Insured either alone or jointly with another party shall not be excluded from the scope of this Agreement merely because no legal liability may arise in respect thereof by reason of the fact that the Company is named as the insured or one of the insured.

ARTICLE NUMBER 5: Bordereau

5.1. The Company shall maintain a record of all cessions hereunder and all renewals and alterations thereto. No bordereaux in respect of such cessions shall however be supplied to the Reinsurer.

ARTICLE NUMBER 6: Errors and/or Omissions

6.1. Any delay, error or omission in connection with this Agreement, or in connection with any risk ceded hereunder, shall not be held to relieve either party from any liability which would attach to it if such delay, error or omission had not been made, provided such delay, error or omission is rectified as soon as possible after discovery.
6.2. It is the intention of this Agreement that the Reinsurer shall, in all matters falling within the scope of this Agreement, follow to the extent of its interest the fortune of the Company.
6.3. Subject to prior arrangement and at the expense of the Reinsurer, the Reinsurer may inspect or obtain copies of the whole or any part of the records, books, accounts and any documents of the Company relating to business ceded under this Agreement.
6.4. The right of inspection of the Reinsurer shall exist for as long as one of the parties hereto has a claim against the other party originating from business covered by this Agreement even after its termination, annulment or invalidation, but where arbitration or legal proceedings are pending between the parties hereto, this right of

inspection shall only be exercised through a representative who is not an employee of the Reinsurer.

ARTICLE NUMBER 7: Premiums and Commissions

7.1. The Company shall pay to the Reinsurer the Reinsurer's proportion of the original gross premiums due to the Company in respect of all risks ceded hereto.
7.2. The Reinsurer shall pay to the Company its proportion of taxes and other charges (other than agents' commission) not recoverable from the original insured or reinsured as the case may be.
7.3. The Reinsurer shall allow to the Company commission at the rate of % (per cent.) on the premium ceded hereunder.
7.4. The Reinsurer shall also pay to the Company a profit commission calculated at the rate of % (per cent.) on the profit arising from all business ceded under this Agreement and included in the accounts for each annual period of this Agreement in accordance with the following formula:—

Income

(1) Premium included in the accounts for the current year.
(2) Unearned proportion (if any) of the premiums ceded hereunder in the previous year.
(3) Outstanding losses (if any) sustained hereunder as estimated by the Company at the close of the previous year.

Items 1 and 2 shall not apply to the first Profit Commission Statement.

Outgo

(1) Commission included in the accounts for the current year.
(2) Taxes and other charges included in the accounts for the current year
(3) Paid Losses and Loss Expenses included in the accounts for the current year including cash losses paid by the Reinsurer during the current year and not brought into account.
(4) Unearned proportion (if any) of the premiums ceded hereunder in the current year.
(5) Outstanding losses (if any) sustained hereunder as estimated by the Company at the close of the current year.
(6) Reinsurer's management expenses calculated at % (per cent.) on the premium included in the accounts for the current year.
(7) Cost of any excess of loss protection effected for the benefit of the Reinsurer (if any).

(8) Deficit hereunder, if any, brought forward and calculated in accordance with the provision shown in paragraph 7.4.1. below.

7.4.1. Any deficit resulting from each year's profit commission calculation shall be carried forward and offset against the profit of the next two years. If at the end of the third year the overall result is still a loss then the loss of the first year and the profits for the second and third years shall be eliminated from any further profit commission calculations. Where the second year is also a loss then the loss carried forward to the fourth year shall be the full loss of the second year less any profit resulting from the combined result of the third year's profit less the first year's loss. Where the third year is a loss then the full loss of that year shall be carried forward and offset against the profit of the next two years in the same manner.
7.4.2. The difference between **Income** and **Outgo** represents the annual result on which (if a profit) any profit commission will be calculated.
7.4.3. The profit commission shall be calculated annually and the profit commission statement shall be submitted to the Reinsurer within three months of the end of the year to which the profit commission relates and any profit commission due shall be included in account.
7.4.4. On termination of this Agreement, the profit commission statement for the final period of duration hereof shall be deferred until all cessions hereunder have expired and all losses hereunder have been settled.

ARTICLE NUMBER 8: Claims

8.1. Preliminary loss advice shall be sent by the Company to the Reinsurer of all losses where the amount of the loss is estimated to exceed £ together with relevant details and an estimate of the probable cost of the claim. The Company shall keep the Reinsurer informed of all developments likely to affect the the cost of any such claims and undertakes insofar as is reasonably possible to consult the Reinsurer with regard to the settlement of such claims.
8.2. All loss settlements made by the Company affecting cessions under this Agreement, whether made under strict policy conditions or by compromise or otherwise, including ex gratia payments, shall be unconditionally binding upon the Reinsurer, and the Reinsurer shall bear its rateable proportion of such settlements and of any expenses relating thereto but excluding office expenses and the salaries of employees of the Company. The Reinsurer shall, nevertheless, share

to the extent of its interest in any sums which may be recovered by the Company.

8.3. The Company may likewise at its sole discretion commence, continue, defend, compromise, settle or withdraw from actions, suits or proceedings, and generally do all such matters and things relating to any claim or loss as in its judgment may be beneficial or expedient and all payments made and costs and expenses incurred therewith shall be shared by the Reinsurer in proportion to its liability for the claim or loss and debited or paid in accordance with the provisions of this Article.

8.4. Where the Reinsurer's share of a loss falling under this Agreement amounts to or exceeds the sum of £ , the Reinsurer shall upon receiving a summarised statement from the Company (detailing the payment made or the amount to be paid forthwith as agreed with the insured or original reinsured as the case may be) remit its share of such loss promptly. When such share is less than the amount stated the amount shall be debited in the accounts.

8.5. The Company shall as soon as practicble and in any event not later than three months after the 31st December of each year send to the Reinsurer a statement of unsettled claims as at the date of submission of such statement showing the amount for which the Reinsurer may be liable.

ARTICLE NUMBER 9: Accounts

9.1. Accounts between the Company and the Reinsurer in respect of the business under this Agreement shall be closed quarterly and rendered to the Reinsurer as soon as possible thereafter but in any event not less than three months after the end of the quarter.

9.2. Accounts shall be confirmed by the Reinsurer within one month of receipt but inadvertent errors or omissions in the account shall not delay the payment of any balance hereunder (unless such error or omission has a major effect on the remittable balance). Any necessary correction shall be made in the next account rendered hereunder, unless such error or omission has a major effect on the remittable balance, in which event it shall be corrected by a supplementary account.

9.3. Balances due to the Company shall be paid at the time of confirmation of the account and balances due to the Reinsurer shall be paid by the Company at the same time as the accounts are rendered.

9.4. Either party may at its discretion offset against any amounts advised to and due from the other party hereunder any amounts which have been previously advised and are due at that time.

9.5. All payments hereunder shall be in Sterling and balances in other currencies shall be converted into Sterling at the rates of exchange ruling at the time they were entered in the books of the Company.

ARTICLE NUMBER 10: Reserve Deposits

10.1. As a security for the Company in respect of the future performance of the Reinsurer for cessions hereunder, the Company shall retain from the Reinsurer a Premium Reserve Deposit in cash calculated at % (per cent.) on the premium ceded to the Reinsurer in the accounts rendered hereunder. Such retained Deposit will be held by the Company and released to the Reinsurer in the corresponding account of the following year.
10.2. The Reinsurer may at any time request the release of the Premium Reserve Deposit retained in cash and its replacement with Bonds and/or Securities acceptable to both parties and the Reinsurer shall receive all dividends, interest and other rights accruing thereon. When a Deposit is constituted in Bonds and/or Securities the Company shall have the right to debit the Reinsurer and retain in cash any deficiency between the Premium Reserve Deposit required and the market value of the Bonds and/or Securities held. The cash deposit so retained shall be held by the Company until covered by Bonds and/or Securities deposited by the Reinsurer.
10.3. The Company shall credit the Reinsurer in the accounts rendered hereunder with interest calculated at the rate of % (per cent.) per annum on the Premium Reserve Deposit retained in cash at any time throughout the relevant period.
10.4. It is hereby expressly agreed and declared that all sums Cash and/or Bonds and/or Securities held by the Company in accordance with the provisions of this Article remain the property of the Reinsurer and are held by the Company as trustees for the Reinsurer and may only be utilised by the Company in the event and up to the amount of the Reinsurer's failure to discharge its liability under this Agreement.

ARTICLE NUMBER 11: Commencement and Termination

11.1. This Agreement shall take effect in respect of all insurances relating to risks covered hereunder issued or renewed on or after the First day of January 19 and shall continue in force for an indefinite period unless otherwise agreed. Either party may, however, terminate this Agreement by giving three months notice in writing to expire on the Thirty First day of December of any year. In the event of either party giving notice of termination then such notice shall be automatically deemed to have been given by both parties.
11.2. In the event of either party giving notice of termination of any

business ceded in the reciprocation (in whole or in part) for this Agreement, then this Agreement shall automatically be deemed to be under notice of termination from the same date notwithstanding that previous notice had not been given in accordance with paragraph 11.1. above.

11.3. Either party shall have the right to terminate this Agreement immediately by giving the other party notice by the quickest means available which shall be deemed to be served upon despatch or where communications between the parties are interrupted upon attempted despatch, where:

> 11.3.1. The performance of the whole or any part of this Agreement be prohibited or rendered impossible de jure or de facto in particular and without prejudice to the generality of the preceding words in consequence of any law or regulation which is or shall be in force in any country or territory in which either party is situated or if any law or regulation shall prevent directly or indirectly the remittance of any payments due to or from either party.
>
> 11.3.2. The other party has become insolvent or unable to pay its debts or has lost the whole or a major part of its paid up capital or has had any authority to transact any class of insurance withdrawn, suspended or made conditional or if there is any material change in the management or control of the other party.
>
> 11.3.3. The country or territory in which the other party resides or has its head office or is incorporated shall be involved in armed hostilities with any other country whether war be declared or not or is partly or wholly occupied by another power or be in a state of civil war.
>
> 11.3.4. The other party shall have failed to comply with any of the terms and conditions of this Agreement.

11.4. The Reinsurer shall remain liable for its share of all cessions made and effective up to and including the termination date of this Agreement, except where this Agreement is terminated in the circumstances provided for in paragraph 11.3. of this Article where the liability of the Reinsurer under current cessions shall cease as from the date of the notice of termination and any relevant adjustment of premium shall be made forthwith.

ARTICLE NUMBER 12: Assumption and/or Withdrawal of Portfolios

Premiums

12.1. At the option of the Company the Reinsurer shall assume liability for its share of all cessions current at the commencement date of this Agreement and in consideration thereof the Company shall credit the Reinsurer in the first account rendered hereunder with a portfolio premium assumption calculated at % (per cent.) of the original gross premiums less commission included in the accounts for the twelve months prior to the inception of this Agreement.

12.2. At the option of the Company the Reinsurer's liability for its share of the risks ceded under this Agreement shall cease at the date of termination of this Agreement and in consideration thereof the Company shall debit the Reinsurer in account with a portfolio premium withdrawal calculated at % (per cent.) of the original gross premiums less commission included in the accounts for the twelve months prior to the date of termination of this Agreement.

Losses

12.3. At the option of the Company the Reinsurer shall assume liability for its share of all losses outstanding at the commencement date of this Agreement and in consideration thereof the Company shall credit the Reinsurer in the first account rendered hereunder with a portfolio loss assumption calculated at % (per cent.) of the Company's estimate of the amount of the losses outstanding at inception of this Agreement.

12.4. At the option of the Company, the Reinsurer's liability for its share of all losses outstanding at the date of termination of this Agreement shall cease at that date and in consideration thereof the Company shall debit the Reinsurer in account with a portfolio loss withdrawal calculated at % (per cent.) of the Company's estimate of the amount of the losses outstanding at the date of termination of this Agreement.

ARTICLE NUMBER 13: Alterations and Interpretation

13.1. This Agreement may be altered at any time by mutual consent of the parties either by Addendum or by exchange of correspondence signed by a responsible official of each of the parties, and such variations shall be deemed to form part of this Agreement and be binding on the parties.

13.2. Any attachments which may be expressly incorporated herein shall be read together with this Agreement as one contract and any word or expression to which a specific meaning has been applied, shall bear such specific meaning wherever it may appear.

13.3. The laws of England shall apply as the proper law of this Agreement.

ARTICLE NUMBER 14: Confidentiality

14.1. Both parties hereto undertake to regard this Agreement as well as all transactions relating hereto as confidential and further agree that neither will at any time during the currency of this Agreement or subsequently make use either directly or indirectly of the information afforded in connection herewith in any manner which shall or may operate to the prejudice or detriment of the other party.

ARTICLE NUMBER 15: Communications

15.1. All documents, advices and communications served in accordance with any of the provisions of this Agreement shall be addressed to the party concerned at its head office or at any other address previously designated by that party.
15.2. All postal, cable, remittance or other similar charges shall be paid by the sender.

IN WITNESS WHEREOF this Agreement has been drawn up and signed in duplicate on behalf of and by the authority of each contracting party,

In this day of 19 for and on behalf of the Company

And in this day of 19 for and on behalf of the Reinsurer in respect of its per cent. share of the liabilities and premiums set forth herein.

PROFIT COMMISSION ON A THREE YEAR AVERAGE BASIS

7.4. The Reinsurer shall also pay to the Company a profit commission on a three year average basis calculated at the rate of % (per cent.) on the profit arising from all business ceded under this Agreement and included in the accounts for each annual period of this Agreement in accordance with the following formula:

Income

(1) Premium included in the account for the current year.
(2) Unearned proportion (if any) of the premiums ceded hereunder in the previous year.
(3) Outstanding losses (if any) sustained hereunder as estimated by the Company at the close of the previous year.

Items 1 and 2 shall not apply to the first Profit Commission Statement.

Outgo

(1) Commission included in the accounts for the current year.
(2) Taxes and other charges included in the accounts for the current year.
(3) Paid Losses and Loss Expenses included in the accounts for the current year including cash losses paid by the Reinsurer during the current year and not brought into account.
(4) Unearned proportion (if any) of the premiums ceded hereunder in the current year.
(5) Outstanding losses (if any) sustained hereunder as estimated by the Company at the close of the current year.
(6) Reinsurer's management expenses calculated at % (per cent.) on the premium included in the accounts for the current year.
(7) Cost of any excess of loss protection effected for the benefit of the Reinsurer (if any).

7.4.1. Any excess of **Income** over **Outgo** shall be deemed to be the profit for the annual period.
7.4.2. In the first year the Reinsurer shall pay profit commission on 100% of that year's profit and in the second year on 50% of each of the profits of the first and second years. Thereafter the Reinsurer shall pay profit commission calculated on 33.33% of the aggregate net profits of the current and two preceding years.
7.4.3. The profit commission shall be calculated annually and the profit commission statement shall be submitted to the

Reinsurer within three months of the end of the year to which the profit commission relates and any profit commission due shall be included in account.

7.4.4. On termination of this Agreement, the profit commission statement for the final period of duration hereof shall be deferred until all cessions hereunder have expired and all losses hereunder have been settled.

FIRST EXCESS OF LOSS TREATY REFERENCE NO.

COMPANY:
OF

REINSURER:
OF

TABLE OF CONTENTS

FIRST EXCESS OF LOSS REINSURANCE AGREEMENT NO.
made between
(hereinafter referred to as the "Company") of the one part
and
(hereinafter referred to as the "Reinsurer") of the other part.

IN CONSIDERATION OF the payment of the premuim as hereinafter provided it is agreed:—

ARTICLE NUMBER 1: The Business Covered

1.1. The Reinsurer shall pay to the Company by way of excess of loss reinsurance the amount of its ultimate net loss (as hereinafter defined) in excess of £ arising out of any one claim or series of claims due to the same cause, under motor insurance policies issued by the Company in any part of the world except the United States of America, provided always that the liability of the Reinsurer shall not exceed £ in all in respect of each such ultimate net loss.
1.2. The Company may effect facultative reinsurance for any risk where such reinsurance is considered to be in the interest of the parties hereto.
1.3. An insurance granted by the Company wherein the Company is named as the Insured either alone or jointly with another party or parties shall not be excluded from this Agreement merely because no legal liability may arise in respect thereof by reason of the fact that the Company be the Insured or one of the Insureds.

ARTICLE NUMBER 2: Exclusions

2.1. This Agreement excludes:—
Loss or liability occasioned by or happening through or in consequence directly or indirectly of war, invasion, acts of foreign enemies, hostilities (whether war be declared or not), civil war, rebellion, revolution, insurrection, military or usurped power or confiscation or nationalisation or requisition or destruction of or damage to property by or under the order of any government or public or local authority.

Nevertheless this exclusion shall not apply to business permitted under the terms of the War and Civil War Exclusion Agreement, 1937, and any amendments thereto.

2.2. This Agreement excludes:—
Nuclear Energy Risks, whether such risks are written directly and/or by way of reinsurance and/or via Pools and/or Associations.

For all purposes of this Agreement, Nuclear Energy Risks shall be defined as all first party and/or third party insurances (other than Worker's Compensation and/or Employer's Liability) in respect of:

2.2.1. Nuclear reactors and nuclear power stations or plant,

2.2.2. Any other premises or facilities whatsoever related to or concerned with:

2.2.2.1. The production of nuclear energy, or

2.2.2.2. The production or storage or handling of nuclear fuel or nuclear waste.

2.2.3. Any other premises or facilities eligible for insurance by any local Nuclear Pool and/or Association but only to the extent of the requirements of the local Pool and/or Association, it being the intention always that the Reinsurer shall follow the fortunes of the Company provided that the Company complies with the requirements of any such local Pool and/or Association.

2.2.4. However this Exclusion shall not apply:—

2.2.4.1. To any insurance or reinsurance in respect of the construction, erection or installation of buildings, plant and other property (including contractor's plant and equipment used in connection therewith):

(a) for the storage of nuclear fuel—prior to the commencement of storage,

(b) as regards reactor installations—prior to the commencement of loading of nuclear fuel into the reactor, or prior to the initial criticality, depending on the commencement of the insurance or reinsurance of the relevant local Nuclear Pool and/or Association.

2.2.4.2. To any machinery breakdown or other engineering insurance or reinsurance not coming within the scope of 2.2.4.1 above, nor affording coverage in the "high radioactivity" zone.

2.3. The Reinsurer shall not be liable for claims arising on policies issued in respect of the following:—

2.3.1. Vehicles other than those running on terra firma.

2.3.2. Vehicles running on rails.

2.3.3. Charabancs, coaches, buses, taxicabs, self-drive hire cars or any vehicle plying for public hire.

2.3.4. Vehicles engaged in racing or speed trials.

2.3.5. Vehicles engaged in the carriage of explosives or inflammable liquids or gases in bulk.

2.3.6. Workmen's Compensation or Employer's Liability risks.

2.3.7. Personal Accident benefits, other than those granted under the standard form of policy without extra charge.

2.3.8. Goods in transit insurances other than those arranged as an extension of motor vehicle policies.
2.3.9. Excess of Loss Insurances and/or Reinsurances and policies with a self-insured deductible exceeding £250.
2.3.10. Obligatory Reinsurances.

ARTICLE NUMBER 3: Net Retained Lines

3.1. This Agreement shall apply only to that portion of any insurance or reinsurance otherwise covered hereunder which the Company, acting in accordance with its established practices, retains net for its own account and in computing the amount in excess of which this Agreement applies, only a loss or losses in respect of that portion of any insurance or reinsurance otherwise covered hereunder which the Company, acting in accordance with its established practices, retains net for its own account shall be included.
3.2. The Reinsurer's liability hereunder shall not be increased due to an error or omission which results in an increase in the Company's net retention nor by the Company's failure to reinsure in accordance with its normal practice.
3.3. The Reinsurer's liablity hereunder shall not be increased by the inability of the Company to collect from any other Reinsurer or Reinsurers, whether specific or general, any amounts which may have become due from them for any reason whatsoever.

ARTICLE NUMBER 4: Ulimate Net Loss

4.1. The term "ultimate net loss" shall be understood to mean the total amount which the Company has actually paid in settlement of all claims or series of claims arising out of any one accident or event which may occur during the period of this Agreement, including any legal costs and professional fees and expenses (excluding salaries of all employees and office expenses of the Company) reasonably incurred in connection therewith. Recoveries including amounts which inure to the benefit of this Agreement shall be first deducted from such amount to arrive at the amount of the liability, if any, hereunder.
4.2. Any salvages, payments or recoveries effected subsequent to a settlement of any such ultimate net loss shall be applied as if effected prior to such settlement and any adjustment as may be necessary shall be made forthwith.
4.3. Nothing in this Article however shall be construed to mean that claims are not recoverable hereunder until the ultimate net loss of the Company has been ascertained.

ARTICLE NUMBER 5: Premiums

5.1. The Company shall pay to the Reinsurer premiums at a rate of per cent. calculated on the annual premium income of the Company in respect of the business covered hereunder. The term "annual premium income" shall mean gross original premiums less returns and cancellations made under the terms and conditions of the original insurances and less premiums paid for reinsurances which inure to the benefit of this Agreement during each annual period hereof.

5.2. In respect of the Company's gross original premiums in currencies other than Sterling the Company shall, for the purposes of determining the "annual premium income", convert such premiums at the rates of exchange ruling at the end of the annual period of the Agreement, or if the Agreement is terminated in any year prior to the end of the annual period then in respect of that year at the rate of exchange ruling on the date of termination

ARTICLE NUMBER 6: Deposit premiums and accounts

6.1. The Company shall pay to the Reinsurer an annual Deposit Premium of £ in four equal quarterly instalments at the 1st January, 1st April, 1st July and 1st October of each annual period of this Agreement or such other amount as may be agreed during the currency of this Agreement.

6.2. As soon as possible after the end of each annual period of this Agreement but in any event within three months thereof the Company shall supply to the Reinsurer a declaration of its annual premium income as defined in Article Number 5 above, fully sub-divided, where applicable, for each class of business and each territory covered by this Agreement. The annual premium due to the Reinsurer under this Agreement shall be calculated in accordance with Article Number 5 and after taking into consideration the Deposit Premium already paid in respect of the same period any premium adjustment due by the Company shall be paid to the Reinsurer at the same time as the premium declaration is rendered.

6.3. The premium adjustments shall be confirmed by the Reinsurer within one month of receipt and any premium adjustment due to the Company shall be paid by the Reinsurer at the time of confirmation.

6.4. The Reinsurer shall not receive less than the Minimum Premium of £ during each annual period of this Agreement.

6.5. Either party may at its discretion offset against any amounts advised to and due from the other party hereunder any amounts which have been previously advised and are due at that time.

ARTICLE NUMBER 7: Claims

7.1. The Company shall notify the Reinsurer immediately of each accident or event with all relevant details where either the sums claimed or the potential loss amounts to or exceeds the sum of £ whether or not the Company considers that it has an adequate defence or that there may be any contribution by a third party, and the Company shall advise the Reinsurer of its estimate of the probable cost of the loss.

7.2. In addition, the following categories of claims or potential claims shall be reported to the Reinsurer immediately, regardless of any questions of the liability of the Insured or the Company:—

7.2.1. Fatal injuries unless it is known that there is no dependency.

7.2.2. Bodily injuries as specified below:—

Brain injuries

Spinal injuries resulting in partial or total paralysis

Total or partial amputations or permanent loss of use of a limb or limbs

Severe burn injuries

Total or partial blindness

Extensive scarring or severe facial disfigurement

All other injuries likely to result in a permanent disability rating of 50% or more.

7.2.3. Bodily injuries resulting in payment of an annuity.

7.2.4. Bodily injuries or property damage for which suit has been filed if the amounts claimed by the plaintiff or plaintiffs exceed the sum stated in paragraph 7.1 above.

7.3. The Company shall keep the Reinsurer informed of all developments likely to affect the cost of any claim or claims hereunder and undertakes insofar as is reasonably possible to cooperate with the Reinsurer or its representative in the conduct and settlement of such claim or claims and in the estimating of claims reserves.

7.4. In calculating the liability of the Reinsurer hereunder all loss payments made by the Company within the conditions of the original insurance and falling within the scope of this Agreement shall be binding on the Reinsurer. The Reinsurer shall be bound also by ex gratia payments made with its consent.

7.5. The Reinsurer shall remit its share of all loss payments within fourteen days of receiving a request from the Company so to do.

7.6. The Company shall as soon as practicable and in any event not later than three months after the 31st December of each year send to the Reinsurer a statement of unsettled claims as at the date of submission of such statement showing the amount for which the Reinsurer may be liable in respect of each individual claim.

ARTICLE NUMBER 8: Inception and Termination

8.1. This Agreement shall take effect from the First day of January 19 and shall continue in force for an indefinite period unless otherwise agreed. Either party may, however, terminate this Agreement by giving three months notice in writing to expire on the Thirty First day of December of any year. In the event of either party giving notice of termination then such notice shall be automatically deemed to have been given by both parties.
8.2. Either party shall have the right to terminate this Agreement immediately by giving the other party notice by the quickest means available which shall be deemed to be served upon despatch or where communications between the parties are interrupted upon attempted despatch, where:—

8.2.1. the performance of the whole or any part of this Agreement be prohibited or rendered impossible de jure or de facto in particular and without prejudice to the generality of the preceding words in consequence of any law or regulation which is or shall be in force in any country or territory in which either party is situated or if any law or regulation shall prevent directly or indirectly the remittance of any payments due to or from either party.
8.2.2. the other party has become insolvent or unable to pay its debts or has lost the whole or a major part of its paid up capital or has had any authority to transact any class of insurance withdrawn, suspended or made conditional or if there is any material change in the management or control of the other party.
8.2.3. the country or territory in which the other party resides or has its head office or is incorporated shall be involved in armed hostilities with any other country whether war be declared or not or is partly or wholly occupied by another power or be in a state of civil war.
8.2.4. the other party shall have failed to comply with any of the terms and conditions of this Agreement.

8.3. The Reinsurer shall remain liable for all losses occurring up to and including the date of termination. Thereafter the liability of the Reinsurer shall cease outright other than so far as outstanding claims are concerned.

ARTICLE NUMBER 9: Errors and/or Omissions

9.1. Bona fide delays, errors or omissions in connection with the operation of this Agreement shall not prejudice the rights of either party hereto but shall be corrected retrospectively upon discovery so that the parties hereto shall be placed in the same position as if the delay and/or error and/or omission had not occurred.

ARTICLE NUMBER 10: Inspection of Records

10.1. Subject to prior arrangement and at the expense of the Reinsurer, the Reinsurer may inspect or obtain copies of the whole or any part of the records, books, accounts and any documents of the Company relating to business covered by this Agreement.
10.2. The right of inspection of the Reinsurer shall exist for as long as one of the parties hereto has a claim against the other party originating from business covered by this Agreement even after its termination, annulment or invalidation, but where arbitration or legal proceedings are pending between the parties hereto, this right of inspection shall only be exercised through a representative who is not an employee of the Reinsurer.

ARTICLE NUMBER 11: Alterations and Interpretation

11.1. This Agreement may be altered at any time by mutual consent of the parties either by Addendum or by exchange of correspondence signed by a responsible official of each of the parties, and such variations shall be deemed to form part of this Agreement and be binding on the parties.
11.2. Any attachments which may be expressly incorporated herein shall be read together with this Agreement as one contract and any word or expression to which a specific meaning has been applied, shall bear such specific meaning wherever it may appear.
11.3. The laws of England shall apply as the proper law of this Agreement.

ARTICLE NUMBER 12: Confidentiality

12.1. Both parties hereto undertake to regard this Agreement as well as all transactions relating hereto as confidential and further agree that neither will at any time during the currency of this Agreement or subsequently make use either directly or indirectly of the information afforded in connection herewith in any manner which shall or may operate to the prejudice or detriment of the other party.

ARTICLE NUMBER 13: Intermediary

13.1.
of
are designated by the parties hereto as the intermediary through whom all communications relating hereto shall be transmitted. Premium settlements and claims recoveries shall also be effected through the intermediary. Settlement to the Reinsurer by the

intermediary shall constitute a full discharge of the obligations of the Company hereunder.

13.2. All postal, cable, remittance or other similar charges shall be paid by the sender.

IN WITNESS WHEREOF this Agreement has been drawn up and signed in duplicate on behalf of and by the authority of each contracting party,

In this day of 19
for and on behalf of the Company

And in this day of
19
for and on behalf of the Reinsurer in respect of its per cent. share of the liabilities and premiums set forth herein.

EXPERIENCE RATING SCALE BASIS

ARTICLE NUMBER 5: Premiums

5.1. The Company shall pay to the Reinsurer premiums at a rate calculated to three decimal places in accordance with the following formula:—

$$\frac{\text{"All amounts both paid and outstanding in respect of losses occurring during the year being rated and for which the Reinsurer is liable hereunder}}{\text{the annual premium income of the Company in respect of the year being rated"}} \times \frac{100}{1} \times \frac{100}{80} = \%$$

on the annual premium income of the Company in respect of the business covered hereunder. The term "annual premium income" shall mean gross original premiums less returns and cancellations made under the terms and conditions of the original insurances and less premiums paid for reinsurances which inure to the benefit of this Agreement during each annual period hereof.

5.2. Provided that the premium rate for any annual period shall not be less than % (per cent.) nor more than % (per cent.).

5.3. In respect of the Company's gross original premiums in currencies other than Sterling the Company shall, for the purposes of determining the "annual premium income", convert such premiums at the rates of exchange ruling at the end of the annual period of the Agreement, or if the Agreement is terminated in any year prior to the end of the annual period then in respect of that year at the rates of exchange ruling on the date of termination.

ARTICLE NUMBER 6: Deposit Premiums and Accounts

6.1. The Company shall pay to the Reinsurer an annual Deposit Premium of £ in four equal quarterly instalments at the 1st January, 1st April, 1st July and 1st October of each annual period of this Agreement or such other amount as may be agreed during the currency of this Agreement.

6.2. As soon as possible after the end of each annual period of this Agreement but in any event within three months thereof the Company shall supply to the Reinsurer a declaration of its annual premium income as defined in Article Number 5 above, fully subdivided, where applicable, for each class of business and each territory covered by this Agreement. The annual premium due to the Reinsurer under this Agreement shall be calculated in accordance

with Article Number 5 and after taking into consideration the Deposit Premium already paid in respect of the same period any premium adjustment due by the Company shall be paid to the Reinsurer at the same time as the premium declaration is rendered.
6.3. The premium adjustments shall be confirmed by the Reinsurer within one month of receipt and any premium adjustment due to the Company shall be paid by the Reinsurer at the time of confirmation.
6.4. Further calculations of premium shall be made annually in respect of each year until all outstanding claims hereunder have been settled and any additional or return premium due after taking into account any premium previously paid for such year shall be settled in the manner set out above.
6.5. The amount to be included in the adjustment statement in respect of outstanding claims hereunder shall be agreed by the Company with the Reinsurer.
6.6. Either party may at its discretion offset against any amounts advised to and due from the other party hereunder any amounts which have been previously advised and are due at that time.

MARINE CARGO QUOTA SHARE TREATY
REFERENCE NO.

COMPANY:
OF

REINSURER:
OF

TABLE OF CONTENTS

QUOTA SHARE REINSURANCE AGREEMENT NO.
made between
(hereinafter referred to as the "Company") of the one part
and
(hereinafter referred to as the "Reinsurer") of the other part.

IN CONSIDERATION OF the payment of the premium as hereinafter provided it is agreed:—

ARTICLE NUMBER 1: The Business Covered

1.1. The Company agrees to cede and the Reinsurer agrees to accept by way of reinsurance a quota share of % (per cent.) of each and every Cargo risk of any description written by the Company in its Marine department in the United Kingdom during the currency of this Agreement, provided that the share so ceded shall not exceed £ in respect of each and every such risk.

1.2. This Agreement excludes:—
Loss or liability occasioned by or happening through or in consequence directly or indirectly of war, invasion, acts of foreign enemies, hostilities (whether war be declared or not), civil war, rebellion, revolution, insurrection, military or usurped power or confiscation or nationalisation or requisition or destruction of or damage to property by or under the order of any government or public or local authority.

Nevertheless this exclusion shall not apply to business permitted under the terms of the War and Civil War Exclusion Agreement 1937, and any amendments thereto. Provided that if the risks of War are insured in conjunction with Marine risks such risks shall not be covered on terms wider than those of the current clauses of the Institute of London Underwriters nor at gross rates below those of the compulsory schedule of minimum rates applying in London.

1.3. This Agreement excludes:—
Nuclear Energy Risks, whether such risks are written directly and/or by way of reinsurance and/or via Pools and/or Associations.

For all purposes of this Agreement, Nuclear Energy Risks shall be defined as all first party and/or third party insurances (other than Worker's Compensation and/or Employer's Liability) in respect of:

1.3.1. Nuclear reactors and nuclear power stations or plant

1.3.2. Any other premises or facilities whatsoever related to or concerned with:

1.3.2.1 The production of nuclear energy, or

1.3.2.2 The production or storage or handling of nuclear fuel or nuclear waste.

1.3.3. Any other premises or facilities eligible for insurance by any local Nuclear Pool and/or Association but only to the extent of the requirements of the local Pool and/or Association, it being the intention always that the Reinsurer shall follow the fortunes of the Company provided that the Company complies with the requirements of any such local Pool and/or Association.

1.3.4. However this Exclusion shall not apply:—

1.3.4.1. To any insurance or reinsurance in respect of the construction, erection or installation of buildings, plant and other property (including contractor's plant and equipment used in connection therewith):

(a) for the storage of nuclear fuel—prior to the commencement of storage,

(b) as regard reactor installations—prior to the commencement of loading of nuclear fuel into the reactor, or prior to the initial criticality, depending on the commencement of the insurance or reinsurance of the relevant local Nuclear Pool and/or Association,

1.3.4.2. To any machinery breakdown or other engineering insurance or reinsurance not coming within the scope of 1.3.4.1 above, nor affording coverage in the "high radioactivity" zone.

1.4. The Reinsurer shall not be liable for claims arising in respect of the following:—

1.4.1. Hulls of vessels and/or aircraft, shipowners' interest and/or freight.

1.4.2. Shipments of Livestock.

1.4.3. Storage risks unless in conjuction with a Marine Risk.

1.4.4. Rejection risks.

1.4.5. Obligatory Reinsurances.

1.5. The Company undertakes to retain for its own account not less than % (per cent.) of the whole business ceded under this Agreement. The Company may however effect excess of loss reinsurance in respect of its net retention on business ceded under this Agreement.

ARTICLE NUMBER 2: The Liability

2.1. The liability of the Reinsurer for amounts ceded under this Agreement shall commence simultaneously with that of the Company and shall be identical in every way with that of the Company.

2.2. The cessions shall be subject to the same conditions as the original insurances and the Reinsurer hereby agrees to all the clauses and conditions contained in the original policies. Unless otherwise provided for the liability of the Reinsurer shall remain in force until the end of the terms of the insurances to which they pertain.
2.3. Subject to the limitations hereunder, the Company shall be at liberty at any time to cancel or alter in any manner it may consider desirable any cession hereunder and to adjust the premium resulting therefrom.
2.4. The Company shall be at liberty to effect reinsurances elsewhere on any risk normally within the scope of this Agreement provided such reinsurance is in the interest of the Reinsurer.
2.5. It is understood that whenever the Company is compelled by law or by Decree to give a priority cession to any Insurance or Reinsurance Institution, state controlled or otherwise, then cessions to the Reinsurer shall be made after requirements for such priority cessions have been fulfilled.
2.6. Cessions made hereunder shall not exceed a period of twelve months plus any odd time, which shall in any case be less than a further twelve months.
2.7. In the event of the Company receiving advice of the occurrence of a loss before cession to this Agreement has been determined, the Reinsurer will be liable for its share of such loss based on the usual underwriting policy of the Company relating to this type of risk. If the Company has ceded to the Reinsurer a larger amount on a risk than provided in this Agreement then in the event of a loss the liability of the Reinsurer shall be calculated after the Company has corrected the amount ceded hereunder in accordance with all the provisions of this Agreement.
2.8. In respect of risks of contracts written in currencies other than the currency used in expressing the limits as specified in this Agreement, the retention of the Company and cessions made to this Agreement are fixed at the date of acceptance of each risk or contract based on the rate of exchange prevailing at that time. The Reinsurer agrees to accept its proportionate share of the liability for risks or contracts ceded in this manner regardless of subsequent fluctuations in rates of exchange. The Company undertakes to correct any anomalies thereby created at the renewal of each risk or contract.

ARTICLE NUMBER 3: Bordereau

3.1. The Company shall maintain a record of all cessions hereunder and of all renewals and alterations thereto. No bordereaux in respect of such cessions shall however be supplied to the Reinsurer.

ARTICLE NUMBER 4: Errors and/or Omissions

4.1. Any delay, error or omission in connection with this Agreement, or in connection with any risk ceded hereunder, shall not be held to relieve either party from any liability which would attach to it if such delay, error or omission had not been made, provided such delay, error or omission is rectified as soon as possible after discovery.
4.2. It is the intention of this Agreement that the Reinsurer shall in all matters falling within the scope of this Agreement, follow to the extent of its interests the fortune of the Company.
4.3. Subject to prior arrangement and at the expense of the Reinsurer, the Reinsurer may inspect or obtain copies of the whole or any part of the records, books, accounts and any documents of the Company relating to business ceded under this Agreement.
4.4. The right of inspection of the Reinsurer shall exist for as long as one of the parties hereto has a claim against the other party originating from business covered by this Agreement even after its termination, annulment or invalidation, but where arbitration or legal proceedings are pending between the parties hereto, this right of inspection shall only be exercised through a representative who is not an employee of the Reinsurer.

ARTICLE NUMBER 5: Premiums and Commissions

5.1. The rates of premium payable to the Reinsurer shall be the same as those received by the Company in respect of all risks ceded hereto after deduction of all brokerage discounts, agency commissions and allowances, provided that such deductions from the original gross rates shall not exceed % (per cent.) in all.
5.2. The Reinsurer shall pay to the Company its proportion of taxes and other charges (other than agents' commission) not recoverable from the original insured or reinsured as the case may be.
5.3. The Reinsurer shall allow to the Company an overriding commission at the rate of %) per cent.) on the premium ceded hereunder.
5.4. The Reinsurer shall also pay to the Company a profit commission calculated at the rate of % (per cent.) on the profit arising from all business ceded under this Agreement and included in the accounts for each annual period of this Agreement in accordance with the following formula:—

Income

(1) Premium included in the accounts for the current year

(2) Unearned proportion (if any) of the premiums ceded hereunder in the previous year.
(3) Outstanding losses (if any) sustained hereunder as estimated by the Company at the close of the previous year.

Items (1) and (2) shall not apply to the first Profit Commission Statement.

Outgo

(1) Commission included in the accounts for the current year.
(2) Taxes and other charges included in the accounts for the current year.
(3) Paid Losses and Loss Expenses included in the accounts for the current year including cash losses paid by the Reinsurer during the current year and not brought into account.
(4) Unearned proportion (if any) of the premiums ceded hereunder in the current year.
(5) Outstanding losses (if any) sustained hereunder as estimated by the Company at the close of the current year.
(6) Reinsurer's management expenses calculated at % (per cent.) on the premium included in the accounts for the current year.
(7) Cost of any excess of loss protection effected for the benefit of the Reinsurer (if any).
(8) Deficit hereunder, if any, brought forward and calculated in accordance with the provision shown in paragraph 7.4.1. below.

5.4.1. Any deficit resulting from each year's profit commission calculation shall be carried forward and offset against the profit of the next two years. If at the end of the third year the overall result is still a loss then the loss of the first year and the profits for the second and third years shall be eliminated from any further profit commission calculations. Where the second year is also a loss then the loss carried forward to the fourth year shall be the full loss of the second year less any profit resulting from the combined result of the third year's profit less the first year's loss. Where the third year is a loss then the full loss of that year shall be carried forward and offset against the profit of the next two years in the same manner.
5.4.2. The difference between **Income** and **Outgo** represents the annual result on which (if a profit) any profit commission will be calculated.

5.4.3. The profit commission shall be calculated annually and the profit commission statement shall be submitted to the Reinsurer within three months of the end of the year to which the profit commission relates and any profit commission due shall be included in account.
5.4.4. On termination of this Agreement, the profit commission statement for the final period of duration hereof shall be deferred until all cessions hereunder have expired and all losses hereunder have been settled.

ARTICLE NUMBER 6: Claims

6.1. Preliminary loss advice shall be sent by the Company to the Reinsurer of all losses where the amount of the loss is estimated to exceed £ together with relevant details and an estimate of the probable cost of the claim. The Company shall keep the Reinsurer informed of all developments likely to affect the cost of any such claims and undertakes insofar as is reasonably possible to consult the Reinsurer with regard to the settlement of such claims.
6.2. All loss settlements made by the Company affecting cessions under this Agreement, whether made under strict policy conditions or by compromise or otherwise, including ex gratia payments, shall be unconditionally binding upon the Reinsurer, and the Reinsurer shall bear its rateable proportion of such settlements and of any expenses relating thereto but excluding office expenses and the salaries of employees of the Company. The Reinsurer shall, nevertheless, share to the extent of its interest in any sums which may be recovered by the Company.
6.3. The Company may likewise at its sole discretion commence, continue, defend, compromise, settle or withdraw from actions, suits or proceedings, and generally do all such matters and things relating to any claim or loss as in its judgment may be beneficial or expedient and all payments made and costs and expenses incurred therewith shall be shared by the Reinsurer in proportion to its liability for the claim or loss and debited or paid in accordance with the provisions of this Article.
6.4. Where the Reinsurer's share of a loss falling under this Agreement amounts to or exceeds the sum of £ , the Reinsurer shall upon receiving a summarised statement from the Company (detailing the payment made or the amount to be paid forthwith as agreed with the insured or original reinsured as the case may be) remit its share of such loss promptly. When such share is less than the amount stated the amount shall be debited in the accounts.

6.5. The Company shall as soon as practicable and in any event not later than three months after the 31st December of each year send to the Reinsurer a statement of unsettled claims as at the date of submission of such statement showing the amount for which the Reinsurer may be liable.

ARTICLE NUMBER 7: Accounts

7.1. Accounts between the Company and the Reinsurer in respect of the business under this Agreement shall be closed quarterly and rendered to the Reinsurer as soon as possible thereafter but in any event not less than three months after the end of the quarter.
7.2. Accounts shall be confirmed by the Reinsurer within one month of receipt but inadvertent errors or omissions in the account shall not delay the payment of any balance hereunder (unless such error or omission has a major effect on the remittable balance). Any necessary correction shall be made in the next account rendered hereunder, unless such error or omission has a major effect on the remittable balance, in which event it shall be corrected by a supplementary account.
7.3. Balances due to the Company shall be paid at the time of confirmation of the account and balances due to the Reinsurer shall be paid by the Company at the same time as the accounts are rendered.
7.4. Either party may at its discretion offset against any amounts advised to and due from the other party hereunder any amounts which have been previously advised and are due at that time.
7.5. All payments hereunder shall be in Sterling and balances in other currencies shall be converted into Sterling at the rates of exchange ruling at the time they were entered in the books of the Reinsured.

ARTICLE NUMBER 8: Reserve Deposits

8.1. As security for the Company in respect of the future performance of the Reinsurer for cessions hereunder, the Company shall retain from the Reinsurer a Premium Reserve Deposit in cash calculated at % (per cent.) on the premium ceded to the Reinsurer in the accounts rendered hereunder. Such retained Deposit will be held by the Company and released to the Reinsurer in the corresponding account of the following year.
8.2. The Reinsurer may at any time request the release of the Premium Reserve Deposit retained in cash and its replacement with Bonds and/or Securities acceptable to both parties and the Reinsurer shall receive all dividends, interest and other rights accruing thereon. When a Deposit is constituted in Bonds and/or Securities the

Company shall have the right to debit the Reinsurer and retain in cash any deficiency between the Premium Reserve Deposit required and the market value of the Bonds and/or Securities held. The cash deposit so retained shall be held by the Company until covered by Bonds and/or Securities deposited by the Reinsurer.

8.3. The Company shall credit the Reinsurer in the accounts rendered hereunder with interest calculated at the rate of % (per cent.) per annum on the Premium Reserve Deposit retained in cash at any time throughout the relevant period.

8.4. It is hereby expressly agreed and declared that all sums Cash and/or Bonds and/or Securities held by the Company in accordance with the provisions of this Article remain the property of the Reinsurer and are held by the Company as trustees for the Reinsurer and may only be utilised by the Company in the event and up to the amount of the Reinsurer's failure to discharge its liability under this Agreement.

ARTICLE NUMBER 9: Commencement and Termination

9.1. This Agreement shall take effect in respect of all insurances relating to risks covered hereunder issued or renewed on or after the First day of January 19 and shall continue in force for an indefinite period unless otherwise agreed. Either party may, however, terminate this Agreement by giving three months notice in writing to expire on the Thirty First day of December of any year. In the event of either party giving notice of termination then such notice shall be automatically deemed to have been given by both parties.

9.2. In the event of either party giving notice of termination of any business ceded in the reciprocation (in whole or in part) for this Agreement, then this Agreement shall automatically be deemed to be under notice of termination from the same date notwithstanding that previous notice had not been given in accordance with paragraph 9.1. above.

9.3. The acceptance of War risks under this Agreement is at all times subject to seven days notice of termination given by either party.

9.4. Either party shall have the right to terminate this Agreement immediately by giving the other party notice by the quickest means available which shall be deemed to be served upon despatch or where communications between the parties are interrupted upon attempted despatch, where

9.4.1. The performance of the whole or any part of this Agreement be prohibited or rendered impossible de jure or de facto in particular and without prejudice to the generality of the preceding words in consequence of any law or regulation which is or shall be in force in any country or territory in which either party is situated or if any law or regulation shall prevent directly or indirectly the remittance of any payments due to or from either party.

9.4.2. The other party has become insolvent or unable to pay its debts or has lost the whole or a major part of its paid up capital or has had any authority to transact any class of insurance withdrawn, suspended or made conditional or if there is any material change in the management or control of the other party.

9.4.3. The country or territory in which the other party resides or has its head office or is incorporated shall be involved in armed hostilities with any other country whether war be declared or not or is partly or wholly occupied by another power or be in a state of civil war

9.4.4. The other party shall have failed to comply with any of the terms and conditions of this Agreement.

9.5. The Reinsurer shall remain liable for its share of all cessions made and effective up to and including the termination date of this Agreement, except where this Agreement is terminated in the circumstances provided for in paragraph 9.4. of this Article where the liability of the Reinsurer under current cessions shall cease as from the date of the notice of termination and any relevant adjustment of premium shall be made forthwith.

ARTICLE NUMBER 10: Assumption and/or withdrawal of portfolios

Premiums

10.1. At the option of the Company the Reinsurer shall assume liability for its share of all cessions current at the commencement date of this Agreement and in consideration thereof the Company shall credit the Reinsurer in the first account rendered hereunder with a portfolio premium assumption calculated at % (per cent.) of the premiums included in the accounts for the twelve months prior to the inception of this Agreement.

10.2. At the option of the Company the Reinsurer's liability for its share of the risks ceded under this Agreement shall cease at the date of termination of this Agreement and in consideration thereof the Company shall debit the Reinsurer in account with a portfolio premium withdrawal calculated at % (per cent.) of the premiums included in the accounts for the twelve months prior to the date of termination of this Agreement.

Losses

10.3. At the option of the Company the Reinsurer shall assume liability for its share of all losses outstanding at the commencement date of this Agreement and in consideration thereof the Company shall credit the Reinsurer in the first account hereunder with a portfolio loss assumption calculated at % (per cent.) of the Company's estimate of the amount of the losses outstanding at inception of this Agreement.
10.4. At the option of the Company, the Reinsurer's liability for its share of all losses outstanding at the date of termination of this Agreement shall cease at that date and in consideration thereof the Company shall debit the Reinsurer in account with a portfolio loss withdrawal calculated at % (per cent.) of the Company's estimate of the amount of the losses outstanding at the date of termination of this Agreement.

ARTICLE NUMBER 11: Alterations and Interpretation

11.1. This Agreement may be altered at any time by mutual consent of the parties either by Addendum or by exchange of correspondence signed by a responsible official of each of the parties, and such variations shall be deemed to form part of this Agreement and be binding on the parties.
11.2. Any attachments which may be expressly incorporated herein shall be read together with this Agreement as one contract and any word or expression to which a specific meaning has been applied, shall bear such specific meaning wherever it may appear.
11.3. The laws of England shall apply as the proper law of this Agreement.

ARTICLE NUMBER 12: Confidentiality

12.1. Both parties hereto undertake to regard this Agreement as well as all transactions relating hereto as confidential and further agree that neither will at any time during the currency of this Agreement or subsequently make use either directly or indirectly of the information afforded in connection herewith in any manner which shall or may operate to the prejudice or detriment of the other party.

ARTICLE NUMBER 13: Intermediary

13.1.
of
are designated by the parties hereto as the intermediary through whom all communications relating hereto shall be transmitted.

Premium settlements and claims recoveries shall also be effected through the intermediary. Settlement to the Reinsurer by the intermediary shall constitute a full discharge of the obligations of the Company hereunder.

13.2. All postal, cable, remittance or other similar charges shall be paid by the sender.

IN WITNESS WHEREOF this Agreement has been drawn up and signed in duplicate on behalf of and by the authority of each contracting party,

In this day of 19
for and on behalf of the Company

and in this day of 19
for and on behalf of the Reinsurer in respect of its per cent. share of the liabilities and premiums set forth herein.

RETROCESSION TREATY REFERENCE NO.

REINSURED:
OF

RETROCESSIONAIRE:
OF

TABLE OF CONTENTS

QUOTA SHARE RETROCESSION AGREEMENT NO.
made between ....
(hereinafter referred to as the "Reinsured") of the one part
and
(hereinafter referred to as the "Retrocessionaire") of the other part.

IN CONSIDERATION OF the payment of the premium as hereinafter provided it is agreed:—

ARTICLE NUMBER 1: The Business Covered

1.1. The Reinsured shall cede and the Retrocessionaire shall accept a % share of the Reinsured's acceptance of the fire reinsurance treaty (hereinafter referred to as the "original treaty") as specified in the treaty schedule attached hereto (hereinafter referred to as the "Schedule").
1.2. The Reinsured may effect catastrophe retrocession to protect its net retained account.
1.3. The liability of the Retrocessionaire shall be subject to all the stipulations clauses waivers and modifications of the original business and of any endorsement thereto except insofar as they are contrary to the terms of this Agreement. However the liability of the Retrocessionaire hereunder in respect of any claim shall not be increased by reason of the inability of the Reinsured to recover amounts from any other Retrocessionaires for any reason whatsoever.

ARTICLE NUMBER 2: Inspection of Records and Errors and Omissions

2.1. Subject to prior arrangement and at the expense of the Retrocessionaire, the Retrocessionaire may inspect or obtain copies of the whole or any part of the records, books, accounts and any documents of the Reinsured relating to business covered by this Agreement.
2.2. The right of inspection of the Retrocessionaire shall exist for as long as one of the parties hereto has a claim against the other party originating from business covered by this Agreement even after its termination, annulment or invalidation, but where arbitration or legal proceedings are pending between the parties hereto, this right of inspection shall only be exercised through a representative who is not an employee of the Retrocessionaire.
2.3. The Retrocessionaire shall in all circumstances follow the fortunes of the Reinsured in respect of the insurances ceded and of any further alterations or modifications thereof and shall in every case accept as binding any decision which might be made by the Reinsured concerning the original business.

2.4. Bona fide delays errors or omissions in connection with the operation of this Agreement shall not prejudice the rights of either party hereto but shall be corrected retrospectively upon discovery so that the parties hereto shall be placed in the same position as if the delay and/or error and/or omission had not occurred.

ARTICLE NUMBER 3: Bordereau

3.1. The Reinsured shall not be required to furnish the Retrocessionaire with copies of any bordereau or loss advice lists which it may receive under the original treaty.

ARTICLE NUMBER 4: Accounts

4.1. The Retrocessionaire shall receive from the Reinsured its proportion of all premiums less ceding commission, returns and cancellations as received by the Reinsured and shall pay its proportion of the original losses and all charges allowed by the Reinsured in respect of the business retroceded hereunder.
4.2. The Retrocessionaire shall allow to the Reinsured an overriding commission of   % (per cent.) of the net premiums retroceded hereunder.
4.3. The accounts between the Reinsured and the Retrocessionaire shall be rendered as soon as possible after the receipt by the Reinsured of the original accounts.
4.4. Accounts shall be confirmed by the Retrocessionaire within one month of receipt but inadvertent errors or omissions in the account shall not delay the payment of any balance hereunder (unless such error or omission has a major effect on the remittable balance). Any necessary correction shall be made in the next account rendered hereunder, unless such error or omission has a major effect on the remittable balance, in which event it shall be corrected by a supplementary account.
4.5. Balances due to the Reinsured shall be paid at the time of confirmation of the account and balances due to the Retrocessionaire shall be paid by the Reinsured at the same time as the accounts are rendered.
4.6. The Retrocessionaire shall on demand pay to the Reinsured its due share of all cash losses paid by the Reinsured under the terms of the original treaty.
4.7. All payments hereunder shall be in Sterling and balances in other currencies shall be converted into Sterling at the rates of exchange ruling at the time they were entered in the books of the Reinsured.
4.8. Either party may at its discretion set off against any amounts

due from the other party hereunder or under any other Agreement between the parties hereto any amounts which are due under this or such other Agreement.

ARTICLE NUMBER 5: Premium Reserve Deposits

5.1. As security for the due performance of the obligations of the Retrocessionaire under this Agreement the Reinsured shall be entitled to retain as a premium reserve out of any monies due to the Retrocessionaire a sum equal to % (per cent.) of the annual net premiums credited to the Retrocessionaire. The calculation of the premium reserve shall be made in each quarterly account and shall be calculated on the net premiums of the relative quarter and of the three preceding quarters after deducting the reserve of the corresponding quarter of the previous year.

5.2. The Reinsured shall pay to the Retrocessionaire interest on such premium reserve at a rate of % (per cent.) per annum less tax, such interest to accrue from the dates on which the respective amounts are credited to the premium reserve.

5.3. It is further understood and agreed that in respect of any business requiring the Reinsured to set up loss reserves in cash to any ceding company then in respect of any loss involving the Retrocessionaire hereunder the Retrocessionaire agrees to contribute its appropriate share of such loss reserve subject to payment of interest at the rate received by the Reinsured on such loss reserve.

ARTICLE NUMBER 6: Inception and Termination

6.1. This Agreement shall take effect from the First day of January 19 and shall continue in force for an indefinite period unless otherwise agreed. Either party may, however, terminate this Agreement by giving notice of termination in writing to take effect on the Thirty First day of December of any year, such notice to be mailed by the Retrocessionaire not later than four calendar months prior to such date or by the Reinsured not later than two calendar months prior to such date. In the event of either party giving notice of termination in accordance with these provisions then such notice shall be automatically deemed to have been given by both parties.

6.2. In the event of either the Reinsured or its ceding company giving notice of termination of the original treaty it is understood that this Agreement shall likewise be deemed to be under notice of termination from the same date notwithstanding that previous notice had not been given in accordance with paragraph 6.1. above.

6.3. In the event of the Retrocessionaire giving notice of termination to the Reinsured of any reinsurance or retrocession treaty in consideration for which this Retrocession Agreement has been made then this Agreement shall automatically be deemed to be under notice of termination from the same date notwithstanding that previous notice had not been given in accordance with paragraph 6.1. above.

6.4. Either party shall have the right to terminate this Agreement immediately by giving the other party notice by the quickest means available which shall be deemed to be served upon despatch or where communications between the parties are interrupted upon attempted despatch, where:—

6.4.1. The performance of the whole or any part of this Agreement be prohibited or rendered impossible de jure or de facto in particular and without prejudice to the generality of the preceding words in consequence of any law or regulation which is or shall be in force in any country or territory in which either party is situated or if any law or regulaton shall prevent directly or indirectly the remittance of any payments due to or from either party.

6.4.2. The other party has become insolvent or unable to pay its debts or has lost the whole or a major part of its paid up capital or has had any authority to transact any class of insurance withdrawn, suspended or made conditional or if there is any material change in the management or control of the other party.

6.4.3. The country or territory in which the other party resides or has its head office or is incorporated shall be involved in armed hostilities with any other country whether war be declared or not or is partly or wholly occupied by another power or be in a state of civil war.

6.4.4. The other party shall have failed to comply with any of the terms and conditions of this Agreement.

6.5. The Retrocessionaire shall remain liable for its share of all cessions made and effective up to and including the termination date of this Agreement, except where the Agreement is terminated in the circumstances provided for in paragraph 6.4. of this Article where the liability of the Retrocessionaire under current cessions shall cease as from the date of the notice of termination and any relevant adjustment or premium shall be made forthwith.

ARTICLE NUMBER 7: Portfolio withdrawal

7.1. In the event of termination of this Agreement the Retrocessionaire shall remain liable for its share of all retrocessions hereunder in force on the effective date of termination as long as the liability of the Reinsured continues under the original treaty, provided however that the Reinsured shall have the option to withdraw the portfolio of current cessions as at that date and to debit the Retrocessionaire with

% (per cent.) of the net premiums credited to the Retrocessionaire in the four quarterly accounts immediately preceding such date, without any deduction for overriding commission.
7.2. In the event of the portfolio being so withdrawn the Reinsured shall credit the Retrocessionaire with the premium reserve set up in accordance with Article No. 5 and shall debit the Retrocessionaire with an amount for outstanding losses as shown in the books of the Reinsured, and such amount shall be retained by the Reinsured until all the obligations of the Retrocessionaire under this Agreement have been fully discharged.

ARTICLE NUMBER 8: Alterations and Interpretation

8.1. This Agreement may be altered at any time by mutual consent of the parties either by Addendum or by exchange of correspondence signed by a responsible official of each of the parties, and such variations shall be deemed to form part of this Agreement and be binding on the parties.
8.2. Any attachments which may be expressly incorporated herein shall be read together with this Agreement as one contract and any word or expression to which a specific meaning has been applied, shall bear such specific meaning wherever it may appear.
8.3. The laws of England shall apply as the proper law of this Agreement.

ARTICLE NUMBER 9: Confidentiality

9.1. Both parties hereto undertake to regard this Agreement as well as all transactions relating hereto as confidential and further agree that neither will at any time during the currency of this Agreement or subsequently make use either directly or indirectly of the information afforded in connection herewith in any manner which shall or may operate to the prejudice or detriment of the other party.

ARTICLE NUMBER 10: Intermediary

10.1
of
are designated by the parties hereto as the intermediary through whom all communications relating hereto shall be transmitted. Premium settlements and claim recoveries shall also be effected through the intermediary. Settlement to the Retrocessionaire by the intermediary shall constitute a full discharge of the obligations of the Reinsured hereunder.

10.2. All postal, cable, remittance or other similar charges shall be paid by the sender.

IN WITNESS WHEREOF this Agreement has been signed in duplicate on behalf of and by the authority of each contracting party.

at this day of 19
For and on behalf of the Reinsured

And at this day of 19
for and on behalf of the Retrocessionaire in respect of its per cent. share of the liabilities and premiums set forth herein.

SCHEDULE ATTACHING TO RETROCESSION AGREEMENT NO.
TERMS AND CONDITIONS OF THE ORIGINAL TREATY

CEDING COMPANY

ADDRESS

TREATY REFERENCE

TYPE OF TREATY

CLASS OF BUSINESS

GEOGRAPHICAL SCOPE

LIMITS

PREMIUM

CEDING COMMISSION

OTHER DEDUCTIONS

PROFIT COMMISSION

ACCOUNTS

This is the Arbitration Agreement 1985, agreed by the British Insurance Brokers Association Reinsurance Committee and the Reinsurance Offices Association, and it is recommended by them to complete this as a separate agreement in this manner.

ARBITRATION AGREEMENT between
of the one part
and
of the other part.

(1) All matters in difference between the parties in relation to the contract to which this Agreement is attached (REINSURANCE AGREEMENT NO.), including formation and validity, and whether arising during or after the period of that contract, shall be referred to an arbitration tribunal in the manner hereinafter set out.

(2) Unless the parties agree upon a single arbitrator within thirty days of one receiving a written request from the other for arbitration, the claimant (the party requesting arbitration) shall appoint his arbitrator and give written notice thereof to the respondent. Within thirty days of receiving such notice the respondent shall appoint his arbitrator and give written notice thereof to the claimant, failing which the claimant may apply to the appointer hereinafter named to nominate an arbitrator on behalf of the respondent.

(3) Before they enter upon a reference the two arbitrators shall appoint a third arbitrator. Should they fail to appoint such a third arbitrator within thirty days of the appointment of the respondent's arbitrator then either of them or either of the parties may apply to the appointor for the appointment of the third arbitrator. The three arbitrators shall decide by majority. If no majority can be reached the verdict of the third arbitrator shall prevail. He shall also act as Chairman of the Tribunal.

(4) Unless the parties otherwise agree the arbitration tribunal shall consist of persons with not less than ten years' experience of insurance or reinsurance.

(5) The arbitration tribunal shall have the power to fix all procedural rules for the holding of the arbitration including discretionary power to make orders as to any matters which it may consider proper in the circumstances of the case with regard to pleadings, discovery, inspection of the documents, examination of witnesses and any other matter whatsoever relating to the conduct of the arbitration and may receive and act upon such evidence whether oral or written strictly admissible or not as it shall in its discretion think fit.

(6) The appointor shall be the Secretary General for the time being of the Court of Arbitration of the International Chamber of Commerce.
(7) All costs of the arbitration shall be at the discretion of the arbitration tribunal who may direct to and by whom and in what manner they shall be paid.
(8) The seat of the arbitration shall be in London and the arbitration tribunal shall apply the laws of England as the proper law of this Agreement and of the contract to which this Agreement is attached.
(9) The award of the arbitration tribunal shall be in writing and binding upon the parties who convenant to carry out the same. If either of the parties should fail to carry out any award the other may apply for its enforcement to a court of competent jurisdiction in any territory in which the party in default is domiciled or has assets or carries on business.

IN WITNESS WHEREOF this Agreement has been drawn up and signed in duplicate on behalf of and by the authority of each contracting party.

In this day of
19
for and on behalf of

And in this day of
19
for and on behalf of

TREATY ADMINISTRATION
PROPORTIONAL TREATY REINSURANCE ACCOUNT

Statement of Account for the 2nd Quarter 19

From the Insurance Company Limited

In Respect of 1st Surplus Treaty No.

19 Treaty Year

These figures are in respect of 100% placement.

INCOME		
Premiums Ceded for the Quarter	£	
Premium Reserve Deposit Released (being amount debited in corresponding quarter of previous year)	£	
Interest thereon	£	
Cash Losses (previously paid)	£	
LESS OUTGO		
Losses Paid during the Quarter		£
Ceding Commission on premiums ceded during the quarter		£
Taxes, Licence Fees, Fire Brigade Charges and other allowed expenses for the quarter		£
Premium Reserve Deposit retained (being amount debited in respect of the unexpired risks of the current year)		£
BALANCE DUE TO/(FROM) THE REINSURER		

ESTIMATED OUTSTANDING LOSSES AS AT THE END OF THE QUARTER £

BALANCE DUE TO/(FROM) £ REINSURANCE COMPANY LIMITED

IN RESPECT OF THEIR % SHARE OF THE ABOVE.

INDEX

A

B

C

D

E

F

G

H

I

L

Q

R

S

U

V

W

Z